Ecological Studies

Analysis and Synthesis

Edited by

W. D. Billings, Durham (USA) F. Golley, Athens (USA)
O. L. Lange, Würzburg (FRG) J. S. Olson, Oak Ridge (USA)

Volume 32

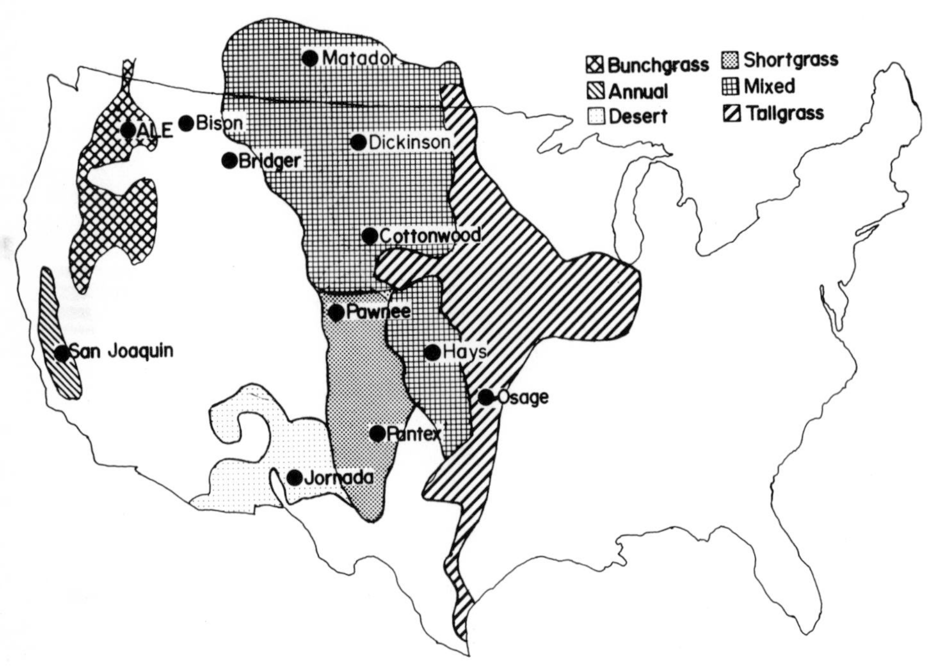

Distribution of North American grasslands. Adapted from: Dodd, J. L. The biotic structure of grassland ecosystems: Producers. *In* J. E. Ellis (ed.) Grassland ecosystems of North America: Structure and function. Dowden, Hutchinson, and Ross, Inc., Stroudsburg, Penn. (In press).

Perspectives in Grassland Ecology

Results and Applications of the US/IBP Grassland Biome Study

Edited by

Norman R. French

With 60 Figures

Springer-Verlag New York Heidelberg Berlin

Library of Congress Cataloging in Publication Data
Main entry under title:
Perspectives in grassland ecology.
(Ecological studies; v.32)
Bibliography: p.
Includes index.
1. Grassland ecology—North America. 2. Range management—North America. I. French, Norman R. II. International Biological Programme. III. US/IBP grassland biome study. IV. Series.
QH102.P36 574.5′264 78-13971

Printed in the United States of America.

9 8 7 6 5 4 3 2 1

ISBN 0-387-90384-4 Springer-Verlag New York
ISBN 3-540-90384-4 Springer-Verlag Berlin Heidelberg

Preface

This volume is a result of the summary and synthesis of data collected in the Grassland Biome Program, which is part of the American contribution to the International Biological Program (IBP). The purpose of this volume is to present a summary of quantitative ecological investigations of North American grasslands and to present a set of broad comparisons of their characteristics and functions as well as the results of some models and experiments that lead to practical considerations of the management of grasslands.

Synthesis is a continuing activity in science. Early in the Grassland Biome Program there was a synthesis of literature data on grasslands, edited by R. L. Dix and R. G. Beidleman (1969). Results of the first year of field data collection under this program were synthesized in a volume edited by N. R. French (1971). Development of the large-scale model constructed to depict the processes and the dynamics of state variables in grassland ecosystems was presented by Innis (1978). Soon to appear will be two volumes integrating studies of American grasslands with IBP studies in other grasslands of the world (Coupland, in press) and the application of systems analysis to understanding grassland function and utilization (Breymeyer and Van Dyne, in press). The present volume presents current results and comparisons of field investigations and experimental studies that were conducted under this program. Both efforts—the modeling and theoretical studies and the quantitative studies and experimental investigations—were planned to be conducted simultaneously with interactive feedback between the two efforts. Together, these volumes comprise the current summary of results of a large-scale cooperative and interdisciplinary research effort that involved many scientists from several different institutions and government agencies.

The program was organized using a conceptual model of the grassland ecosystem as a framework for conducting field studies. State variable dynamics were measured at a number of sites representing different grassland types, while intensive studies of grassland ecosystem processes were concentrated at the shortgrass prairie site near Colorado State University. The relationship of process rates or flows in the ecosystem to system-driving variables was to be determined by the process studies at the Intensive Site, and these were to be compared and extended by models utilizing the state variable dynamics as measured in field studies at other grassland sites. This plan was conceived to maximize utility of information derived from the effort invested in research on grasslands.

The Grassland Biome study truly was a large-scale cooperative interdisciplinary research program. A great many research scientists had their horizons broadened and their understanding enhanced by participating in this effort. Perhaps the greatest impact on future science will be through the large number of graduate students who participated in the program and, while actively contributing to the data base upon which all scientists drew, formulated their own personal views and philosophies of ecosystem science. Through their teaching and future contributions to science, the influence of interdisciplinary programs such as this will have an inestimable impact on future science.

Another substantial benefit derived from participation in the Grassland Biome Study was the high degree of communication fostered on a national and international scale. Comparison and contrast with results from studies of other grasslands in the world, to be reported in two IBP synthesis volumes on grasslands from Cambridge University Press, have resulted in unexpected insights into the functioning of organisms and processes characteristic of different grassland ecosystems. It is difficult to focus attention on processes that are unimportant or organisms that do not occur in a particular grassland until one observes the importance of these in a related ecosystem. The broadening of our views of total grassland ecosystems has enhanced our understanding of native grasslands. Other ecosystem studies conducted under the IBP have taken different approaches to field experimentation and modeling. Some have been reported in this series (volumes 2, 7, 16, and 17). These contrasts, too, have helped to broaden our understanding and sharpen our insight. Each has been a different experiment in large-scale environmental investigation.

The general objective of the Grassland Biome Program was to enhance our understanding of, and our ability to manage, grassland as a renewable resource through quantitative investigation and modeling guided by a systems analysis approach to study. To carry out this program, a core of coordinators, data managers, and modelers was assembled at the Natural Resource Ecology Laboratory of Colorado State University. They coordinated the efforts and compiled the results of many cooperating investigators studying different grassland types and working at different institutions. This type of organization resulted in a central data bank which has been used as a base for analysis and synthesis of that information in a variety of modes by a number of participants.

The management design and principal motivation for the Grassland Biome effort came primarily from George M. Van Dyne who conceived and carried out the plan through its formative and productive stages, and who outlined the procedures for synthesis and summary of results. The cooperation of many grassland scientists, whose names appear in the chapters and references to follow, made the plan both fruitful and stimulating. The authors and editor, of course, bear the responsibility for the analysis and interpretation of results reported herein. Following the introduction, in which the types and general characteristics of North American grasslands are presented, there are ten chapters which focus on four general categories of grassland ecosystem studies: primary production and factors controlling it (Chapters 1–4), the effects of aboveground and belowground consumers in the grassland ecosystems (Chapters 4–6), nutrient cycling and the application of simulation modeling in grasslands (Chapters 7–9), and the most important subsystem interactions in grasslands (Chapter 10). These chapters present our current concepts of grassland ecosystem structure and function.

This book reports on work supported primarily by National Science Foundation Grants GB-31862X, GB-31862X2, GB-41233X, BMS73-02027 A02, and DEB73-02027 A03 and A04 to the Grassland Biome, U.S. International Biological Program, for "Analysis of Structure, Function, and Utilization of Grassland Ecosystems." The Pawnee site, the field research facility of the Natural Resource Ecology Laboratory, Colorado State University, is located on the United States Department of Agriculture (USDA) Science and Education Administration Central Plains Experimental Range in northeastern Colorado.

Norman R. French
February 7, 1979

Volumes synthesizing results of US/IBP Grassland Biome studies:

Dix, R. L. and R. G. Beidleman (eds.). 1969. *The Grassland Ecosystem: A Preliminary Synthesis*. Range Science Department Science Series No. 2. Fort Collins: Colorado State University. 437 p.

French, N. R. (ed.). 1971. *Preliminary Analysis of Structure and Function in Grasslands*. Range Science Department Science Series No. 10. Fort Collins: Colorado State University. 387 p.

Innis, G. S. (ed.). 1978. *Grassland Simulation Model*. Ecological Studies, 26. New York: Springer-Verlag. 298 p.

Coupland, R. T. (ed.). In press. *Grassland Ecosystems of the World: Analysis of Grasslands and Their Uses*. International Biological Programme, 18. Cambridge: Cambridge University Press.

Breymeyer, A. I. and G. M. Van Dyne (eds.). In press. *Grasslands, Systems Analysis and Man*. International Biological Programme, 19. Cambridge: Cambridge University Press.

Contributors

DETLING, J. K.	Natural Resource Ecology Laboratory, Colorado State University, Fort Collins, Colorado 80523, USA
DODD, J. L.	Natural Resource Ecology Laboratory, Colorado State University, Fort Collins, Colorado 80523, USA
FRENCH, N. R.	Natural Resource Ecology Laboratory, Colorado State University, Fort Collins, Colorado 80523, USA
LAUENROTH, W. K.	Natural Resource Ecology Laboratory, Colorado State University, Fort Collins, Colorado 80523, USA
LAYCOCK, W. A.	USDA-SEA Forage and Range Management, Crops Research Laboratory, Colorado State University, Fort Collins, Colorado 80523, USA
LEETHAM, J. W.	Natural Resource Ecology Laboratory, Colorado State University, Fort Collins, Colorado 80523, USA
PARTON, W. J.	Natural Resource Ecology Laboratory, Colorado State University, Fort Collins, Colorado 80523, USA
REDETZKE, K. A.	Natural Resource Ecology Laboratory, Colorado State University, Fort Collins, Colorado 80523, USA Present address: Biology Department, University of Texas, El Paso, Texas 79910, USA
RISSER, P. G.	Department of Botany, University of Oklahoma, Norman, Oklahoma 73069, USA
SCOTT, J. A.	Natural Resource Ecology Laboratory, Colorado State University, Fort Collins, Colorado 80523, USA Present address: 60 Estes Street, Lakewood, Colorado 80226, USA
STEINHORST, R. K.	Natural Resource Ecology Laboratory, Colorado State University, Fort Collins, Colorado 80523, USA Present address: Department of Agricultural Economics, University of Idaho, Moscow, Idaho 83843, USA
SWIFT, D. M.	Natural Resource Ecology Laboratory, Colorado State University, Fort Collins, Colorado 80523, USA
VAN DYNE, G. M.	Natural Resource Ecology Laboratory, Colorado State University, Fort Collins, Colorado 80523, USA Present address: Department of Range Science, Colorado State University, Fort Collins, Colorado 80523, USA
WOODMANSEE, R. G.	Natural Resource Ecology Laboratory, Colorado State University, Fort Collins, Colorado 80523, USA Present address: Department of Range Science, Colorado State University, Fort Collins, Colorado 80523, USA

Contents

Introduction

W. A. Laycock

The chapters in this volume are the result of research and synthesis efforts of the Grassland Biome study of the U.S. International Biological Program (IBP) which originated as part of the Analysis of Ecosystems program in the American contribution to the IBP. The focal point of the Grassland Biome studies was improvement of our understanding of an entire ecosystem. No matter how narrow or detailed a single given project or study may have been, the relationship to the whole system was the dominant theme. The first grant in support of these studies from the National Science Foundation was received in the summer of 1968, with supplemental funding from the U.S. Atomic Energy Commission. Fieldwork started in 1969 on the Intensive Site in northeastern Colorado.

Types of Grassland

Beginning in 1970 the Grassland Biome study established a network of sites in the major types of grassland found in the U.S. (Frontispiece). These included:

1. Tallgrass (true) prairie—Osage site (Oklahoma). The tallgrass prairie is an assemblage of three grassland types in which *Andropogon* is the dominant genus, and three deciduous forest ecotone types which have tallgrass communities as understory.
2. Shortgrass prairie—Pawnee site (Colorado) and Pantex site (Texas). The shortgrass prairie is dominated by *Buchloe dactyloides* and *Bouteloua gracilis*, and they often become more prevalent with intensive grazing by large herbivores.
3. Mixed-grass prairie—Cottonwood site (South Dakota). The mixed-grass prairie includes nine types and varies from areas dominated by *Andropogon scoparius* in Texas to *Agropyron*- and *Stipa*-dominated prairies in western North and South Dakota. *Bouteloua gracilis*, *B. curtipendula*, and *Buchloe dactyloides* are either codominant or important secondary species throughout most of the area of the mixed-grass prairie. This is a biotically rich prairie and grades into tallgrass to the east and shortgrass to the west.
4. Shrub steppe—ALE site (Washington). The shrub steppe includes an aggregation of vegetation types characterized by *Agropyron spicatum* and often *Festuca idahoensis* populations occurring with various species of *Artemisia*.

5. Annual grassland—San Joaquin site (California). In North America, annual grasslands have developed in an area in California that was originally dominated by perennial midgrasses. These annual grasslands have developed throughout the world where there is a Mediterranean climate characterized by hot, dry summers and wet, relatively warm winters. The uncultivated portions of the grasslands currently are species-rich mixtures of introduced annual grasses such as *Avena, Bromus,* and *Festuca,* with a complement of perennial forbs.

6. Desert (arid) grassland—Jornada site (New Mexico). Desert grasslands include those arid ecosystems of Texas, Arizona, New Mexico, and southern Utah where *Hilaria* is either dominant or codominant with species of *Bouteloua.* Shrubs such as *Larrea divaricata, Prosopis,* or *Yucca* are usually associated with this type and are often dominant. The composition of the desert grasslands varies from mixtures of herbaceous species and few shrubs to nearly pure shrub combinations.

7. High mountain grassland—Bridger site (Montana). High mountain grasslands constitute the high-elevation mountain meadows below timberline. The grasses *Agropyron* and *Festuca* are the dominant genera in the northern Rocky Mountains. These grasslands generally include a rich and important assembly of forbs such as *Lupinus* and *Delphinium.*

Final Year of Grassland Biome Studies

In 1977 the Natural Resource Ecology Laboratory at Colorado State University entered the final year of effort under National Science Foundation support for the Grassland Biome studies. The previous year was primarily one of synthesis, and this effort is the stimulus for this volume. This synthesis effort will continue toward the preparation of a major volume which will consider the structure and functional aspects of the grassland ecosystems of North America. Other major efforts underway to summarize the Biome program are the grassland-type synthesis volumes being prepared by some of the scientists who have been studying the grassland types outlined above under this program.

1. Grassland Primary Production: North American Grasslands in Perspective

William K. Lauenroth

Introduction

Interest in primary production on a global scale has flourished in the past two decades (Westlake 1963, Bazilevich et al 1971, Lieth 1973, Cooper 1975, Lieth and Whittaker 1975, Rodin et al 1975). Although reviews are available for forests (Kira 1975), grazing lands (Caldwell 1975), tundra (Wielgolaski 1975), and aquatic ecosystems (Bunt 1975, Likens 1975), no similar review is available in English for grasslands. The work presented here is an initial step towards a synthesis of grassland primary production. Before proceeding to the detailed examination of North American grasslands in the succeeding chapters, it is well to place their production in perspective with other grasslands and with other ecosystems.

From the many available estimates of net primary production in the biosphere, two were chosen in order to represent a range of values. The most recent estimate is by Whittaker and Likens (1975); the estimate providing greatest detail with respect to vegetation types is by Bazilevich et al (1971). Whittaker and Likens' estimate of net primary production for land-plant communities is 1.17×10^{11} tons $\cdot$ yr^{-1}. The corresponding estimate from Bazilevich et al (1971) is 1.72×10^{11} tons $\cdot$ yr^{-1}. It is assumed that the true value falls within this range.

According to both calculations, forests are the most productive vegetation type. Whittaker and Likens estimate that forests account for 63% of total net primary production, while the Bazilevich study attributes 74% of land-surface primary production to forests. Whittaker and Likens provide production for five categories of forest; the tropical rain forest is by far the most productive. Bazilevich et al. divide forests into four thermal belts and several precipitation regimes; their data also indicate that tropical humid forest is by far the most productive type.

Grassland and savanna rank second in contribution to total net primary production. Whittaker and Likens' estimate of grassland production is 1.89×10^{10} tons $\cdot$ yr^{-1} representing 16% of the total. Bazilevich et al. submitted estimates of 2.87×10^{10} tons $\cdot$ yr^{-1} and 17%, respectively.

Thus, forests and grasslands account for 79% of the primary production of the earth's land surface using the calculations of Whittaker and Likens and 91% by the account of Bazilevich et al. One source of difference between the two estimates is that the Bazilevich study included agricultural land in their estimates for forests and grasslands; their estimates therefore represent net primary production of potential natural vegetation types.

Whittaker and Likens provide estimates for woodland and shrubland, tundra, deserts, agricultural lands and swamps and marshes in accounting for the remaining 21% of total land-surface primary production. Of this remaining percentage, agricultural lands account for 8%, woodlands and shrublands, 5%, swamps and marshes, 5%, tundra and alpine, 1%, and desert, 3%. Bazilevich et al estimate the contribution to total net primary production by bogs at 8%, deserts at 1%, and tundra at 1%.

Grassland

General Characteristics

Grassland—here including savanna and shrub steppe—is the potential natural vegetation on 33 million km^2, or 25% of the earth's land surface (Shantz 1954, Figure 1.1). These are the climatically determined grasslands. They occur in areas having a period of the year when soil water availability falls below the requirements for forests, yet they receive sufficient precipitation during part of the year to sustain grasses *(Gramineae)* as the dominant or, at least, major component of vegetation. Most of these areas occur either between deserts and forests or in the rain shadow of major mountain ranges. An example of the former is the grassland and savanna of Africa occurring between the desert of

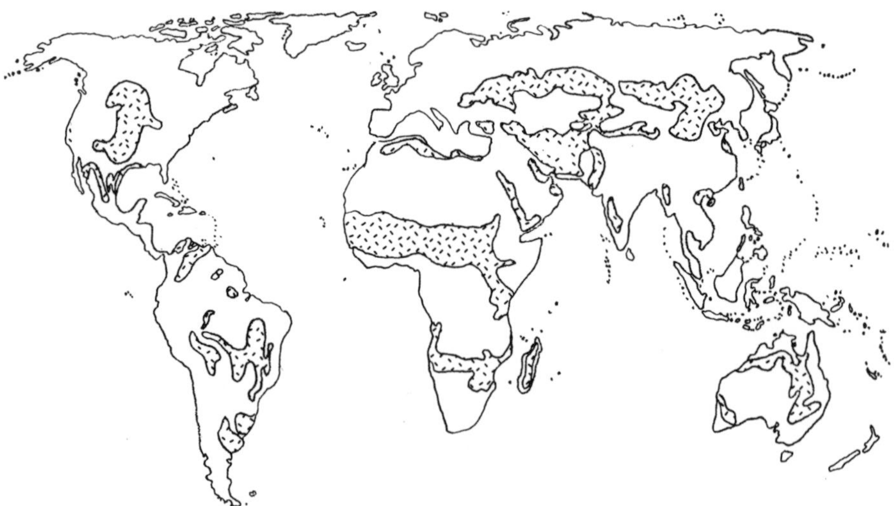

Figure 1.1. Distribution of grassland over the earth. Adapted from Hammond World Atlas, Maplewood, N.J.: Hammond, Inc., 1971.

northern Africa and the forest of the Congo Basin. An example of the latter is the grassland occurring in the rain shadow of the Rocky Mountains in North America.

Figure 1.2 presents the relationship between temperature and precipitation among the major vegetation types of the earth and illustrates the position of climatically determined grassland with respect to forest, tundra, and desert (Lieth 1975). Grasslands occur in areas receiving 250 to 1000 mm annual precipitation and having mean annual temperatures between 0 and 26°C. It is clear that forests are found over a wide range of environmental conditions. As an index for comparing the ranges, forests are found over approximately 20% of the temperature × precipitation space depicted in Figure 1.2 while grasslands cover approximately 5% of the area.

In addition to the climatically determined grasslands, two other categories can be distinguished. Successional grasslands result from removal of the original forest vegetation and are maintained by either grazing, mowing, or burning. Many of the grasslands of India (Singh 1968) and essentially all grasslands in Japan (Numata 1961) fall into this category. These grasslands are very productive largely because of the high precipitation which sustained the original forest vegetation. The second category includes agricultural grasslands: those which have been planted and maintained by intensive agronomic practices. The vegetation is composed of a few species either of improved varieties of native grasses or of introduced grasses. Management of agricultural grasslands usually includes irrigation, fertilization, or both. These grasslands occur in areas that would support natural grasslands as well as where the original forest or shrub vegetation has been removed. Great Britain, Europe, and Australia have extensive areas of agricultural grasslands.

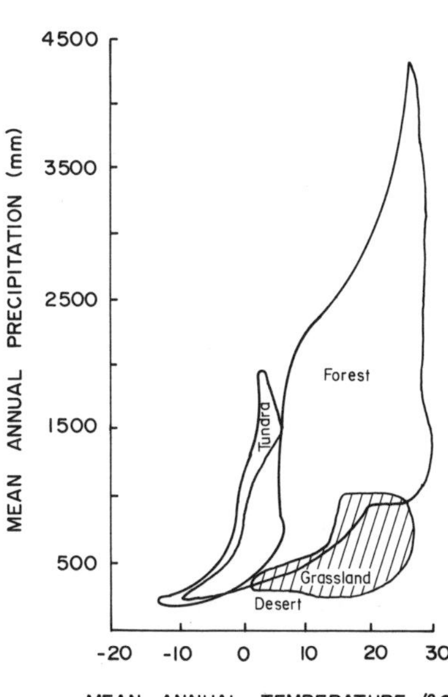

Figure 1.2. Relationship of forest, grassland, tundra and desert on an annual temperature and precipitation plane. Adapted from Lieth (1975).

Of concern here is the category of climatically determined grasslands, and successional types. Agricultural grasslands have been excluded because they are not natural assemblages of species and because it is difficult to compare production resulting from large input of mineral fertilizer with those areas not receiving artificial fertilization.

Characteristics of the Primary Production Data Set

Estimates of aboveground net primary production in grams dry weight · m^{-2} were taken from 52 sites throughout the world (Table 1.1, Figure 1.3). Thirty-two of the sites were from the United States and the remaining 20 from 15 other countries. A total of 271 estimates of aboveground production was available from the 52 sites. Since the number of estimates varied widely among sites, an average was used to compare production among sites.

Although the data used for analysis do not represent grasslands on an area basis, they do include estimates from a wide range of annual production classes, ranging from 100 to 1700 g · m^{-2} · yr^{-1}. Production is skewed towards the lower classes because a large number of sites from semiarid midcontinental North America were included.

Grasslands can exist over a remarkably wide range of temperature and precipitation conditions (Figure 1.4). The range of mean annual temperature represented in Figure 1.4 is 4.6 to 28.8°C and the annual precipitation range is 136 to 1810 mm. There is a general trend of increased production with increasing

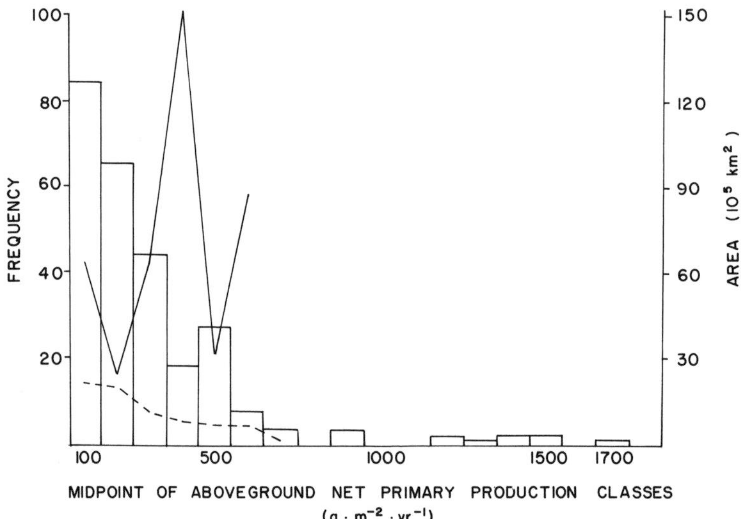

Figure 1.3. Frequency distribution of 271 estimates of aboveground net primary production among 100 g · m^{-2} · yr^{-1} productivity classes. The solid line plotted over the bars represents the number of km^2 of world grassland falling into the various classes (Bazilevich et al 1971). The dashed line represents average production of the 52 sites analyzed.

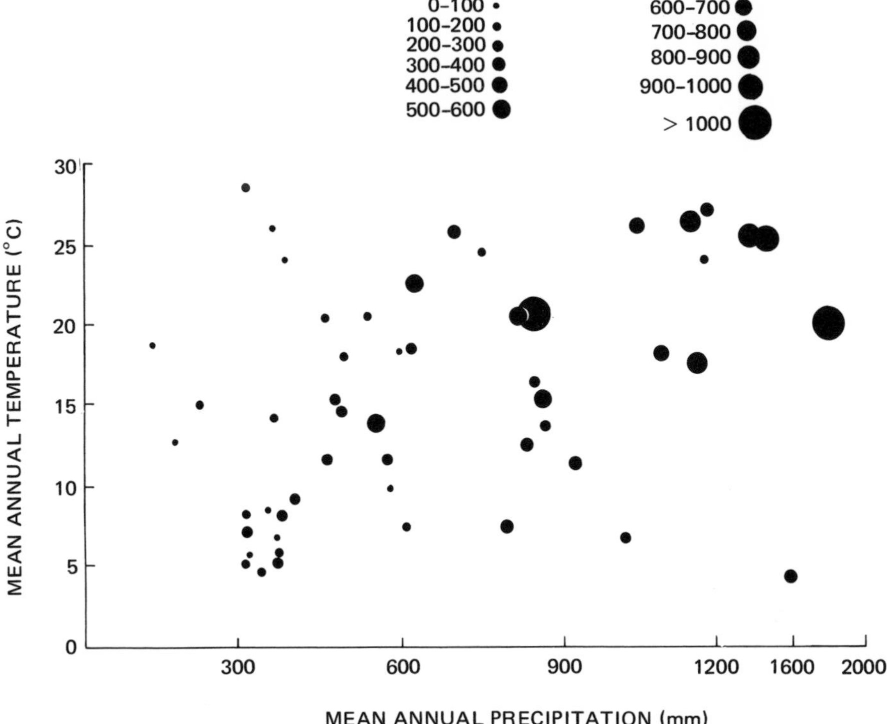

Figure 1.4. Distribution of the 52 grassland sites on a mean annual precipitation and mean annual temperature plane. Dot size indicates the magnitude of annual aboveground net primary production in g · m^{-2} · yr^{-1}.

precipitation and temperature. The least productive sites occur where precipitation is low and temperature high. The most productive sites occur where mean annual precipitation is greater than 800 mm and mean annual temperature above 15°C.

Linear regression analysis failed to indicate a relationship between mean annual temperature and grassland production (Figure 1.5). This is not interpreted as a lack of relationship, but emphasizes the interaction of temperature with precipitation. The importance of precipitation in determining grassland production is suggested in Figure 1.6. In general, the greater the mean annual precipitation of a site, the greater is the aboveground production. Sites represented by dots removed from the regression line indicate that mean annual precipitation is not always the most important factor determining the magnitude of net production. At any level of precipitation such variables as temperature, distribution of precipitation, soil fertility, amount of disturbance, and successional status can significantly influence productivity. The increased spread of the data at higher precipitation values suggests that the relative importance of site-specific factors increase as a function of precipitation.

Table 1.1. Macroclimatic Group Designation, Location, Annual Precipitation (mm), Annual Temperature (°C), and Aboveground Net Primary Production ($g \cdot m^{-2} \cdot yr^{-1}$) for 52 Grassland Sites

Macro-climatic	Sites: City, state	Sites: Country	Mean annual precipitation	Mean annual temperature	Aboveground net production	Number of estimates	Reference
1	Las Cruces, New Mexico	USA	225	15.1	115	4	IBP[1]
	Garies, Cape of Good Hope	S. Africa	136	18.9	99	1	Bourlière and Hadley 1970
	Richland, Washington	USA	183	12.8	90	4	IBP
2	St. Lanatius, Montana	USA	324	7.3	230	1	IBP
	Boulder, Colorado	USA	470	11.8	298	4	Moir 1969
	Albion, Montana	USA	329	5.9	42	4	Branson 1956
	Dickinson, N. Dakota	USA	380	5.1	224	6	Goetz 1969, Lauenroth and Whitman 1977 and IBP
	New Town, N. Dakota	USA	350	4.8	144	20	Redmann 1975
	Long Valley, S. Dakota	USA	410	9.2	250	2	Larson and Whitman 1942
	Bismarck, N. Dakota	USA	385	5.7	203	15	Lorenz and Rogler 1972, Rogler and Lorenz 1957
	Sidney, Montana	USA	313	5.3	122	4	Black 1968
	Sundance, Wyoming	USA	380	6.8	76	16	Cosper et al 1967
	Cottonwood, S. Dakota	USA	387	8.2	282	3	IBP
	Ardmore, S. Dakota	USA	360	8.5	86	3	Cosper and Thomas 1961
	Nunn, Colorado	USA	311	8.2	145	9	IBP
3	Mao	Chad	318	28.8	158	4	Bourlière and Hadley 1970
	Jodhpur, Rajasthan	India	362	26.0	99	6	Gupta et al 1972
	St. Louis	Senegal	400	24.1	60	1	Bourlière and Hadley 1970
	Santa Rita, New Mexico	USA	503	18.0	144	1	Freeman and Humphrey 1956
	Allahabad, Utkar Pradesh	India	1063	26.4	458	8	Singh 1968, Choudhary 1972, Ambasht et al 1972
	Udaipur Rajasthan	India	764	24.5	177	3	Vyas et al 1972, Shrimal and Vyas 1975
	Zeerust	S. Africa	601	18.4	92	1	Bourlière and Hadley 1970
	Lusaka	Zambia	835	20.6	550	1	Brockington 1960
	Shabani	Rhodesia	541	20.7	145	1	Bourlière and Hadley 1970

4	Mishmar, Hayarden	Israel	466	20.6	162	15	Ofer and Seligman 1969
	San Jose, California	USA	368	14.2	166	8	McNaughton 1968
	San Joaquin, California	USA	484	15.3	224	34	Duncan and Woodmansee 1975
	Berkeley, California	USA	568	14.0	552	3	Hervey 1949, Ratliff and Heady 1962
	Hopland, California	USA	886	13.9	228	16	Jones and Evans 1960, Heady 1965, Murphy 1970
5	Accra	Ghana	714	25.9	306	2	Lansbury et al 1965
	Imakindu	Tanzania	632	22.7	520	1	Bourlière and Hadley 1970
	Calobozo Guanico	Venezuela	1196	27.1	353	3	San Jose and Medina 1975
	Tschaurou	Nigeria	1120	26.7	510	2	Bourlière and Hadley 1970
6	Minneapolis, Minnesota	USA	627	7.6	160	1	Bray et al 1959
	Hays, Kansas	USA	588	11.9	234	5	Hulett and Tomanek 1969, 1974
	Amarillo, Texas	USA	499	14.9	257	3	IBP
	Sapporoa, Hokkado	Japan	1040	6.9	1170	1	Oshima 1961
	Kirigamine, Nagano	Japan	1684	4.6	315	2	Iwaki et al 1964
	Manhattan, Kansas	USA	851	12.8	387	16	Owensby and Anderson 1967
	Cresco, Iowa	USA	810	7.6	369	1	Ehrenreich and Aikman 1963
	Vermillion, S. Dakota	USA	597	10.0	353	5	Beebe and Hoffman 1968
	Throckmorton, Texas	USA	631	18.5	280	2	Mathis et al 1971
	Columbia, Missouri	USA	1172	17.8	634	9	Kucera et al 1967, Koelling and Kucera 1965
	Aiken, S. Carolina	USA	1106	18.4	485	1	Golley and Gentry 1965
	Pasukuska, Oklahoma	USA	880	15.5	567	3	IBP
	Norman, Oklahoma	USA	853	16.7	265	5	Kelting 1954, Penfound 1964
	Urbana, Illinois	USA	940	11.6	373	3	Old 1969
	San Jose	Costa Rica	1810	20.2	1387	1	Daubenmire 1972
	Miami, Florida	USA	1199	24.1	183	1	Porter 1967
	Sassandra	Ivory Coast	1404	25.6	711	3	Lamotte 1975
	Kumasi	Ghana	1500	25.5	870	1	Bourlière and Hadley 1970
	Mbarara	Dem. Rep. Congo	880	20.6	1112	2	Bourlère and Hadley 1970

[1] US/IBP Grassland Biome data bank.

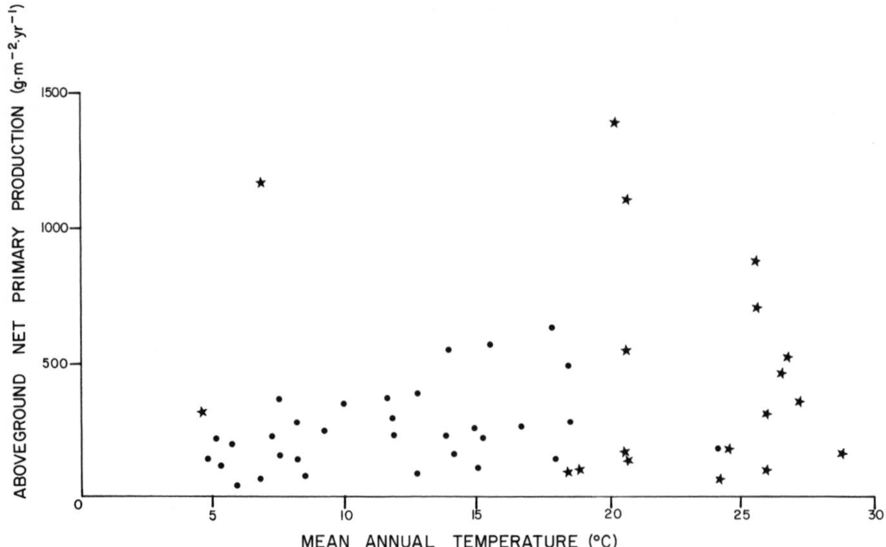

Figure 1.5. Relationship between aboveground net primary production and mean annual temperature for 52 grassland sites. North American grasslands are represented by dots, others by stars.

One should not expect a linear relationship between production and precipitation over a wide range of precipitation values. At some point production would reach an asymptote, indicating precipitation in excess of the amount which current vegetation can utilize. At this point these sites would be vulnerable to invasion by forest.

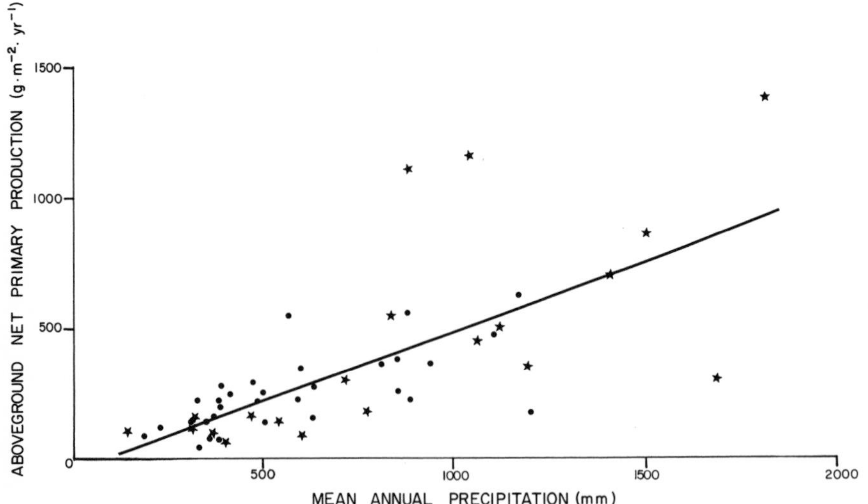

Figure 1.6. Relationship between aboveground net primary production and mean annual precipitation for 52 grassland sites. North American grasslands are represented by dots, others by stars. ANP = 0.5(annual precipitation)−29: r^2 = 0.51.

Method of Analysis

To facilitate comparison of grassland sites occurring over a wide range of climatic conditions, a method combining similar sites into groups was required. The method chosen used a climatic diagram for each of the 52 grassland sites as the basic unit of comparison (Walter 1973). An example of a climatic diagram is presented in Figure 1.7. The desirable qualities of climatic diagrams for a macroclimatic analysis are derived from the scales chosen to graph temperature and precipitation, and the interpretations of the diagrams from Walter's practical experience. Information utilized in the analysis included the humid, drought, and moderate drought periods. This information was quantified by dividing the area of each diagram into 20 equal parts and estimating the proportions of the humid and drought periods within each division. Each unit was assigned coordinates, and a vector of period types was established for each site. A similarity matrix of correlation coefficients was then constructed and site grouping was accomplished with a hierarchical clustering algorithm (Johnson 1967).

Both climatic diagrams and cluster analysis have been used by other authors to classify climates (DiCastri 1973, Walter et al 1975, Russell and Moore 1976). French (in press) used climatic diagrams to group North American grassland sites according to amount and distribution of precipitation, and showed that

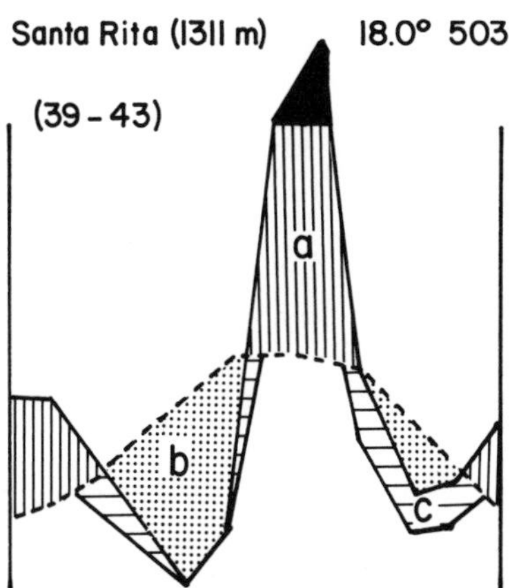

Figure 1.7. Example of a climatic diagram (Santa Rita, Arizona, USA). The top line of the diagram consists of the station location, mean elevation above sea level (m), mean annual temperature (°C), and mean annual precipitation (mm). Numbers in parentheses below the station location indicate the number of years of observations that the means are based upon (temperature-precipitation). The abscissa is a linear scale of months (January–December in northern hemisphere and July–June in southern hemisphere) and the ordinate is a dual scale of temperature and precipitation. Mean monthly temperature (°C, dashed line) and mean monthly precipitation (mm, solid line) are graphed at a ratio of 1°: 2 mm. Vertical shaded area (a) represents a humid period defined by precipitation > temperature at the 2:1 scale. The stippled area (b) is a drought period defined by temperature > precipitation at the 2:1 scale. The area shaded by horizontal dashes (c) represents a moderate drought period defined by graphing precipitation and temperature at a 1°: 3 mm ratio. The solid area plots precipitation on a scale reduced by a factor of 100.

incoming solar radiation at the sites showed an approximately inverse relation to precipitation. DiCastri used climatic diagrams to compare the mediterranean climates of Chile and western North America. His analysis involved quantifying the duration and area of the humid and drought periods. Admitting to the arbitrary nature of this method, he concluded that it facilitated comparisons in a meaningful way. Walter et al. employed climatic diagrams to classify the climates of the earth into nine ecological zones. Russell and Moore used a hierarchical clustering scheme to classify climates of 300 stations from Africa and Australia. They concluded that cluster analysis shows promise as a method for climatic classification. Although the intentions in this chapter are not to classify climates per se, it is useful to group objectively macroclimatically similar grassland sites.

Results

Site Grouping

The cluster analysis of macroclimatic characteristics resulted in defining six major groups of sites. Negative correlation was the criterion used to distinguish between groups. Thus, sites within a group are positively correlated with sites in the same group and negatively correlated with sites in other groups.

Group 1 consists of three dry sites, two from North America and one from Africa (Figure 1.8, Table 1.1). Using Köppen's criterion (in Riley and Spolton 1974), two are *arid* (Las Cruces and Garies) and the other is *semiarid*. According to Trewartha's (1968) classification, they fall within the *tropical arid* (Garies), *subtropical arid* (Las Cruces), and *temperate semiarid* (Richland) categories. The important factors determining thier grouping by cluster analysis are low precipitation and prolonged duration of drought conditions.

The Group 2 sites include 12 semiarid sites from the Great Plains of North American (Figure 1.8, Table 1.1). Under Trewartha's scheme, these sites would be classified as *temperate semiarid*. Their grouping is the result of low temperature, relatively low precipitation, a single peak in precipitation during the early summer, and severe to moderate drought conditions following the peak precipitation.

The sites within Group 3 are from three continents and, according to Köppen's aridity criterion, include arid, semiarid, and subhumid types (Figure 1.8, Table 1.1). The important feature for grouping is a single peak in precipitation occurring during the warmest months of the year, preceded and followed by a period of severe drought. Trewartha classified these areas as *tropical* and *subtropical semiarid*.

Group 4 sites have *mediterranean* or *subtropical summer dry* climates. Aridity index values place them in subhumid to humid categories. The distinguishing characteristics for their grouping by cluster analysis are winter concentration of precipitation and summer drought.

The sites comprising Group 5 are from tropical latitudes where mean monthly temperatures are essentially constant. Because of precipitation periodicity they

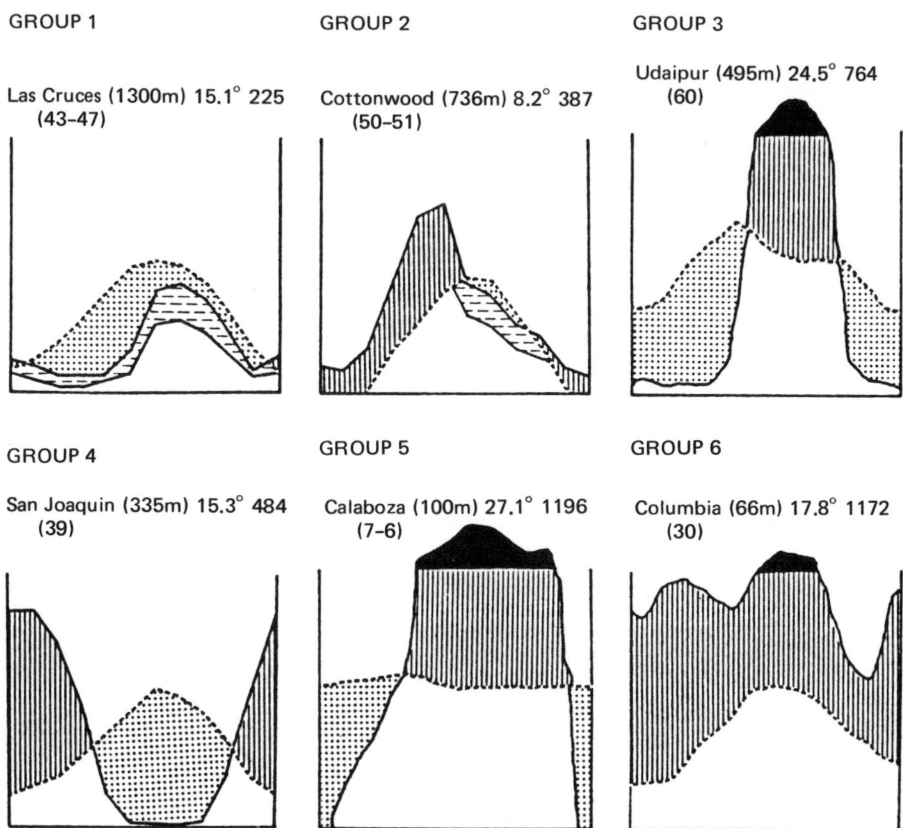

Figure 1.8. Example climatic diagrams from each of the six groups of grasslands distinguished by hierarchical cluster analysis.

Representative sites are: Group 1-Las Cruces, New Mexico, USA; Group 2-Cottonwood, South Dakota, USA; Group 3-Udaipur, Rajasthan, India; Group 4-San Joaquin, California, USA; Group 5-Calabozo, Guanico, Venezuela, Group 6-Columbia, Missouri, USA.

are *tropical wet-dry* climatic types. The important features for grouping here are the constancy of temperature, and the pattern and amount of precipitation.

Group 6 includes a range from *semiarid* to *humid* and *tropical wet-dry, subtropical humid,* and *temperate continental* climatic types. The distinguishing characteristic for their grouping by cluster analysis is almost complete absence of drought.

Aboveground Net Primary Production

For discussion and comparison of production at the sites, site groups determined by cluster analysis were plotted on a precipitation and temperature plane (Figures 1.9–1.14). This tends to emphasize the importance of the magnitude of both precipitation and temperature in determining both grouping by cluster analysis

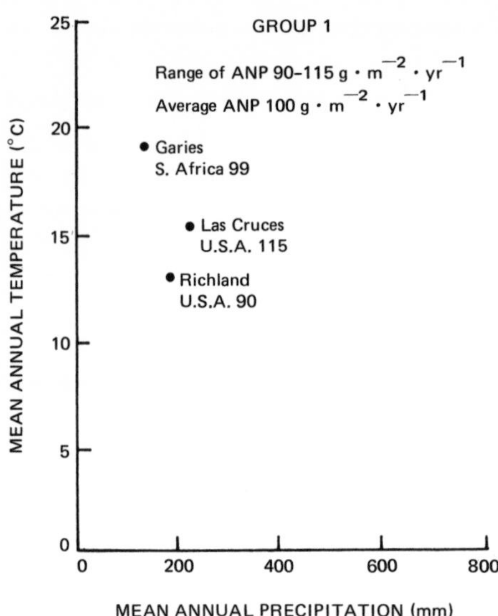

Figure 1.9. Position of Group 1 grassland sites on a precipitation and temperature plane. Numbers following site locations are net aboveground primary production estimates (g · m^{-2} · yr^{-1}).

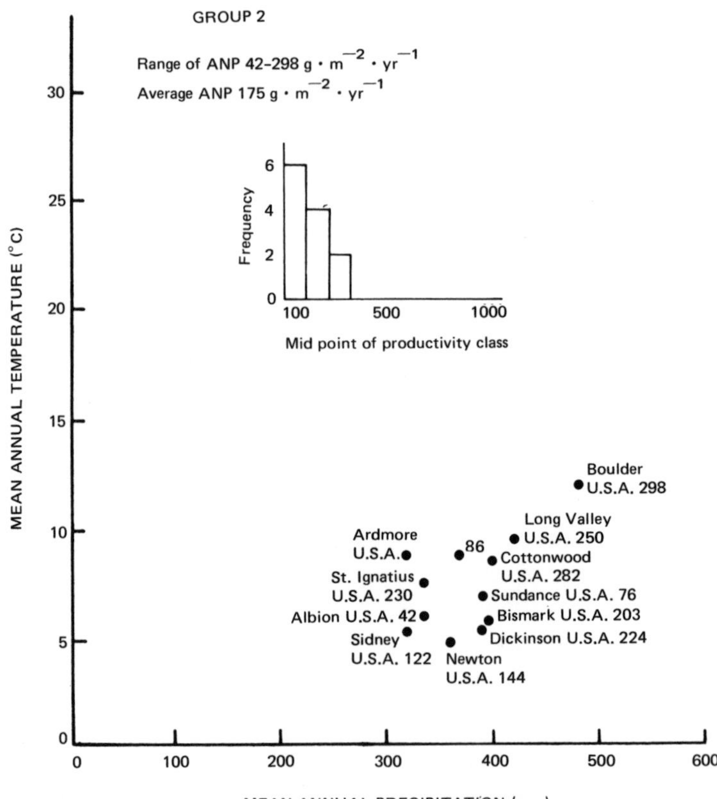

Figure 1.10. Position of Group 2 grassland sites on a precipitation and temperature plane. Numbers following site locations are net aboveground primary production estimates (g · m^{-2} · yr^{-1}).

Inset indicates the distribution of production among 100 g · m^{-2} · yr^{-1} classes.

and production in the case of the drier and warmer sites, and the diminished importance of these two variables at the wetter sites.

The extremely dry Group 1 sites may be considered grasslands occurring within an area of predominantly desert vegetation, or grasslands including a significant desert shrub component. Of the two North American sites included in this group, one is of each type. Average production at these sites is 100 g · m^{-2} with a range of 90–115. Bazilevich et al (1971) indicate comparable categories for dry steppe and steppe-like desert with average production of 250 g · m^{-2}.

Group 2 grassland sites are exclusively from midcontinental North America. They have a semiarid climate with average annual aboveground production of 175 g · m^{-2}. If data were available from the steppes of central Asia one would expect them to fall within this group. Bazilevich et al (1971) classified these as subboreal, semiarid grasslands with average production of 290 g · m^{-2} with a range of 25–450.

Grasslands within Group 3 include only a single site from North America: Santa Rita, Arizona. The remaining sites are from tropical and subtropical semiarid regions of Africa and India. At least one, Allahabad, is a successional

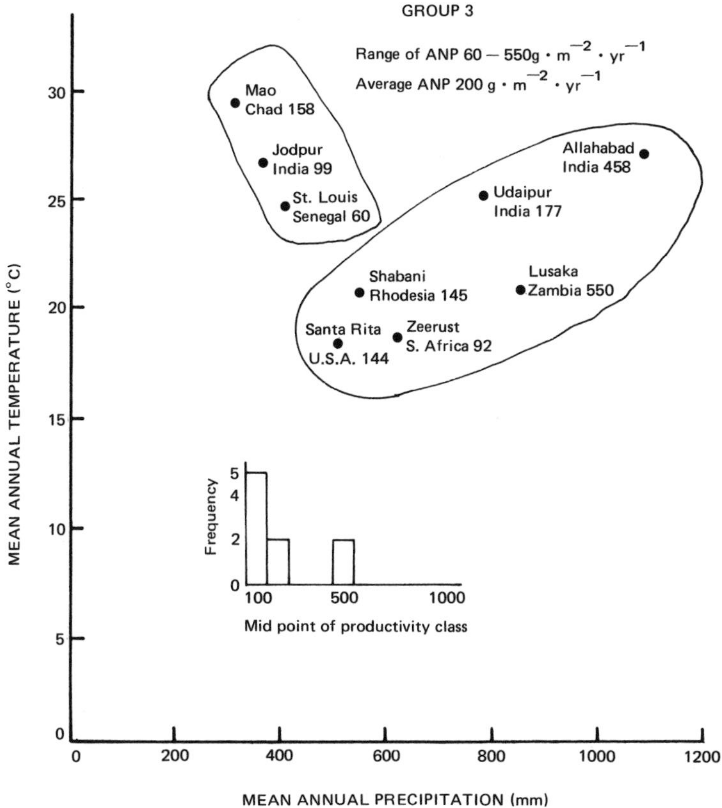

Figure 1.11. Position of Group 3 grassland sites on a precipitation and temperature plane. Numbers following site locations are net aboveground primary production estimates (g · m^{-2} · yr^{-1}).

grassland maintained by mowing and grazing. Within this group, two subgroups were identified. The first includes three sites with very high mean annual temperatures and low precipitation; average production for these sites is 100 g $\cdot$ m^{-2}. The cooler or wetter subgroup has an average production of 250 g $\cdot$ m^{-2}. Average production for the entire group is 200 g $\cdot$ m^{-2}. Bazilevich et al estimated production of this category of sites to be 350 g $\cdot$ m^{-2}.

Group 4 grasslands include four sites from the inland valleys of California and one site from northern Israel. All sites are dominated by a mixture of annual species. Average production is 260 g $\cdot$ m^{-2} with a range of 160–550. Bazilevich et al. estimated production of these grasslands at 290 g $\cdot$ m^{-2}.

The sites included in Group 5 are from South America and Africa. North American grasslands are not included here because of the lack of analogous climates. The average production of these sites is 425 g $\cdot$ m^{-2} with a range of 306–520. The Bazilevich et al. estimate of production for this group is 450 g $\cdot$ m^{-2} with a range of 250–575.

Group 6 includes the most productive grasslands and also the widest range of climates and production estimates. The single unifying characteristic of these sites is lack of a significant drought period at any time during the year. Average

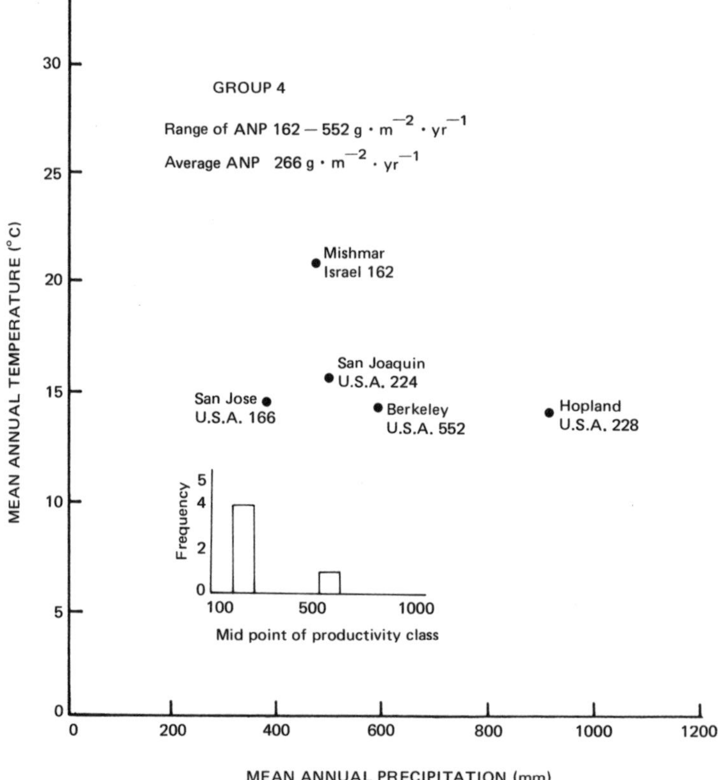

Figure 1.12. Position of Group 4 grassland sites on a precipitation and temperature plane. Numbers following site locations are net aboveground primary production estimates (g $\cdot$ m^{-2} $\cdot$ yr^{-1}).

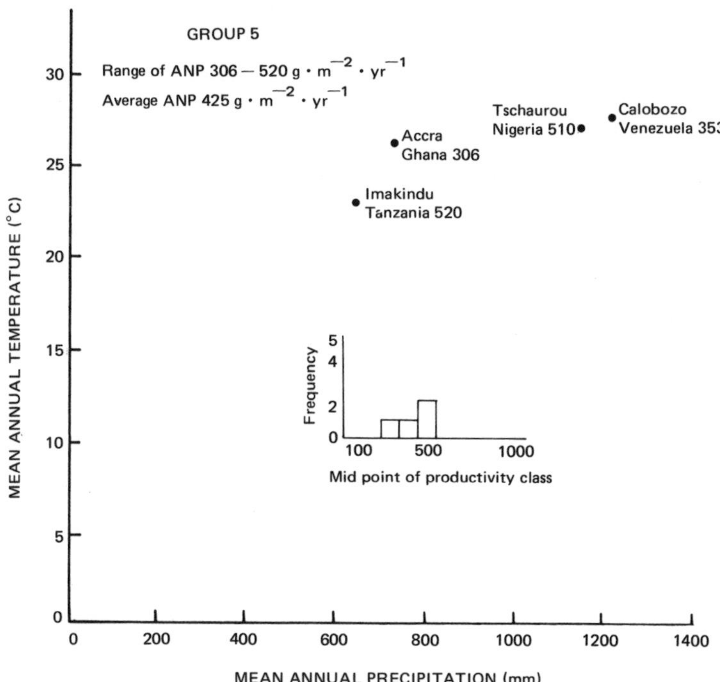

Figure 1.13. Position of Group 5 grassland sites on a precipitation and temperature plane. Numbers following site locations are net aboveground primary production estimates (g · m^{-2} · yr^{-1}).

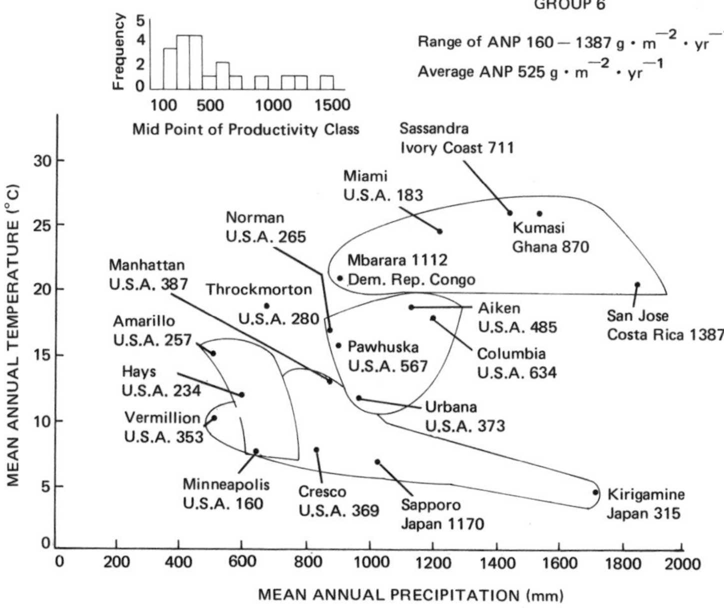

Figure 1.14. Position of Group 6 grassland sites on a precipitation and temperature plane. Numbers following site locations are net aboveground primary production estimates (g · m^{-2} · yr^{-1}).

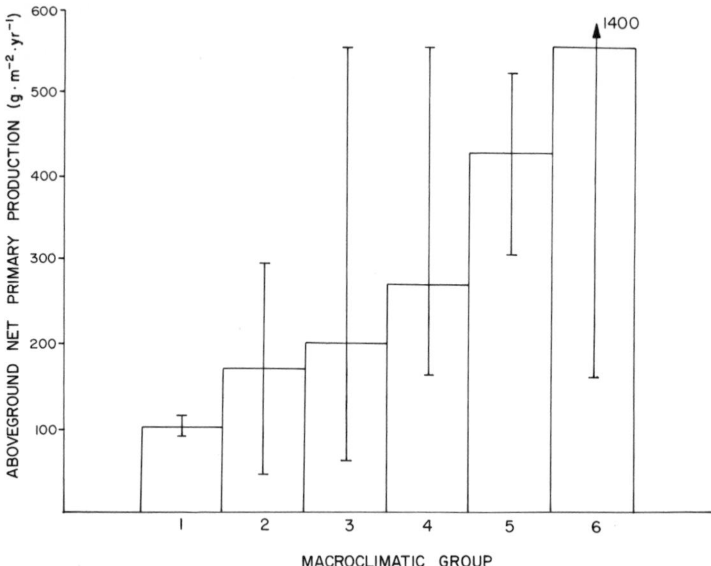

Figure 1.15. Net aboveground primary production of grasslands as a function of macroclimatic group.

production is 525 g · m^{-2} with a range of 160–1387. Four subgroups can be identified among these sites. The first subgroup consists of five warm humid sites from tropical areas, including a single North American site, a subtropical prairie near Miami, Florida. The second subgroup includes tallgrass prairie sites from North America and two bamboo grasslands from mountainous areas in Japan. The final subgroup includes a shortgrass prairie from west Texas, a mixed prairie from central Kansas, a successional tallgrass prairie from Minnesota. A single site from Texas which falls outside the subgroupings is also included in Group 6.

Figure 1.15 summarizes the relationship between aboveground net primary production and macroclimatic groupings. Bars indicate average production of each group while vertical lines indicate the range of values. The upper limit of the range for Group 6 is actually 1400 g · m^{-2}. If one accepts that the climates represented by the various groups are different, the gradient across groups can be interpreted as real and the range of values then provides emphasis for the importance of site specific factors in determining the production at any specific site. If sufficient data were available, one would expect the range of values within each group to increase across this gradient since it generally represents sites from arid to humid conditions.

North American Grasslands in Perspective

How do North American grasslands compare to grasslands of the world? First, we must establish general production relationships for North American grasslands. This task is greatly facilitated by the general grassland classification accepted for North America, and by recent intensive investigations of grasslands under the US/IBP Grassland Biome Program, the results of which are summarized in Chapters 3 and 4.

Table 1.2 presents average aboveground net primary production estimates for the six major North American grassland types; two production estimates are presented for each. The first is based upon the 32 North American sites used in earlier sections of this chapter. The second draws upon results from the Grassland Biome Program. In both cases, production estimates have been rounded to the nearest 100 g · m^{-2}. The major differences stemming from the IBP efforts relate to increased estimates of production for three of the seven grassland types which resulted from more refined methods of measurement. Previous to the IBP research effort, production estimates were largely based upon a single harvest at the end of the growing season. IBP research emphasized seasonal dynamics of dry-matter production and assessed the contribution of individual species or functional groups to annual production. This resulted in increasing the production estimate of the annual grassland from 300 to 400 g · m^{-2} · yr^{-1}, of the mixed prairie from 200 to 300 g · m^{-2} · yr^{-1}, and of the tallgrass prairie from 400 to 500 g · m^{-2} · yr^{-1}. The ranges associated with these averages are perhaps ± 50%.

When it is assumed that these averages are of comparable reliability to those of Bazilevich et al (1971), they can be used to compare North American grassland production to production of grasslands on a worldwide scale (Table 1.3). Estimates derived from either data set for North America indicate that the North American grasslands are among the lower production classes. IBP data indicate that 40% of North American grassland area has average production of 200 g · m^{-2} · yr^{-1} or less and 75% of the area is within or below the 300 g · m^{-2} yr^{-1} class. By comparison, only 36% of the grassland area on a worldwide scale falls into or below the 300 g · m^{-2} · yr^{-1} class. The IBP data set indicates a lack of sites in the 600 g · m^{-2} · yr^{-1} class and the aggregate North American data indicate a lack of sites in the 500 and 600 g · m^{-2} · yr^{-1} classes. Regardless of which interpretation is accepted, in comparison to grasslands on a worldwide

Table 1.2. Production of North American Grassland Types

Grassland type	Area[1] 10⁴ km²	Area[1] %	Aboveground net production (g · m^{-2} · yr^{-1}) All data	Aboveground net production (g · m^{-2} · yr^{-1}) US/IBP
Annual	9.7	3	300	400
Shortgrass	27.9	7	200	200
Mixed	142.7	38	200	300
Tallgrass	84.3	23	400	500
Shrub steppe	59.3	16	100	100
Desert	50.1	13	100	100
	374.0	100		

[1] Estimates taken from Van Dyne et al (in press) and Coupland (1961).

Table 1.3. Distribution by Production Classes of North American Grasslands and World Grasslands

Production class	North America (% area)		World (% area)
($g \cdot m^{-2} \cdot yr^{-1}$)	US/IBP	All data	Bazilevich et al (1971)
<150	29	29	15
150-250	7	45	6
250-350	38	3	15
350-450	3	23	36
450-550	23	0	7
550-650	–	0	20

basis, North American grasslands are poorly represented in the higher production classes.

What percentage of global grassland production is contributed by North American grasslands? Utilizing the data from Tables 1.2 and 1.3, it appears that total aboveground production of North American grasslands is 9.14×10^8 tons $\cdot$ yr^{-1}. Estimates of global aboveground net production of grasslands from Bazilevich et al and Whittaker and Likens are 1.03×10^{10} tons $\cdot$ yr^{-1} and 6.8×10^9 tons $\cdot$ yr^{-1}. The difference between these two estimates is partially explained by differences in estimates of the total area covered by grasslands—3.23×10^7 km^2 for the Bazilevich study and 2.4×10^7 km^2 for Whittaker and Likens—and partially by the estimates of production employed. Bazilevich et al indicate a global average aboveground net production of 320 g $\cdot$ m^{-2} while Whittaker and Likens' data average 280 g $\cdot$ m^{-2}. Since the estimation of regional production is a tenuous endeavor and the differences obtained relatively small, it is assumed here that the two estimates of global grassland production define a range within which the true value lies. Thus, North American grasslands comprise between 12 and 16% of the total grassland area of the world, and they contribute between 9 and 16% of the total grassland aboveground net primary production of the world.

Summary

The primary production of 52 grassland sites is compared, and sites are grouped according to proportional distribution of humid and drought conditions. Precipitation and temperature are important determinants of the average annual production of grasslands, but increasing variations among sites within groups toward the mesic end of the spectrum indicates the relatively greater importance of other factors characteristic of these sites when released from the constraints of aridity. Increased estimates of average annual production for North American grasslands have resulted from studies under the International Biological Program. These values range from approximately 100 to approximately 500 g $\cdot$ m^{-2} $\cdot$ yr^{-1}, whereas values for other grasslands range up to 1400 g $\cdot$ m^{-2} $\cdot$ yr^{-1}. North American grasslands are among the lower production classes. Total aboveground production of North American grasslands is estimated to be 9.14×10^8 tons · yr^{-1}. This is 9 to 16% of the world grassland primary production.

References

Ambasht, R. S., A. N. Maurya, and U. N. Singh. 1972. Primary production and turnover in certain protected grasslands of Varanasi, India. *In* P. M. Golley and F. B. Golley (eds.), *Symposium on Tropical Ecology with Emphasis on Organic Productivity,* pp. 43–50. Athens: Univ. of Georgia Institute of Ecology.

Bazilevich, N. I., L. Y. Rodin, and N. N. Rozov. 1971. Geographical aspects of biological productivity. *Soviet Geogr. Rev. Trans.* **12**:293–317.

Beebe, J. D. and G. R. Hoffman. 1968. Effects of grazing on vegetation and soils in southeastern South Dakota. *Am. Midl. Nat.* **80**:96–110.

Black, A. L. 1968. Nitrogen and phosphorus fertilization for production of crested wheatgrass and native grass in northeastern Montana. *Agron. J.* **60**:213–216.

Bourlière, F. and M. Hadley. 1970. The ecology of tropical savannas. *Annu. Rev. Ecol. Syst.* **1**:25–52.

Branson, F. A. 1956. Range forage production changes on a water spreader in southeastern Montana. *J. Range Manag.* **9**:187–191.

Bray, J. R., D. B. Lawrence, and L. C. Pearson. 1959. Primary production in some Minnesota terrestrial communities for 1957. *Oikos* **10**:38–49.

Brockington, N. R. 1960. Studies of the growth of a *Hyparrhenia* dominant grassland in northern Rhodesia. I. Growth and reaction to cutting. *Br. Grassl. Soc. J.* **15**:323–338.

Bunt, J. S. 1975. Primary productivity of marine ecosystems. *In* H. Lieth and R. H. Whittaker (eds.), *Primary Productivity of the Biosphere,* Ecological Studies, 14 pp. 169–183. New York: Springer-Verlag.

Caldwell, M. M. 1975. Primary production of grazing lands. *In* J. P. Cooper (ed.), *Photosynthesis and Productivity in Different Environments,* IBP Vol. 3 pp. 41–73. New York: Cambridge University Press.

Choudhary, V. B. 1972. Seasonal variation in standing crop and net aboveground production in *Dichanthium annulatum* grassland at Varanasi. *In* P. M. Golley and F. B. Golley (eds.) *Symposium on Tropical Ecology with Emphasis on Organic Productivity,* pp. 51–57. Athens: Univ. of Georgia Institute of Ecology.

Cooper, J. P. (ed.). 1975. *Photosynthesis and Productivity in Different Environments,* IBP Vol. 3. New York: Cambridge Univ. Press.

Cosper, H. R. and J. R. Thomas. 1961. Influence of supplemental runoff water and fertilizer on production and chemical composition of native forage. *J. Range Manage.* **14**:292–297.

Cosper, H. R., J. R. Thomas, and A. L. Alsayegh. 1967. Fertilization and effects on range improvement in the northern Great Plains. *J. Range Manage.* **20**:216–222.

Coupland, R. T. 1961. A reconsideration of grassland classification in the northern Great Plains of North America. *J. Ecol.* **49**:135–167.

Daubenmire, R. 1972. Standing crops and primary production in savanna derived from semi-deciduous forest in Costa Rica. *Bot. Gaz.* **133**:395–401.

DiCastri, F. 1973. Climatographic comparisons between Chile and the west coast of North America. *In* F. DiCastri and H. A. Mooney (eds.), *Mediterranean-type Ecosystems,* pp. 21–36. New York: Springer-Verlag.

Duncan, D. and R. G. Woodmansee. 1975. Forecasting forage yield from precipitation in California's annual rangeland. *J. Range Manag.* **28**:327–329.

Ehrenreich, J. H. and J. M. Aikman. 1963. An ecological study of the effect of certain management practices on native prairie in Iowa. *Ecology* **33**:113–130.

Freeman, B. N. and R. R. Humphrey. 1956. The effects of nitrates and phosphates upon forage production of a southern Arizona desert grassland range. *J. Range Manag.* **9**:176–181.

French, N. R. In Press. Introduction. *In* R. T. Coupland (ed.), *Grassland Ecosystems of the World,* pp. 41–48. New York: Cambridge Univ. Press.
Goetz, H. 1969. Composition and yield of native grasslands fertilized with different rates of nitrogen. *J. Range Manag.* **22**:384–390.
Golley, F. B. and J. B. Gentry. 1965. A comparison of variety and standing crop of vegetation on a 1-year and 12-year abandoned field. *Oikos* **15**:185–199.
Gupta, R. K., S. K. Saxena, and S. K. Sharm. 1972. Aboveground productivity of grasslands at Jodhpur, India. *In* P. M. Golley and F. B. Golley (eds.), *Symposium on Tropical Ecology with Emphasis on Organic Productivity,* pp. 75–93. Athens: Univ. of Georgia Institute of Ecology.
Hammond, Inc. 1971. *Hammond Medallion World Atlas.* Maplewood, New Jersey: Hammond, Inc.
Heady, H. F. 1965. The influence of mulch on herbage production in an annual grassland. *In* Proc. 9th International Grassland Congress, pp. 391–94. Sao Paulo, Brazil:
Hervey, D. F. 1949. Reaction of a California annual plant community to fire. *J. Range Manag.* **2**:116–121.
Hulett, G. K. and G. W. Tomanek. 1969. Forage production on a clay upland range site in western Kansas. *J. Range Manag.* **22**:270–276.
Hulett, G. K. and G. W. Tomanek. 1974. Productivity in a Kansas mixed prairie grassland. *In* Proc. 12th International Grassland Congress, Vol. **1**:725–733. Moscow.
Iwaki, H., B. Midorikawa, and K. Hogetsu. 1964. Studies on the productivity and nutrient element circulation in Kirigamine grasslands, central Japan. II. Seasonal change in standing crop. *Bot. Mag.* (Tokyo) **77**:447–457.
Johnson, S. C. 1967. Hierarchial clustering schemes. *Psychrometrica* **32**:241–254.
Jones, M. B. and R. A. Evans. 1960. Botanical composition changes in annual grassland as affected by fertilization and grazing. *Agron. J.* **52**:459–461.
Kelting, R. W. 1954. Effects of moderate grazing on the composition and plant production of a native tallgrass prairie in central Oklahoma. *Ecology* **35**:200–207.
Kira, T. 1975. Primary production of forests. *In* J. P. Cooper (ed.), *Photosynthesis and Productivity in Different Environments.* IBP Vol. 3, pp. 5–40. New York: Cambridge Univ. Press.
Koelling, M. R. and C. L. Kucera. 1965. Productivity and turnover relationships in native tallgrass prairie. *Iowa St. J. Sci.* **39**:387–392.
Kucera, C. L., R. C. Dahlman, and M. R. Koelling. 1967. Total net productivity and turnover on an energy basis for tallgrass prairie. *Ecology* **48**:536–541.
Lamotte, M. 1975. The structure and function of a tropical savannah ecosystem. *In* F. B. Golley and E. Medina (eds.), *Tropical Ecological Systems: Trends in Terrestrial and Aquatic Research,* pp. 179–222. New York: Springer-Verlag.
Lansbury, T. J., R. R. Innes, and G. L. Mabey. 1965. Studies on Ghana grasslands: Yield and composition on the Accra plains. *Trop. Agric.* **42**:1–18.
Larson, F. and W. Whitman. 1942. A comparison of used and unused grassland mesas in the Badlands of South Dakota. *Ecology* **23**:438–445.
Lauenroth, W. K., and W. C. Whitman. 1977. Dynamics of dry matter production in a mixed-grass prairie in western North Dakota. *Oecologia* **27**:339–351.
Lieth, H. 1973. Primary production; Terrestrial ecosystems. *Human Ecol.* **1**:303–332.
Lieth, H. 1975. Modeling the primary productivity of the world. *In* H. Lieth and R. H. Whittaker (eds.), *Primary Productivity of the Biosphere,* Ecological Studies, 14, pp. 237–63. New York: Springer-Verlag.
Lieth, H. and R. H. Whittaker (eds.). 1975. *Primary Productivity of the Biosphere,* Ecological Studies, 14. New York: Springer-Verlag.
Likens, G. E. 1975. Primary productivity of inland aquatic ecosystems. *In* H. Lieth and R. H. Whittaker (eds.), *Primary Productivity of the Biosphere.* Ecological Studies, 14, pp. 185–202. New York: Springer-Verlag.
Lorenz, R. J. and G. A. Rogler. 1972. Forage production and botanical composition of mixed prairie as influenced by nitrogen and phosphorus fertilization. *Agron. J.* **64**:244–249.

Mathis, G. W., M. M. Kothmann, and W. J. Waldrip. 1971. Influence of rootplowing and seeding on composition and forage production of native grasses. *J. Range Manag.* **24**:43–47.

McNaughton, S. J. 1968. Structure and function in California grasslands. *Ecology* **49**:962–972.

Moir, W. H. 1969. Steppe communities in the foothills of the Colorado front range and their relative productivities. *Am. Midl. Nat.* **81**:331–340.

Murphy, A. H. 1970. Predicted forage yield based on fall precipitation in California annual grassland. *J. Range Manag.* **23**:363–365.

Numata, M. 1961. Ecology of grasslands in Japan. *J. Coll. Arts. Sci.,* (Chiba) **3**:327–342.

Ofer, Y. and N. G. Seligman. 1969. Fertilization of annual range in northern Israel. *J. Range Manag.* **22**:337–341.

Old, S. M. 1969. Microclimate, fire and plant production in an Illinois prairie. *Ecol. Monogr.* **39**:355–384.

Oshima, Y. 1961. Ecological studies of sasa communities. II. Seasonal variations of productive structure and annual net production in sasa communities. *Bot. Mag.* (Tokyo) **74**:280–290.

Owensby, C. E. and K. L. Anderson. 1967. Yield response to time of burning in the Kansas flint hills. *J. Range Manag.* **20**:12–16.

Penfound, W. T. 1964. Effects of denudation on the productivity of grasslands. *Ecology* **45**:838–845.

Porter, C. L., Jr. 1967. Composition and productivity of a subtropical prairie. *Ecology* **48**:937–942.

Ratliff, R. D. and H. E. Heady. 1962. Seasonal changes in herbage weight in an annual grass community. *J. Range Manag.* **15**:146–149.

Redmann, R. E. 1975. Production ecology of grassland plant communities in North Dakota. *Ecol. Monogr.* **45**:83–106.

Riley, D. and L. Spolton. 1974. World Weather and Climate. New York: Cambridge Univ. Press.

Rodin, L. E., N. I. Bazilevich, and N. N. Rozov. 1975. Productivity of the world's main ecosystems. *In* D. E. Reichle, J. F. Franklin, and D. W. Goodall (eds.), *Productivity of World Ecosystems,* pp. 13–26. Washington, D.C.: Natl. Acad. Sci.

Rogler, G. A. and R. J. Lorenz. 1957. Nitrogen fertilization of northern Great Plains rangelands. *J. Range Manag.* **10**:156–160.

Russell, J. S. and A. W. Moore. 1976. Classification of climate by pattern analysis with Australian and southern African data as an example. *Agric. Meteorol.* **16**:45–70.

San Jose, J. J. and E. Medina. 1975. Effects of fire on organic matter production and water balance in a tropical savanna. *In* F. B. Golley and E. Medina (eds.), *Tropical Ecological Systems: Trends in Terrestrial and Aquatic Research,* pp. 251–64. New York: Springer-Verlag.

Shantz, H. L. 1954. The place of grasslands in the earth's cover of vegetation. *Ecology* **35**:142–145.

Shrimal, R. L. and L. N. Vyas. 1975. Net primary production in grasslands at Udaipur, India. *In* F. B. Golley and E. Medina (eds.), *Tropical Ecological Systems: Trends in Terrestrial and Aquatic Research,* pp. 265–71. New York: Springer-Verlag.

Singh, J. S. 1968. Net aboveground community productivity in the grasslands of Varansi. *In* P. M. Golley and F. B. Golley (eds.), *Symposium on Recent Advancements of Tropical Ecology,* pp. 631–54. Varanasi, India: ISTE.

Trewartha, G. 1968. *An Introduction to Climate.* New York: McGraw-Hill Book Co., Inc.

Van Dyne, G. M., F. M. Smith, R. L. Czaplewski, and R. G. Woodmansee. In Press. Analysis and synthesis of grassland ecosystem dynamics. *BioEcos.*

Vyas, L. N., R. K. Garg, and S. K. Agarwal. 1972. Aboveground production in the monsoon vegetation at Udaipar. *In* P. M. Golley and F. B. Golley (eds.), *Symposium on Tropical Ecology with Emphasis on Organic Productivity,* pp. 95–99. Athens: Univ. of Georgia Institute of Ecology.

Walter, H. 1973. *Vegetation of the Earth in Relation to Climate and Ecophysiological Conditions*. New York: Springer-Verlag.

Walter, H., E. Harnickell, and D. Mueller-Dombois. 1975. *Climate-Diagram Maps of the Individual Continents and the Ecological Climatic Regions of the Earth*. New York: Springer-Verlag.

Westlake, D. F. 1963. Comparisons of plant productivity. *Biol. Rev.* **38**:385–425.

Whittaker, R. H. and G. E. Likens. 1975. The biosphere and man. *In* H. Lieth and R. H. Whittaker (eds.), *Primary Productivity of the Biosphere*. Ecological Studies, 14, pp. 305–28. New York: Springer-Verlag.

Wielgolaski, F. E. 1975. Primary production of tundra. *In* J. P. Cooper (ed.), *Photosynthesis and Productivity in Different Environments*. IBP Vol. 3, pp. 75–106. New York: Cambridge University Press.

2. Processes Controlling Blue Grama Production on the Shortgrass Prairie

JAMES K. DETLING

Introduction

The dominant grass of the shortgrass prairie of North America is blue grama [*Bouteloua gracilis* (H.B.K.) Lag. ex Steud.], a warm-season perennial species with the C_4 photosynthetic pathway (Williams and Markley 1973). At the Pawnee site in north-central Colorado, C_4 grasses account for over 40% of the annual aboveground net primary production (ANP) of from 59–182 grams dry matter · m^{-2} · yr^{-1} (Table 2.1) and over 80% of the total grass production. Perennial cool-season or C_3 grasses, principally western wheatgrass *(Agropyron smithii)* and needle and thread grass *(Stipa comata)*, contribute only about 10% of ANP. Most of the remaining ANP is accounted for by the C_3 shrubs, fringed sage *(Artemisia frigida)* and snakeweed *(Gutierrezia sarothrae)*, which contribute approximately 40%, while forbs as a group generally constitute less than 10% of the ANP. While Chapters 3 and 4 deal with total herbage biomass or production at the Pawnee site, this chapter concentrates on primary production processes in blue grama grass because of its dominance.

As indicated by the climatic diagram in Chapter 1, the area is semiarid and characterized by warm summers and cold winters (Figure 2.1). Maximum summer daytime temperatures average between 25 and 30°C while the nights are relatively cool, averaging 10 to 13°C. Approximately 75% of the 310 mm average annual precipitation at the Pawnee site occurs from May through September, primarily as irregularly spaced thunder showers (Jameson 1969). Between these periodic rainfall events, soil water potential in the upper 20 cm frequently declines to −50 bars or less (Van Haveren 1973, Ares 1976, Brown and Trlica 1977a) for extended periods of time. Consequently, soil water availability is considered the principal determinant of shortgrass prairie productivity (Lauenroth and Sims 1976).

Although functional roots have been observed to depths of 60 cm or more, approximately 85% of the functional root biomass is concentrated in the upper 20 cm (Singh and Coleman 1974, Clark 1977). Depending upon precipitation intensity and frequency, soil water reserves at this depth and below may not be

Table 2.1. Seasonal Aboveground Net Primary Production (g dry wt · m^{-2} yr^{-1}) Estimates and Percent Contribution to Total for Five Functional Groups on the Shortgrass Prairie at the Pawnee Site, 1970–1975

	Range	Average	Percent
Warm-season grasses	35–78	52	42
Cool-season grasses	5–19	11	9
Warm-season forbs	0–14	3	3
Cool-season forbs	3–16	6	4
Shrubs	9–81	51	42
Total production	59–182	123	100

Data from Dodd and Lauenroth, Chapter 3, this volume.

replenished during the growing season (Van Haveren 1973, Ares 1976). Consequently, during much of the growing season, soil water absorption probably occurs primarily from roots in the upper 10 to 20 cm of soil, and the availability of water in this layer ultimately controls many physiological processes such as photosynthesis, respiration, leaf growth, and translocation.

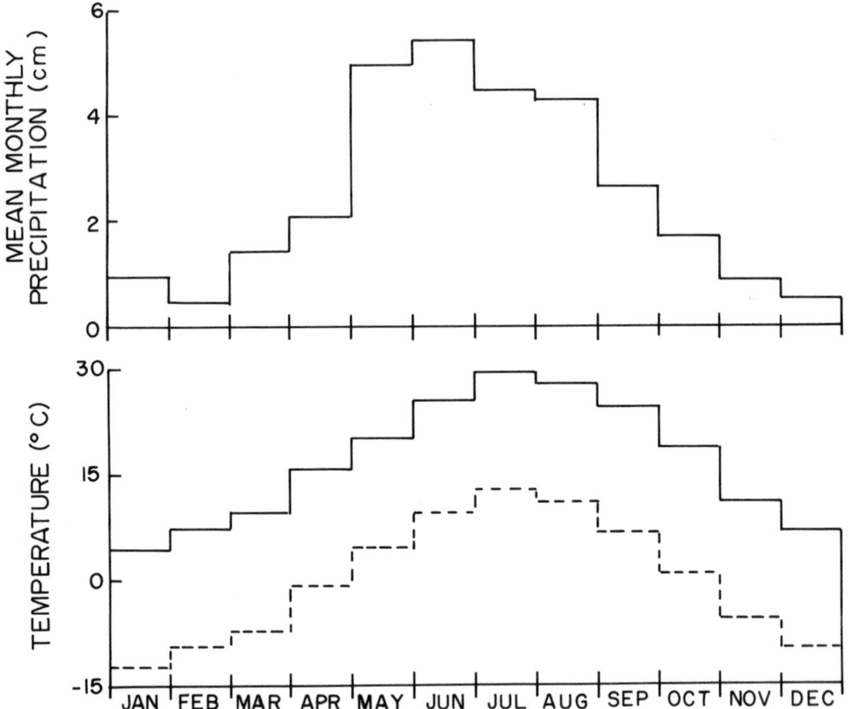

Figure 2.1. Mean monthly precipitation (cm) and mean daily maximum and minimum temperature (°C) at the Pawnee site (data from Jameson 1969).

Processes Controlling Primary Production

A major goal of the US/IBP Grassland Biome Program was the development of an ecosystem level model (ELM) to simulate the intraseasonal carbon, nitrogen, and water dynamics of grassland ecosystems (Innis 1978). Further development has resulted in a new primary producer submodel being constructed to better integrate available knowledge of primary production processes (Detling et al 1978). Since this model represents our current understanding of these processes, it will be used as a vehicle to summarize this information.

For modeling purposes, the plant has been divided into six compartments (Figure 2.2). The root system is divided into three layers (0–4 cm, 4–15 cm, and 15–60 cm), the boundries of which correspond to three of the soil water layers

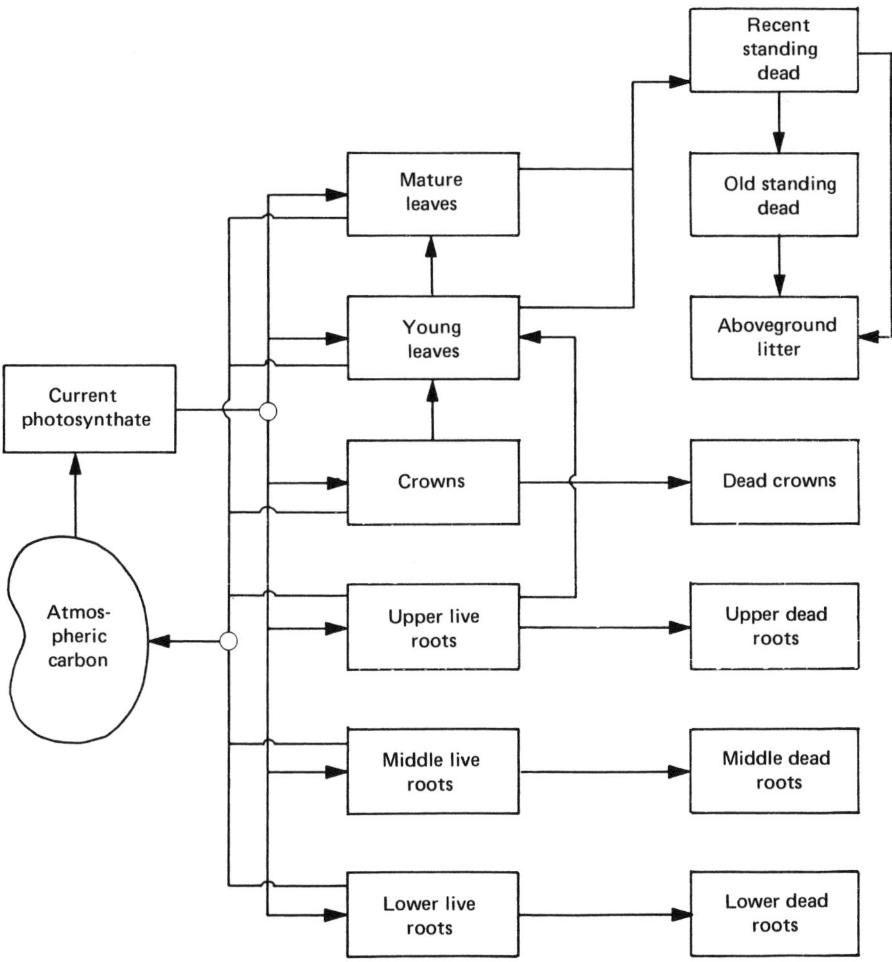

Figure 2.2. Carbon-flow diagram of the primary producer submodel.

simulated in the abiotic submodel of ELM (Parton 1978). Crowns comprise a fourth compartment. Because of differences in photosynthetic rates and source-sink strengths, young expanding leaves and mature fully expanded leaves are considered separately; these comprise the fifth and sixth compartments.

Spring Regrowth

Spring shoot growth of perennial grasses is supported by carbohydrate translocated from crowns and upper live roots to young leaves (Bokhari 1977). The date of initiation of spring regrowth in blue grama is probably determined by temperature (Stubbendieck and Burzlaff 1970). In the model, growth initiation does not occur if the ten-day moving average of soil temperature in the upper 15 cm is less than a critical minimum (10.5°C). Dates of initiation of regrowth calculated in this manner agree closely with observed phenological patterns on the shortgrass prairie (Dickinson and Dodd 1976). Growth of new roots occurs at about the same time as or slightly before resumption of shoot growth (Ares 1976).

Following release from winter dormancy, the rate of spring regrowth is controlled primarily by water availability. Leaf enlargement is commonly believed to be more sensitive to desiccation than most other physiological processes (Chu and McPherson 1977). Leaf water potentials 2 to 4 bars below those of well-watered plants often are sufficient to inhibit leaf growth by 50% (Boyer 1970, Ludlow and Ng 1976). Majerus (1975) correlated leaf growth of blue grama with soil water potential at four depths (5 to 35 cm). He found that while growth occurred when soil water potential at 5 cm (the driest soil layer) was −80 bars or drier, leaf growth ceased entirely when soil water potential at 35 cm (the wettest soil layer) was less than −8 bars. Air temperature is also important in determining rates of regrowth. Knievel and Schmer (1971) and Kemp (1977) have shown shoot production of blue grama is about twice as great at 35°C than at 20°C.

Photosynthesis, Respiration, and Carbon Allocation

Photosynthesis begins as young leaves are formed, and the rate increases to a maximum as the individual leaves approach full leaf expansion. Thereafter, photosynthesis rate declines steadily until senescence and death (Jewiss and Woledge 1967, Woledge and Jewiss 1969, Risser and Johnson 1973; Figure 2.3).

Carbon dioxide exchange rates of blue grama have been determined under a variety of environmental conditions in the laboratory (Williams 1974; Williams and Kemp, 1978; Kemp 1977; Brown and Trlica 1977a) and field (Brown and Trlica 1974, 1977b). While the response to environmental variables including light, water, and temperature was qualitatively similar in laboratory and field-grown plants, overall rates of net photosynthesis were considerably higher in the field (Brown and Trlica 1974, 1977b). Since this pattern has been reported for a number of other species (for example, Bazzaz 1973, Patterson et al 1977), the blue grama CO_2 exchange model (Detling et al 1978) was based on a reanalysis of Brown and Trlica's (1974) field data.

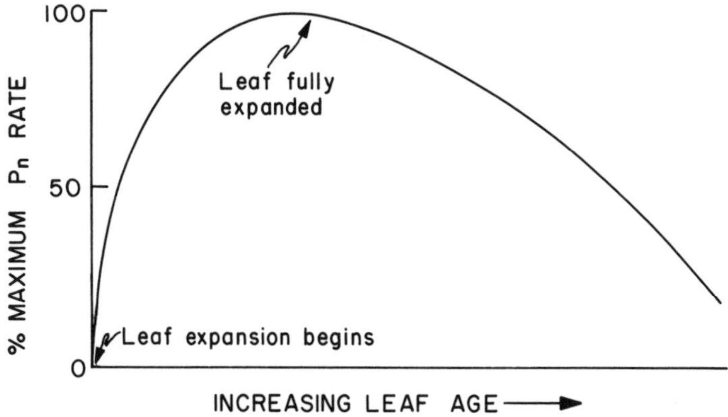

Figure 2.3. Generalized relationship between leaf age and net photosynthesis, P_n (based on Jewiss and Woledge 1967, Woledge and Jewiss 1969, Risser and Johnson 1973, and Catský et al 1976).

Blue grama is represented as having a light response curve (Figure 2.4) typical of C_4 species (Black 1973). The response curve does not exhibit light saturation at full sunlight and shows a high photosynthetic rate under optimal environmental conditions. Evidence exists (Detling et al 1978) that older plants do become light saturated at full sunlight, possibly as a result of reduced leaf chlorophyll content (Bokhari 1976). Williams and Kemp (1978) also found that light saturation

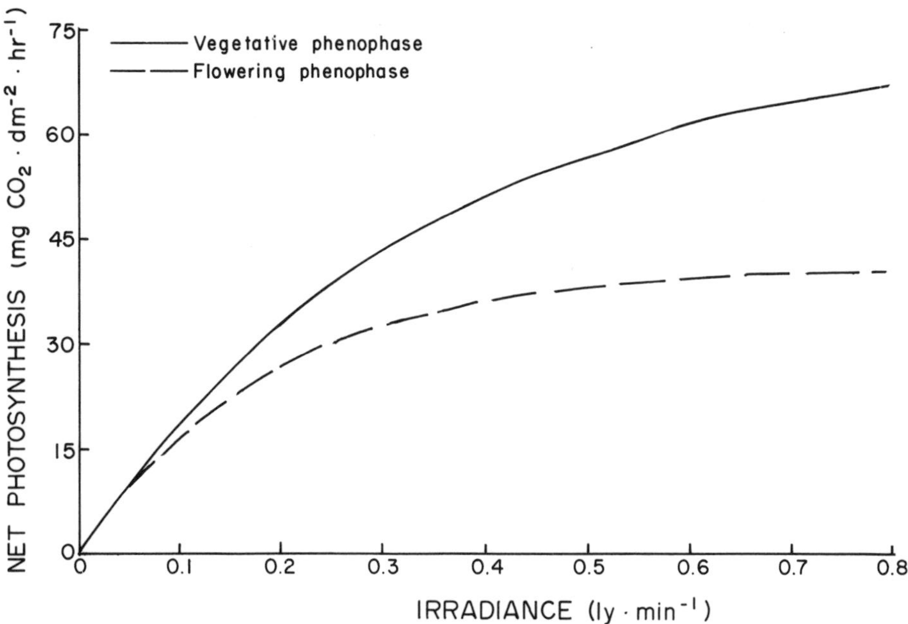

Figure 2.4. The effect of irradiance (400–700 nm) on net photosynthesis of *B. gracilis* (adapted from Detling et al 1978).

occurs in plants grown at suboptimal temperatures or if the light response is measured at suboptimal temperatures.

Although the response of photosynthesis to temperature may change as a result of preconditioning to low temperatures (Williams 1974; Williams and Kemp, 1978) and as a result of water stress (Detling et al 1978), the optimal temperature is near 30°C (Figure 2.5), the average daytime high during midsummer at the Pawnee site. The apparent decrease in optimal air temperature with decreasing soil water potential might result from increased leaf temperatures at given air temperatures when soil water potentials are low, as a consequence of a lower latent-heat term in the surface-energy budget (Conner et al 1974). This shift might also be caused by a more rapid increase in stomatal and mesophyll resistance to CO_2 diffusion at high temperatures in water-stressed plants than in nonstressed plants.

Dark respiration of blue grama exhibits a typical temperature-response curve (Figure 2.6a) with a Q_{10} of about 2.0 over the range of 0 to 45°C. In addition, respiration is reduced as soil water potential decreases (Figure 2.6b). As is typical of C_4 species, measurable photorespiration is negligible in blue grama (Williams and Kemp, 1978).

Brown and Trlica monitored CO_2 exchange of pure *B. gracilis* swards continuously for 24 hours under ambient conditions at monthly intervals during the growing season (1974, 1977b). The 24-hour integrations of measured (1977b) and predicted (Detling et al 1978) aboveground net photosynthesis are shown in Table

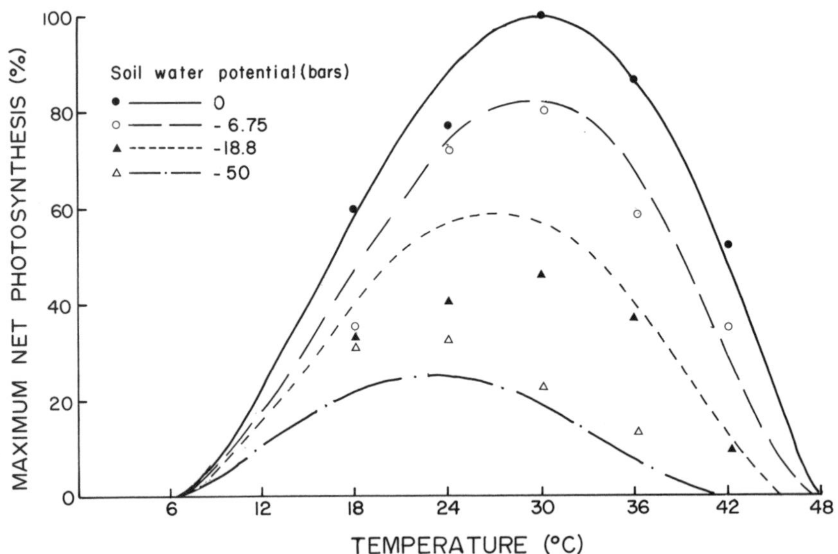

Figure 2.5. The interactive effect of soil water potential at 10 cm depth and temperature on net photosynthesis of *B. gracilis*. Individual data points represent average of all measurements at the indicated soil water potential and temperature (±3°C) recorded for pure swards of *B. gracilis* at the Pawnee site by Brown and Trlica (1974). Lines are predicted rates from the model of Detling et al (1978).

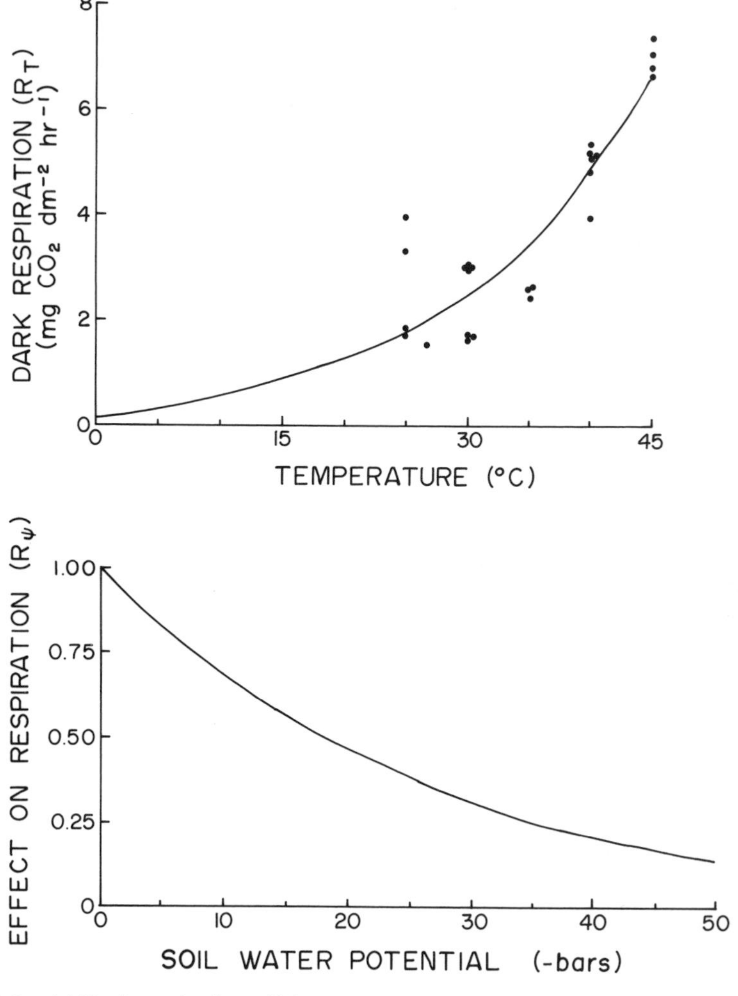

Figure 2.6. (a) Dark respiration of blue grama as influenced by temperature; (b) Effect of soil water potential on dark respiration of blue grama (adapted from data of Brown and Trlica 1974).

2.2. These values appear quite high for a species whose annual aboveground net production averages between 35 and 78 g dry matter · m^{-2} (Table 2.1). Both field measurements (Brown and Trlica 1974, 1977b) and model predictions (Detling et al 1978) reveal that only about 1% of the total daily aboveground net photosynthate is subsequently respired in the shoots during the night. This is probably a result of the low nocturnal temperatures, which averaged between 5 and 12°C on the four days studied. At these temperatures, dark respiration occurs at only 15 to 25% of the rate at 30°C. These low dark respiration rates, combined with high rates of net photosynthesis due to relatively low soil water stress, account for the high productivity measured on three of these four days.

Table 2.2. Daily Aboveground Net Photosynthesis, (P_n)

Date (1972)	Soil water potential (bars)	LAI[1]	P_n (g carbohydrate/m^2 day)	
			Measured[2]	Predicted[2]
28–29 June	−8 to −14	0.39	14.3	12.5
6–7 July	~0	0.43	10.8	14.5
11–12 Aug.	−21 to −32	0.36	1.7	2.6
22–23 Sept.	~0	0.40	5.6	8.6
4-day total			32.4	38.2

[1] LAI values are measured leaf area index of blue grama used in modeling predicted P_n.
[2] Calculated from measured (Brown and Trlica 1977) and predicted (Detling et al 1978) rates of CO_2 exchange over pure swards of blue grama.

Carbon Allocation and Production

Why is aboveground net primary production so low when this species has such high potential photosynthetic capacity? The answer to this question may be found by examining direct and indirect effects of water stress on several physiological processes. As discussed earlier, soil water potential frequently declines to −50 bars for extended periods between infrequent summer thundershowers. The effect of one such 30-day drying period on maximum daily net photosynthetic rates is illustrated in Figure 2.7. Ten days after the rainfall, the maximum daily rate of net photosynthesis had declined to less than 25% of the rate one day following the rainfall. Because of limited growing-season precipitation, there are

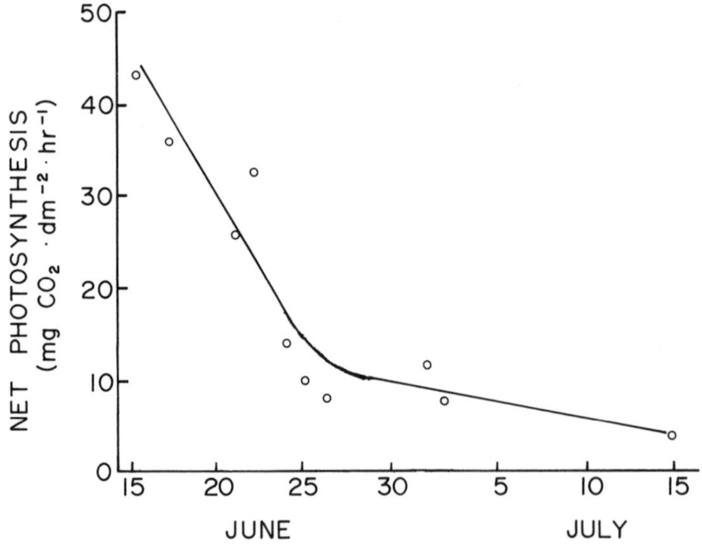

Figure 2.7. Maximum daily rate of net photosynthesis measured over pure *B. gracilis* swards at the Pawnee site during a 30-day drought in 1971 (adapted from Dye 1972).

relatively few days during the growing season when soil water potential, and hence net photosynthetic rate, is as high as on the three highest days listed in Table 2.2.

In spite of reduced net photosynthetic rates during periods of severe water stress, equations developed by Detling et al (1978) suggest that under optimal light and temperature, the net photosynthetic rate of *B. gracilis* varies from 11 to 20 mg $CO_2 \cdot dm^{-2} \cdot hr^{-1}$, depending upon plant age, when soil water potential in the root zone is at -50 bars. These rates are comparable to maximum rates observed for many C_3 species from more productive ecosystems (Black 1973). Thus, the low ANP values observed for this species likely result from allocation of a large proportion of the photosynthetically fixed carbon to belowground organs rather than to the construction of additional photosynthetic tissue. Indeed, results of ^{14}C tracer studies on blue grama-dominated sods indicate that the proportion of the photosynthetically fixed carbon translocated belowground ranged from 70% early in the growing season (May) to 85% in July and September (Singh and Coleman 1977). As a result, the total leaf area index (LAI) of the shortgrass prairie is generally <0.6 (Knight 1973) and the LAI of *B. gracilis* is <0.4 (Knight 1972).

Assuming identical photosynthetic rates, Monsi (1968) calculated that a plant which distributed 70% of its photosynthate to the construction of additional photosynthetic tissue would accumulate about 15 times more biomass after three growing seasons than a plant which distributed 30% of its photosynthate to the photosynthetic system. Similarly, McNaughton (1974) found that although eight different ecotypes of *Typha latifolia* had identical photosynthetic rates per unit of leaf tissue, net production varied greatly among ecotypes because of differences in leaf elongation rates. Sensitivity analysis of a shortgrass prairie simulation model (Parton et al 1978) indicated that decreasing current photosynthate translocation from shoots to the belowground system by 10% resulted in a 36% increase in aboveground production and an 11% increase in belowground production over a single growing season. Studies such as these led Mooney (1972) to conclude that the most productive plants are not only those with the greatest photosynthetic capacity, but also those with the greatest distribution of photosynthate into construction of additional photosynthetic tissue. Therefore, in order to understand carbon balance and net primary production in an ecosystem, it is essential to understand factors influencing leaf growth and carbohydrate allocation in addition to photosynthetic capacity.

Maximum potential leaf growth rates are probably genetically fixed (McNaughton 1974), but actual growth rates are modified by environment. Among the principal factors influencing leaf growth rates and carbon allocation within the plant is water availability. Higher root/shoot ratios are usually observed in water-stressed plants (Bray 1963, Struik and Bray 1970, Davidson 1969). Since water deficit generally limits leaf growth rate more than net photosynthesis (Boyer 1970), the increased root/shoot ratios observed in water-stressed plants may result from a higher proportion of the photosynthate being translocated to belowground organs. Although no specific experiments have been performed to verify this relationship in blue grama, the comparison of

Majerus' (1975) leaf growth data with photosynthesis estimates from the model of Detling et al (1978) tends to support this hypothesis (Figure 2.8). At the soil water potential (15 cm depth) where leaf growth ceased, net photosynthesis continued at about 50% its maximum rate. Since little of this photosynthate can be used in construction of new shoot material, much of it probably is translocated to belowground structures.

Proportionately more carbon is allocated to roots than shoots of nutrient-limited plants, causing higher root/shoot ratios (Hylton et al 1965, Hunt 1975). For example, in a series of nitrogen stress experiments, Benedict and Brown (1944) showed that root/shoot ratios and carbohydrate concentrations of nitrogen-deficient blue grama plants were generally higher than in high-N plants. In N-deficient plants, most nitrogen entering the roots can be rapidly incorporated into organic compounds and utilized in new root construction, thereby minimizing N reaching the shoots, and maintaining the shoot growth potential at a low level. As available N increases, more reaches the shoots where it combines with carbohydrate and results in shoot growth, causing proportionately less carbohydrate translocation to roots (Black 1968).

In view of this information, it is likely that the low ANP recorded for blue grama on the shortgrass prairie is partly due to low photosynthetic rates resulting from frequent prolonged drought. To a large extent, however, low ANP may occur because of an inability of the plants to fully utilize their photosynthetically fixed carbon for construction of shoots as a result of the limiting effects of water and nitrogen on leaf expansion. Thus, the majority of the seasonal photosynthetic production is translocated to belowground structures.

Factors affecting production and carbon utilization in belowground organs are

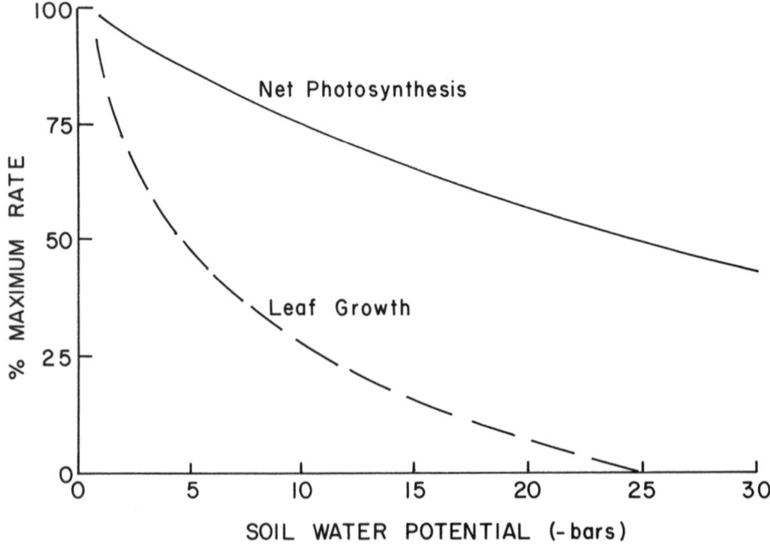

Figure 2.8. Relationship among soil water potential, net photosynthesis (Detling et al 1978) and leaf growth (Majerus 1975) of blue grama.

difficult to study, but considerable progress towards the understanding of blue grama root dynamics was made during the US/IBP Grassland Biome studies. Many of these findings were reviewed by Parton et al (1978). Ares (1976) observed blue grama root dynamics throughout the growing season by means of windows in soil excavations. Root growth activity was highly correlated with wet periods when soil in the upper 20 cm was at or near field capacity. During subsequent dry periods, 30 to 60% of the newly formed roots died. Although root growth in the spring began slightly before leaf growth at the expense of stored carbohydrates, maximum root growth occurred during periods of high soil water potential when leaf expansion was also maximum (Ares 1976).

Rates of root respiration (R_R) estimated from field and hydroponic laboratory techniques differ by a factor of 20 or more. R_R of blue grama estimated from the field data of Clark and Coleman (1972) varied between 0.06 and 0.12 mg $CO_2 \cdot$ g dry $wt^{-1} \cdot h^{-1}$ at 27°C and 12% soil water. These rates are quite close to the R_R determined from field studies on a North American tallgrass prairie (Herman and Kucera 1975, Herman 1977). By contrast, Williams and Kemp (1978) reported R_R rates of about 2.4 mg $CO_2 \cdot$ g dry $wt^{-1} \cdot h^{-1}$ for hydroponically grown blue grama at 20°C. While the latter values are consistent with R_R rates for wheat determined by similar techniques (Osman 1971), results from the simulation modeling exercises reported below and by Parton et al (1978) suggest that insufficient photosynthate is produced in a growing season to meet such high root-respiration demands under natural field conditions. These exercises suggest that the rates reported by Clark and Coleman (1972) are more reasonable estimates for blue grama in natural shortgrass prairie habitat.

Williams and Kemp (1978) reported marked diurnal variations in the R_R of blue grama, with rates at the end of the dark period being less than two-thirds of the rates at the end of the light period. However, in contrast to other studies (Osman 1971, Szaniawski and Adams 1974), R_R was not closely correlated with short-term changes in irradiance or leaf temperature. Increasing water stress generally reduced R_R rates and, under some conditions, water-stressed blue grama roots exhibited net positive CO_2 uptake (Kemp 1977).

Simulated Biomass Dynamics

The concepts described in this chapter have been incorporated into a blue grama primary-producer model (Figure 2.2). A preliminary version of the model was run in conjunction with Parton's (1978) abiotic model to simulate blue grama biomass dynamics under natural, irrigated, and irrigated-plus-fertilized conditions. The simulations were driven by daily maximum and minimum temperatures and precipitation data recorded at the Pawnee site during 1973.

Generally, the model successfully predicted blue grama shoot growth under a wide variety of conditions including a natural (unfertilized and nonirrigated) condition (Figure 2.9a), a plot irrigated to maintain soil water potential at −0.8 bars or greater from mid-May through mid-September (Figure 2.9b), and a similarly irrigated plot receiving N fertilizer at 150 kg $\cdot$ ha^{-1} (Figure 2.9c; see

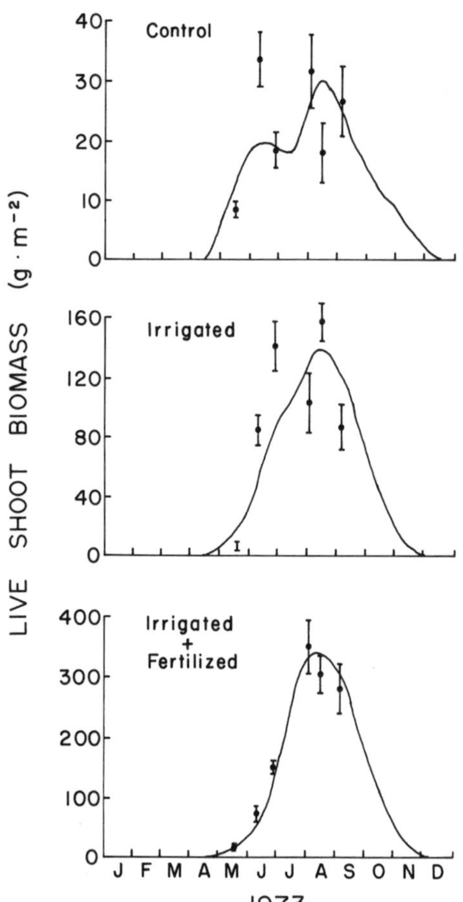

Figure 2.9. Simulated live shoot biomass of *B. gracilis* (continuous line) in the (a) control, (b) irrigated only, and (c) irrigated plus fertilized plots at the Pawnee site for 1973. Points and vertical bars represent mean ±1 standard error of field data.

Chapter 3). The comparison of peak live-shoot biomass under these conditions demonstrates the interactive effects of water and nitrogen on shoot growth. While irrigation caused a four- to five-fold increase in peak biomass, N fertilization in conjunction with irrigation caused a ten-fold increase compared with the untreated control. Therefore, while water is probably the principal factor limiting blue grama growth on the shortgrass prairie, available nitrogen quickly becomes limiting when water stress is alleviated. Indeed, Reuss and Innis (1977) have suggested that, except under conditions of severe temperature or moisture stress, productivity of grasslands is almost universally limited by nitrogen availability.

The simulated live-root biomass dynamics (Figure 2.10) are more difficult to validate since live-dead root separations were not made in the field. The total root biomass (live + dead for all species) was sampled in the upper 10 cm and little seasonal fluctuation was noted. This may be attributable, in part, to the fact that the period of most rapid growth coincides with the period of most rapid decomposition of dead roots (Ares 1976). Consequently, any increase in live-root biomass may have been offset by a corresponding decrease in dead-root biomass. However, the trends in live-root biomass are consistent with the trends in functional-root biomass determined with ^{14}C by Singh and Coleman (1974). The trends in the live-root biomass for the irrigated plot also appear reasonable in light of the data presented in Chapter 3. Although evidence indicates that total root biomass of the irrigated-plus-fertilized treatment exceeded that of the control and irrigated treatments, the model appears to overpredict root biomass under this treatment. Since aboveground production was apparently predicted rather accurately (Figure 2.9c), the overprediction of root biomass may result from an overestimation of net photosynthesis under nonlimiting soil water and nitrogen. The reasons for this are not yet clear, but it is possible that the effects of self-shading actually reduce net photosynthesis to a greater extent than represented in the model.

Results of the simulated carbon dynamics of *B. gracilis* for the 1973 growing season (Table 2.3) provide insight into processes influencing primary production. With gross primary production (P_g) of 378 g dry wt · m^{-2} · yr^{-1}, about 24% was allocated to shoots, and the remaining 76% was distributed belowground to crowns (24%) and roots (52%) in the nonirrigated, nonfertilized simulation. Slightly over one-half (51%) of the P_g was lost via respiration, a value close to that predicted by Mooney (1972) but somewhat higher than the 34% estimated for the lightly grazed, blue grama-dominated shortgrass prairie studied by Coleman

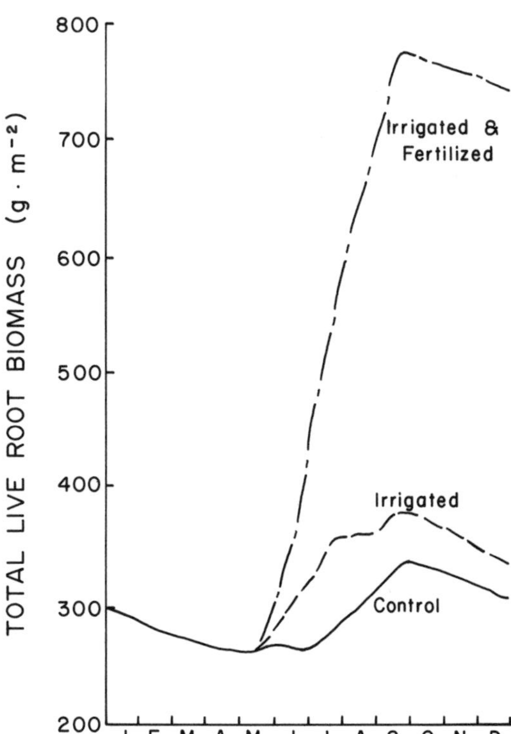

Figure 2.10. Simulated live root biomass of *B. gracilis* in the control, irrigated, and irrigated plus fertilized plots at the Pawnee site.

Table 2.3. Simulated Carbon Budget of *B. gracilis* (g carbohydrate · m^{-2} yr) as Influenced by Irrigation and Fertilization

	Control	Irrigated	Irrigated + fertilized
Gross photosynthesis (P_g)	378	889	2179
Aboveground respiration (R_a)	43	272	593
Light	*35*	*223*	*483*
Dark	*8*	*49*	*110*
Net aboveground photosynthesis ($P_n = P_g - R_a$)	335	617	1586
Translocation to belowground organs (T_b)	287	381	1016
Translocation to crowns (T_c)	*90*	*120*	*319*
Translocation to roots (T_r)	*197*	*261*	*697*
Belowground respiration (R_b)	151	210	308
Crown respiration (R_c)	*50*	*71*	*103*
Root respiration (R_r)	*101*	*139*	*205*
Total plant respiration (R_t)	194	482	901
Net primary production ($NPP = P_g - R_t$)	184	407	1278
Aboveground ($ANP = P_n - T_b$)	*48*	*236*	*570*
Belowground ($BNP = T_b - R_b$)	*136*	*171*	*708*
Crowns ($CNP = T_c - R_c$)	*40*	*49*	*216*
Roots ($RNP = T_r - R_r$)	*96*	*122*	*492*
Root death	69	66	100
Crown death	33	27	40

et al (1976). In further contrast to the studies of Coleman et al (1976), in which they estimated that only about 23% of the total autotrophic respiration occurred in belowground organs, these predictions suggest that approximately 78% occurs belowground in the roots (52%) and crowns (26%). Although the latter values appear to be consistent with the large proportion (86%) of net photosynthate (P_n) which was subsequently translocated belowground, the relative contribution of these organs to total autotrophic respiration under field conditions is poorly understood (Mellinger and McNaughton 1975, Coleman 1976).

The simulated irrigation and irrigation plus fertilization increased gross primary production by 135 and 476%, respectively (Table 2.3). Although less than 50% of P_g was translocated belowground under these conditions, belowground net primary production (BNP) was higher than in the nonirrigated, nonfertilized simulation. Total plant respiration continued to be slightly over 50% of P_g in the irrigated simulation, but accounted for a somewhat lower proportion (41%) in the irrigated-plus-fertilized simulation. However, aboveground respiration was only about 22% of total plant respiration in the control plots whereas it accounted for 56 and 66% of the total in the irrigated and irrigated-plus-fertilized treatments. This appears reasonable in view of the increased construction and maintenance costs associated with the proportionately greater aboveground plant biomass under these conditions.

It is interesting to note that although the control treatment has only 20% as much ANP as the irrigated treatment and 8% as much as the irrigated-plus-fertilized treatment, it had a considerably higher ratio of gross photosynthesis to aboveground respiration ($P_g/R_a = 8.8$) than the irrigated and irrigated-plus-fertilized treatments (3.7 and 3.3, respectively). This situation resulted largely from aboveground respiration increasing in proportion to shoot biomass, whereas photosynthesis per unit of leaf biomass declined beyond a certain LAI value as a result of limiting nitrogen in the irrigated treatment and self-shading in both the irrigated and irrigated-plus-fertilized treatments. Thus, the most productive plants may not always have the highest P_g/R_a ratios, and caution should be exercised when attempting to compare the potential production of different systems on the basis of such ratios.

Bouteloua gracilis appears to be especially well adapted as the dominant grass of shortgrass prairie. It is able to avoid permanent wilting and maintain positive net photosynthesis periods of prolonged drought when soil water potential in the root zone is −50 bars or less. By allocating up to 85% of its annual net photosynthate to the construction and maintenance of belowground organs, including an extensive fibrous root system, leaf area is kept low. Thus, transpirational water loss is minimized and water is conserved in the upper 20 cm where over 85% of the functional roots occur (Singh and Coleman 1974). It is likely that both ANP and BNP would be greater if a larger proportion of current photosynthate were utilized in shoot growth. However, during periods of protracted drought, soil water depletion would probably occur more rapidly, thus exposing the plants to severe water stress for longer periods and jeopardizing their long-term survival.

Summary

Blue grama *(Bouteloua gracilis),* the dominant grass of the North American shortgrass prairie, has the C_4 photosynthetic pathway. This species fails to become light saturated at full sunlight and has an optimal temperature of about 30°C, which is the average daytime high at the Pawnee site. Although water is considered the principal factor limiting primary production, it is able to maintain net photosynthesis at about 20% of maximum when soil water potential in the root zone is −50 bars, if other environmental factors are optimal. Since leaf expansion is more sensitive to water stress than is photosynthesis, productivity of blue grama may be most limited by its inability to utilize photosynthate for development of a full leaf canopy during frequent periods of water stress.

Output from a simulation model suggests that during a typical year, up to 85% of the net carbon fixed in photosynthesis is subsequently translocated belowground. Approximately 50% of the carbohydrate fixed in photosynthesis is respired during the growing season, and over 75% of the total respiration occurs belowground in the crowns and roots.

Simulated results of irrigation and irrigation plus fertilization had the effect of increasing total gross primary production by 135 and 476%, respectively. Under these conditions, a smaller proportion of the photosynthate, but a greater total amount, was translocated belowground. Although aboveground net primary production was increased nearly five times by irrigation and ten times by irrigation plus fertilization, the ratio of photosynthesis to shoot respiration was lower in these treatments than in the untreated simulation.

References

Ares, J. 1976. Dynamics of the root system of blue grama. *J. Range Manag.* **29**:208–213.

Bazzaz, F. A. 1973. Photosynthesis of *Ambrosia artemisiifolia* L. plants grown in greenhouse and in the field. *Am. Midl. Nat.* **90**:186–190.

Benedict, H. M. and G. B. Brown. 1944. The growth and carbohydrate responses of *Agropyron smithii* and *Bouteloua gracilis* to changes in nitrogen supply. *Plant Physiol.* (Lancaster) **19**:481–494.

Black, C. A. 1968. *Soil Plant Relationships.* New York: John Wiley and Sons, Inc.

Black, C. C. 1973. Photosynthetic carbon fixation in relation to net CO_2 uptake. *Annu. Rev. Plant Physiol.* **24**:253–286.

Bokhari, U. G. 1976. The influence of stress conditions on chlorophyll content of two range grasses with contrasting photosynthetic pathways. *Ann. Bot.* **40**:969–979.

Bokhari, U. G. 1977. Regrowth of western wheatgrass utilizing ^{14}C-labeled assimilates stored in belowground parts. *Plant and Soil* **48**:115–127.

Boyer, J. S. 1970. Leaf enlargement and metabolic rates in corn, soybean, and sunflower at various leaf water potentials. *Plant Physiol.* **46**:233–235.

Bray, J. R. 1963. Root production and the estimation of net productivity. *Can. J. Bot.* **41**:65–72.

Brown, L. F. and M. J. Trlica. 1974. Photosynthesis of two important grasses of the shortgrass prairie as affected by several ecological variables, *US/IBP Grassland Biome Tech. Rep. No. 244,* Fort Collins: Colorado State Univ.

Brown, L. F. and M. J. Trlica. 1977a. Interacting effects of soil water, temperature and irradiance on CO_2 exchange rates of two dominant grasses of the shortgrass prairie. *J. Appl. Ecol.* **14**:197–204.

Brown, L. F. and M. J. Trlica. 1977b. Carbon dioxide exchange of blue grama swards as influenced by several ecological variables in the field. *J. Appl. Ecol.* **14**:205–213.

Catský, J., I. Tichá, and J. Solarová. 1976. Ontogenetic changes in the internal limitations to bean leaf photosynthesis. I. Carbon dioxide exchange and conductance for carbon dioxide transfer. *Photosynthetica* **10**:394–402.

Chu, A. C. P. and H. G. McPherson. 1977. Sensitivity to desiccation of leaf extension in prairie grass. Aust. J. Plant Physiol. **4**:381–387.

Clark, F. E. 1977. Internal cycling of ^{15}nitrogen in shortgrass prairie. *Ecology* **58**:1322–1333.

Clark, F. E., and D. C. Coleman. 1972. Secondary productivity below ground in Pawnee Grassland, 1971, *US/IBP Grassland Biome Tech. Rep. No. 169.* Fort Collins: Colorado State Univ.

Coleman, D. C. 1976. A review of root production processes and their influence on soil biota in terrestrial ecosystems. *In* J. M. Anderson and A. Macfadyen (eds.), *The Role of Terrestrial and Aquatic Organisms in Decomposition Processes,* pp. 417–34. Oxford: Blackwell Scientific Publishers.

Coleman, D. C., R. Andrews, J. E. Ellis, and J. S. Singh. 1976. Energy flow and partitioning in man-managed and natural ecosystems. *Agro-Ecosystems* **3**:45–54.

Conner, D. J., L. F. Brown, and M. J. Trlica. 1974. Plant cover, light interception, and photosynthesis of shortgrass prairie. A functional model. *Photosynthetica* **8**:18–27.

Davidson, R. L. 1969. Effects of soil nutrients and moisture on root/shoot ratios in *Lolium perenne* L. and *Trifolium repens* L. *Ann. Bot.* **33**:571–577.

Detling, J. K., W. J. Parton, and H. W. Hunt. 1978. An empirical model for estimating CO_2 exchange of *Bouteloua gracilis* (H.B.K) Lag. in the shortgrass prairie. *Oecologia* **33**:137–147.

Dickinson, C. E., and J. L. Dodd. 1976. Phenological pattern in the shortgrass prairie. *Am. Midl. Nat.* **96**:367–378.

Dye, A. J. 1972. Caron dioxide exchange of blue grama swards in the field (Ph.D. diss.). Fort Collins: Colorado State Univ.

Herman, R. P. 1977. Root contribution to "total soil respiration" in a tallgrass prairie. *Am. Midl. Nat.* **98**:227–232.

Herman, R. P. and C. L. Kucera. 1975. Vegetation management and microbial function in a tallgrass prairie. *Iowa St. J. Res.* **50**:255–260.

Hunt, R. 1975. Further observations on root/shoot equilibrium in perennial ryegrass (*Lolium perenne* L.). *Ann. Bot.* **39**:745–755.

Hylton, L. O., A. Ulrich, and D. R. Cornelius. 1965. Comparison of nitrogen constituents as indicators of the nitrogen status of Italian ryegrass, and relation of top to root growth. *Crop Sci.* **5**:21–22.

Innis, G. S. (ed.). 1978. *Grassland Simulation Model,* Ecological Studies, 26. New York: Springer-Verlag.

Jameson, D .A. 1969. General description of the Pawnee Site, *US/IBP Grassland Biome Tech. Rep. No. 1.* Fort Collins: Colorado State Univ.

Jewiss, O. R., and J. Woledge. 1967. The effect of age on the rate of apparent photosynthesis in leaves of tall fescue *(Festuca Arundinacea* Schreb.) *Ann. Bot.* **31**:661–671.

Kemp, P. R. 1977. Niche divergence between *Agropyron smithii,* C_3, and *Bouteloua gracilis,* C_4: A study of the role of differing photosynthetic pathways in the shortgrass prairie ecosystem (Ph.D. diss.). Pullman: Washington State Univ.

Knievel, D. P. and D. A. Schmer. 1971. Preliminary results of growth characteristics of buffalograss, blue grama, and western wheatgrass, and methodology for translocation studies using ^{14}C as a tracer, *US/IBP Grassland Biome Tech. Rep. No. 86.* Fort Collins: Colorado State Univ.

Knight, D. H. 1972. Leaf area dynamics on the Pawnee Grassland, 1970–1971, *US/IBP Grassland Biome Tech. Rep. No. 164.* Fort Collins: Colorado State Univ.

Knight, D. H. 1973. Leaf area dynamics of a shortgrass prairie in Colorado. *Ecology* **54**:891–896.

Lauenroth, W. K. and P. L. Sims. 1976. Evapotranspiration from a shortgrass prairie subjected to water and nitrogen treatments. *Water Resour. Res.* **12**:437–442.

Ludlow, M. M., and T. T. Ng. 1976. Effect of water deficit on carbon dioxide exchange and leaf elongation rate of *Panicum maximum* var. *trichoglume. Aust. J. Plant Physiol.* **3**:401–413.

Majerus, M. E. 1975. Response of root and shoot growth of three grass species to decreases in soil water potential. *J. Range Manag.* **28**:473–476.

Mellinger, M. F. and S. J. McNaughton. 1975. Structure and function of successional vascular plant communities in Central New York. *Ecol. Monogr.* **45**:161–182.

McNaughton, S. J. 1974. Developmental control of net productivity in *Typha latifolia* ecotypes. *Ecology* **55**:864–869.

Monsi, N. 1968. Mathematical models of plant communities. *In* F. Eckardt (ed.), *Functioning of Terrestrial Ecosystems at the Primary Production Level,* pp. 131–49. Paris: UNESCO.

Mooney, H. A. 1972. Carbon balance of plants. *Annu. Rev. Ecol. Syst.* **3**:315–346.

Osman, A. M. 1971. Root respiration of wheat plants as influenced by age, temperature, and irradiation of shoots. *Photosynthetica* **5**:107–112.

Parton, W. J. 1978. Abiotic section of ELM. *In* G. S. Innis (ed.), *Grassland Simulation Model,* Ecological Studies 26, pp. 31–53. New York: Springer-Verlag.

Parton, W. J., J. S. Singh, and D. C. Coleman. 1978. A model of production and turnover of roots in shortgrass prairie. *J. Appl. Ecol.* (in press).

Patterson, D. T., J. A. Bunce, R. S. Alberte, and E. van Volkenburgh. 1977. Photosynthesis in relation to leaf characteristics of cotton from controlled and field environments. *Plant Physiol.* **59**:384–387.

Reuss, J. O. and G. S. Innis, 1977. A grassland nitrogen flow simulation model. *Ecology* **58**:379–388.

Risser, P. G. and F. L. Johnson. 1973. Carbon dioxide exchange characteristics of some prairie grass seedlings. *Southwest. Nat.* **18**:85–91.

Singh, J. S. and D. C. Coleman. 1974. Distribution of photoassimilated ^{14}carbon in the root system of a shortgrass prairie. *J. Ecol.* **62**:359–365.

Singh, J. S. and D. C. Coleman. 1977. Evaluation of functional root biomass and translocation of photoassimilated ^{14}C in a shortgrass prairie ecosystem. *In* J. K.

Marshall (ed.), *The Belowground Ecosystem: A Synthesis of Plant-Associated Processes,* Range Sci. Dep. Sci. Ser. No. 26, pp. 123–32. Fort Collins: Colorado State Univ.

Stubbendieck, J. and D. F. Burzlaff. 1970. Effects of temperature and daylength on auxillary bud and tiller development in blue grama. *J. Range Manag.* **23**:63–66.

Struik, G. J., and J. R. Bray. 1970. Root/shoot ratios of native forest herbs and *Zea mays* at different soil moisture levels. *Ecology* **51**:892–893.

Szaniawski, R. K., and M. S. Adams. 1974. Root respiration of *Tsuga canadensis* seedlings as influenced by intensity of net photosynthesis and dark respiration of shoots. *Am. Midl. Nat.* **91**:464–468.

Van Havern, B. P. 1973. Soil-water relations of a shortgrass prairie (M.S. thesis). Fort Collins: Colorado State Univ.

Williams, G. J., III. 1974. Photosynthetic adaptation to temperature in C_3 and C_4 grasses. A possible ecological role in the shortgrass prairie. *Plant Physiol.* **54**:709–711.

Williams, G. J., III and P. R. Kemp. 1978. Simultaneous measurement of leaf and root gas exchange of shortgrass prairie species. Bot. Gaz. **139**:150–157.

Williams, G. J., III and J. L. Markley. 1973. The photosynthetic pathway type of North American shortgrass prairie species and some ecological implications. *Photosynthetica* 7:262–270.

Woledge, J. and O. R. Jewiss. 1969. The effect of temperature during growth on the subsequent rate of photosynthesis in leaves of tall fescue (*Festuca arundinacea* Schreb.). *Ann. Bot.* **33**:897–913.

3. Analysis of the Response of a Grassland Ecosystem to Stress

JERROLD L. DODD and WILLIAM K. LAUENROTH

Introduction and Area Description

As indicated in Chapter 1, the shortgrass prairie of the piedmont of north-central Colorado is a semiarid grassland with an average annual precipitation of about 312 mm (Hyder et al 1975). More than 70% of the precipitation occurs as rain from late April through early August, with the largest quantities occurring in May and June. Year-to-year fluctuations in quantity and seasonal distribution of rainfall are great. In a recent 31-year period, annual precipitation was as low as 110 mm and as high as 582 mm. Average monthly temperatures range from −4°C in January to 21°C in July.

The soils of this area are derived from granitic outwash from the Rocky Mountains and are weakly developed zonal soils of loam to sandy-loam texture and relatively low fertility. The vegetation on most soil types of the area is dominated by shortgrasses, succulents, and half-shrubs. The main species of these groups for our study site are *Bouteloua gracilis* (H.B.K.) Lag., *Opuntia polyacantha* Haw., and *Artemisia frigida* Willd., respectively. Based on time-weighted means of total standing crop, more than 90% of the total aboveground plant biomass is about equally divided between these three major groups of plants (Figure 3.1). Cool-season grasses and sedges and cool- and warm-season forbs collectively account for less than 10% of the total standing crop. The relative proportions of these six groups vary with annual fluctuations of the weather. For example, *Opuntia* increases dramatically in drought years while the other groups decrease (Dodd and Lauenroth 1975, Hyder et al 1975).

Previous studies of this grassland, especially those conducted by Dr. Don Hyder and his colleagues (1975) at the Agricultural Research Service's Central Plains Experimental Range, have shown that primary production is limited mainly by spring and summer precipitation and to a lesser extent by the availability of soil mineral nitrogen during shorter periods of the season when soil water is at or near optimal levels for plant growth.

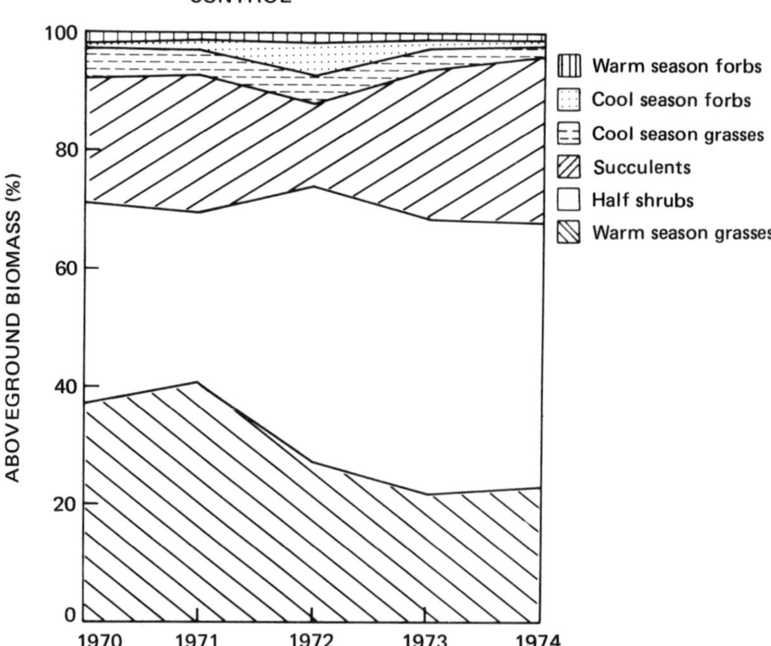

Figure 3.1. Interseasonal vegetation changes in functional group composition for control area of ecosystem stress experiment, 1970 to 1975 (based on time-weighted mean total biomass).

Experiment on Ecosystem Stress

Objective

The objective of this study was to determine the effect of the removal of soil water and soil mineral nitrogen deficiencies on the shortgrass prairie ecosystem. It was hypothesized that the elevation of the soil water and mineral nitrogen levels to well above those levels that the system naturally experiences would induce stress. A measurable system response would be considered confirmation of the hypothesis.

Stress in biology is normally used in reference to responses of organisms or populations to levels of environmental factors that disrupt their normal functions. Environmental factors inducing stress do so either at lower levels than required or at excessive toxic levels. Esch et al (1975) advanced a definition of stress that is appropriate when speaking of stress at the ecosystem level. They define stress as the effect of any force which tends to extend any homeostatic or stabilizing process beyond its normal limit at any level of biological organization. It is this definition of stress that we use in this paper.

Design

The design of the experiment consisted of a factorial combination of two replications each of nitrogen and water treatments (Figure 3.2). Each of the eight contiguous cells of the design was a one-hectare plot of shortgrass prairie (Figure 3.3). Prior to the initiation of the study, the plots had a long history of light summer grazing by cattle. Livestock were excluded the year prior to and during the course of this study.

In the nitrogen and water-plus-nitrogen treatments, soil mineral nitrogen levels were maintained at levels at least 50 kg N · ha^{-1} greater than the control by spring application of ammonium-nitrate fertilizer. Ammonium nitrate was first applied at the rate of 150 kg N · ha^{-1} and subsequently only as needed to maintain the 50 kg N · ha^{-1} differential. More nitrogen was required to maintain the differential in the water-plus-nitrogen treatment than in the nitrogen treatment without water.

Water was applied to the appropriate treatments from early May to mid-September through a programmable sprinkler irrigation system. The objective of watering was to maintain soil matric potential between 0 and −0.8 bars at the 10 cm soil depth through the growing season, May to September. Daily observations of water tension were made with ceramic tensiometers, and water was applied as often as needed to maintain the desired water level. Unfortunately, occasional mechanical problems with the sensors and with the irrigation system prevented the watering objective from being strictly adhered to in all periods of the experiment. Annual total application of water ranged from 460 to 650 mm for

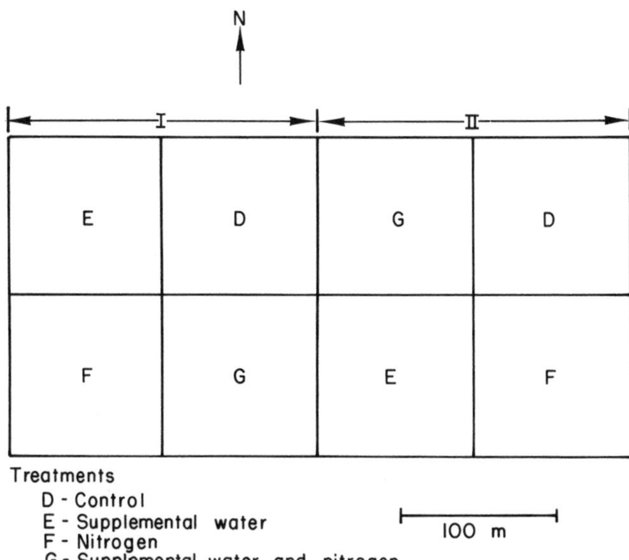

Figure 3.2. Experimental design of shortgrass prairie ecosystem stress study.

Figure 3.3. Aerial view showing six of the experimental plots after four years of treatment.

The darkest plots are those treated with nitrogen and water. Plots in the upper left and lower right received water only, and the one in the lower left, nitrogen only. Plot in the upper center is control. White spots are soil test pits.

the water treatment and from 550 to 710 mm for the water-plus-nitrogen treatment.

Methods

Soil water dynamics were determined by weekly measurements of soil water content in the 0 to 120 cm layer using a neutron probe. Seasonal biomass dynamics were determined by the technique of frequent harvest. Standing-crop estimates of plant biomass were made by harvesting 10 to 12 circular plots of 0.5 m^2 each per treatment several times each year. From 1970 through 1972 total standing crop, by species, was determined and from 1973 through 1975 the harvested material was separated, according to species, into "current year's live" "current year's dead," and "previous years' dead" categories with a fourth category of "perennial live" being used for those plants such as the half-shrubs and succulents that have perennial organs aboveground.

In compiling estimates of aboveground net primary production (ANP), the species information was combined into six functional groups: warm-season grasses, cool-season grasses, warm-season forbs, cool-season forbs, half-shrubs, and succulents. The characteristics of warm-season and cool-season plants are given in Chapters 2 and 10, and the classification of species into these categories follows Sims et al (1978).

Sampling intensity was not sensitive enough to detect the intraseasonal dynamics of the succulents and, therefore, there is no valid estimate of their contribution to ANP. While standard errors for the standing crop estimates of other plant groups ranged from 10 to 25% of the mean, they often exceeded 50% for the succulent group.

For the 1970-to-1972 period, ANP was derived by adding the seasonal peaks of total standing crop for each group except half-shrubs. Since current year's production was not separated from previous years' production, it was necessary to assume that previous years' production was negligible at peak standing crop. The difference between the peak standing crop and the previous low value for the season was considered to be the best estimate of the half-shrub contribution to ANP.

From 1973 to 1975, peak standing crop of the total live plus current dead (current year's production) was used as the estimate of contribution to ANP. Again, the difference between the peak and the seasonal low preceding the peak was used as the estimate for half-shrub contribution to ANP. ANP estimates for 1973 to 1975 were also derived by the same technique as used for the 1970-to-1972 period and were found to be within 10% of the estimates based on current production peaks for all year × treatment combinations, except the water-plus-nitrogen treatment in 1975. In this case, the seasonal peak of total warm-season grass exceeded the peak of live plus current year's dead warm-season grass by 75 $g \cdot m^{-2}$, and the estimate of ANP by summing peaks of total standing crop exceeded by 130 $g \cdot m^{-2}$ the ANP estimate derived by summing peaks of live plus current year's dead standing crop. The latter is assumed to be the most accurate.

In each one-hectare area, a grid of 42 live traps 9 m apart on the rows and 15 m apart on the columns was used for mark-release-recapture of small mammals (Grant et al 1977). In each plot, five consecutive nights of trapping at intervals of 6 weeks were done during the growing season for the first four years. During 1975 and 1976, trapping was on a monthly schedule during the growing season and every six weeks during the winter. Animals were individually marked by toe-clipping, and records were maintained of species, sex, age class, reproductive condition, and location of capture.

Aboveground arthropods were sampled with quick traps. A mesh-covered trap was dropped over a 0.5-m^2 area and surface insects and loose debris were removed with a strong vacuum. The insects were then separated from the debris with a Berlese funnel. Soil microarthropod samples were taken from the 0 to 10-cm surface layer of the soil with a 5-cm diameter soil coring tool. Microarthropods were separated from soil by a modified Berlese process. For both groups of arthropods, 10 to 12 samples per treatment were taken for each of 5 to 10 sample dates per season. Details of arthropod sampling and extraction procedures are presented by Leetham (1975).

Results

Aboveground Net Primary Production

During 6 years of study, ANP on the control ranged from a high of 180 $g \cdot m^{-2}$ (dry weight) in 1970 to a low of 60 $g \cdot m^{-2}$ in 1974, and averaged about 125 $g \cdot m^{-2}$ for the study period (Figure 3.4). ANP was closely related to average soil water content in early summer. Although there is no soil water data for 1970, monthly precipitation records indicate that the average soil water content in early and late summer of 1970 was probably comparable to the same periods in 1971. ANP in the nitrogen treatment equaled or exceeded that of the control in all years and was highest in 1972, the year with the best early summer soil water conditions. Overall ANP of the nitrogen treatments varied with early summer water in the same manner as ANP for the control, being highest in years with wetter early

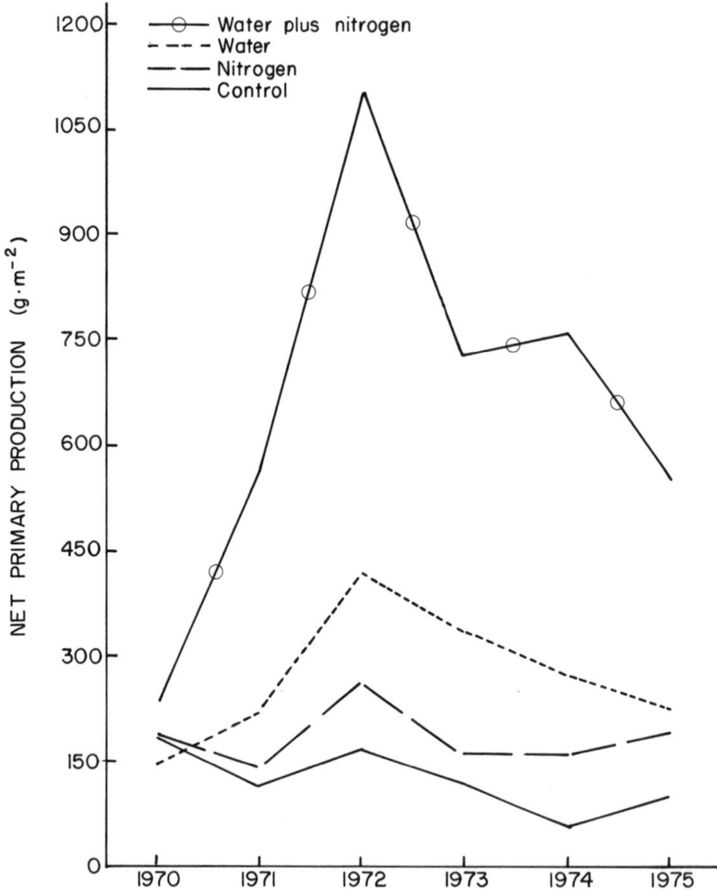

Figure 3.4. Aboveground net primary production for water and nitrogen stress experiment, 1970 to 1975.

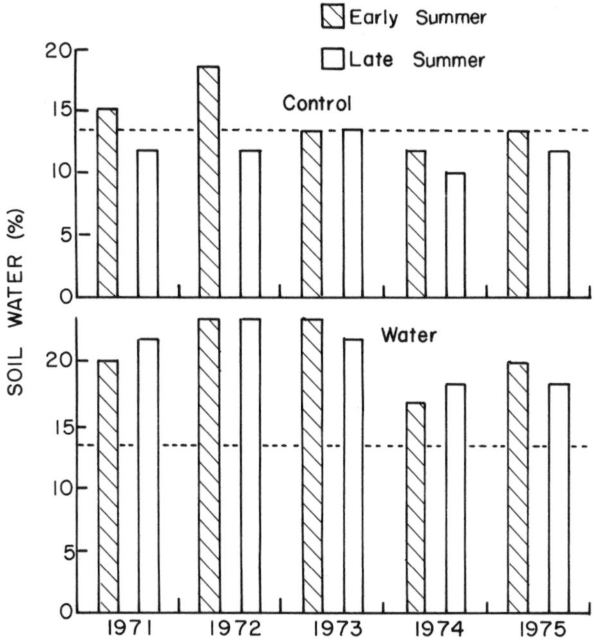

Figure 3.5. Average soil water content (% volume) for early summer (May and June) and late summer (July and August), 0 to 60 cm depth (dotted line is a reference for comparison only).

summers and lowest in years with drier summers. As mentioned earlier, difficulties were encountered in maintaining the soil water regime defined as the objective (Figure 3.5). Although much wetter conditions were maintained on the two water treatments than on the control and nitrogen-without-water treatments, the 0 to −0.8 bar objective was achieved consistently only in 1972. In 1971 and 1973, soil water content of the water treatments averaged slightly lower than the objective, and in 1974 and 1975 water content was well below the objective. Soil nitrogen status varied from year to year, but the differences stated as the objective was maintined. Table 3.1 shows the soil mineral nitrogen status for the spring of 1976. Following these analyses, 100 kg N · ha^{-1} was added to the water-plus-nitrogen treatment to insure the 50 kg N · ha^{-1} differential for the 1976 growing season.

The water treatment showed a greater increase in ANP than did the nitrogen treatment. ANP on the water treatment was equal to the control in 1970, since this was the year prior to application of water. During the 1971-to-1975 period,

Table 3.1. Soil Mineral Nitrogen ($NO_3 - N$ + Exchangeable $NH_4 - N$), April, 1976 (kg · ha^{-1})

Depth	Control	Water	Nitrogen	Water + nitrogen
0–30 cm	104	70	261	146

ANP varied with soil water content. It is suspected that, had equivalent soil water levels been maintained in all years as in 1972, interseasonal variation in ANP from 1972 to 1975 would have been minimal.

ANP on the water-plus-nitrogen treatment showed interactive effects of water and nitrogen on primary production. Interseasonal variation in ANP for this treatment was also dependent upon soil water. It appears that lower production in 1971 was partially due to lower soil water, but a time-lag effect between treatment and full response was also evident. It is likely that lower levels of production in 1973 through 1975 were responses to drier soil conditions, especially in late summer.

These results confirm that primary production in the shortgrass prairie is more sensitive to alterations of available water than to mineral nitrogen. They also point out that, while water is critical to primary production, once it is freely available, nitrogen availability is limiting.

Functional Group Composition

A number of interesting points pertaining to changes or lack of changes in botanical and functional group composition throughout the study can be made. These are summarized below, and shown in the comparison of Figures 3.6 through 3.10.

1. The main warm-season grass, blue grama, maintained its major role in the community in all three treatments (Figure 3.6). The same was true for fringed sagebrush, the major half-shrub (Figure 3.7). In the interaction treatment, exotic

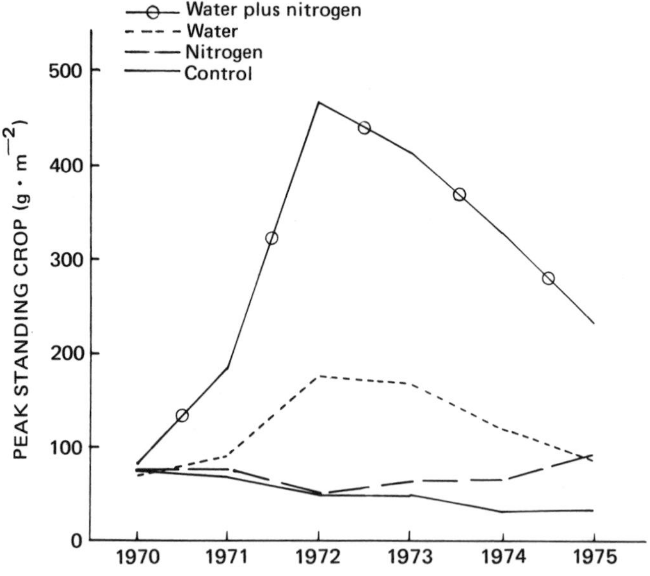

Figure 3.6. Warm-season grass biomass at the time of peak standing crop.

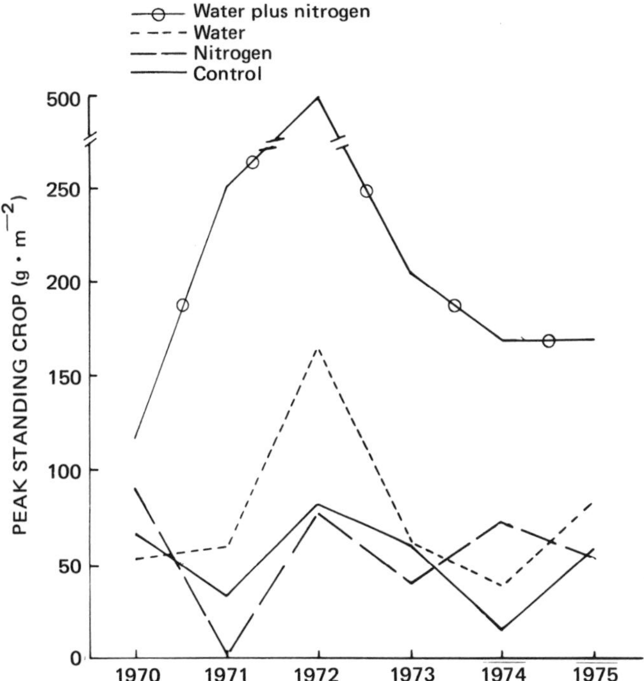

Figure 3.7. Shrub biomass at the time of peak standing crop.

species of warm-season forbs [*Salsola kali* L. and *Cirsium arvense* (L.) Scop.] increased greatly and, according to 1977 observations, appeared to be on the way to complete replacement of the warm-season grass component (Figure 3.8).

2. Legumes, which are always present but usually in low quantities in short-grass prairie, remained low on the nitrogen and nitrogen-plus-water treatments, but increased by a factor of 30 to 40 on the water treatment where they have a competitive advantage over species not capable of symbiotic N fixation (Figure 3.9).

3. Succulents increased greatly on the nitrogen treatment, decreased on the control and water treatments, and were virtually eliminated on the water-plus-nitrogen treatment (Figure 3.10). Elimination was probably brought about by insect injury and shading (Dodd and Lauenroth 1975).

Belowground Plant Biomass

The water and the nitrogen treatments brought about changes in belowground, plant-biomass standing crop (Table 3.2). Belowground standing-crop estimates in late summer from 1972 to 1974 indicate for all treatments a 10 to 25% greater mass of roots than on the control area. However, by 1975 the difference between the control and the treatments was reduced by a large increase in belowground

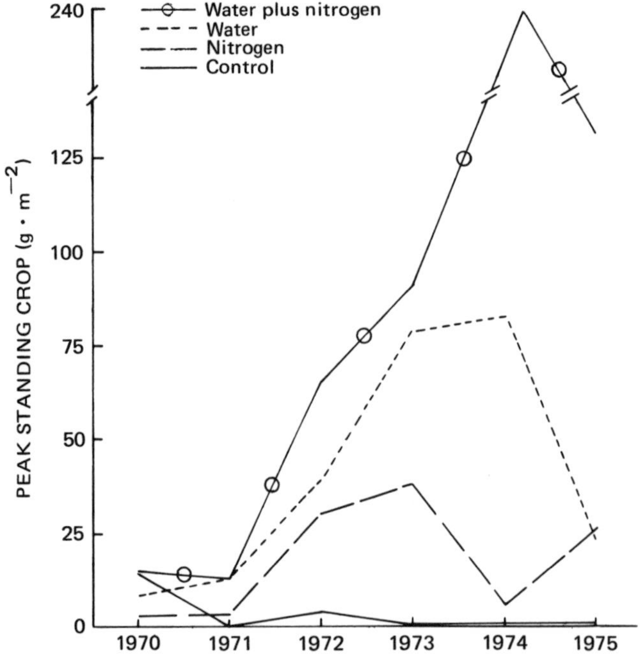

Figure 3.8. Warm-season forb biomass at the time of peak standing crop.

plant biomass on the control area. There is no ready explanation for these differences, but the discussion in Chapter 2 of photosynthate translocation to belowground organs offers intriguing insight into potentially important mechanisms.

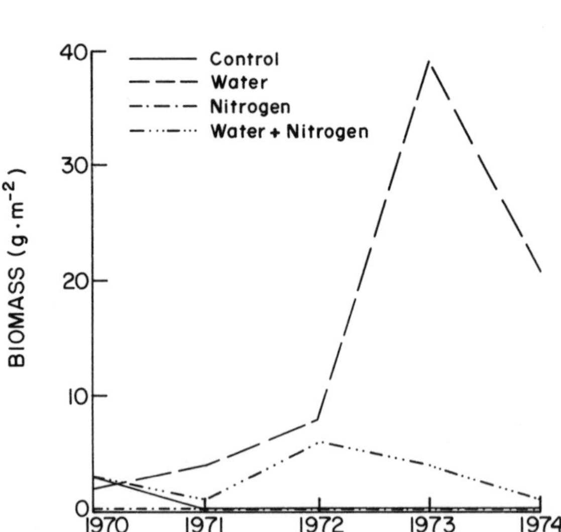

Figure 3.9. Time-weighted mean biomass (g · m^{-2}) of total legumes.

Table 3.2. Belowground Plant Biomass ($g \cdot m^{-2}$, ash-free) for 0–10 cm Depth Between August 18 and September 10 (mean with standard error)

Treatment	1972	1973	1974	1975
Control	689 ± 42	630 ± 29	583 ± 48	829 ± 81
Water	881 ± 54	744 ± 37	659 ± 46	761 ± 54
Nitrogen	789 ± 43	814 ± 56	643 ± 54	954 ± 76
Water + nitrogen	940 ± 75	838 ± 50	738 ± 81	873 ± 53

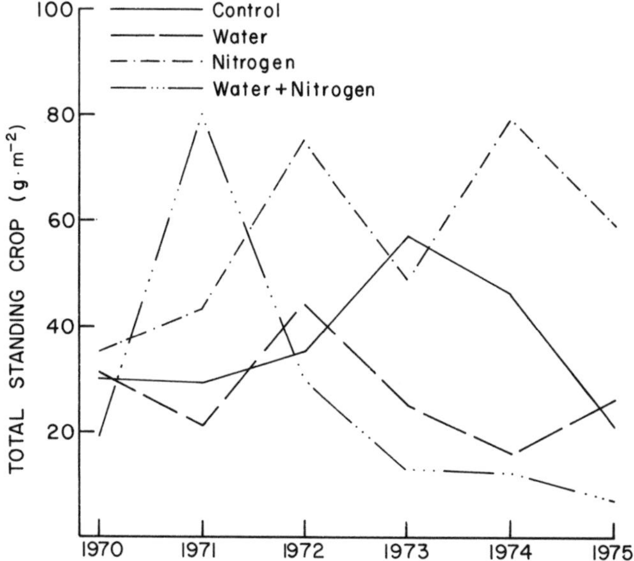

Figure 3.10. Average total standing crop of succulents.

Litter

Late-season standing-crop estimates for aboveground litter ranged from less than 150 $g \cdot m^{-2}$ (ash-free, dry weight) on the control to greater than 600 $g \cdot m^{-2}$ on the water-plus-nitrogen treatment (Table 3.3). The standing crop of litter averaged around 200 $g \cdot m^{-2}$ for the control, water, and nitrogen treatments from 1972 to 1975 and changed little in response to the singular treatments of water or nitrogen. However, the combination of water plus nitrogen resulted in a large increase in litter standing crop.

Table 3.3. Litter Standing Crop ($g \cdot m^{-2}$, ash-free) Between August 18 and September 10 (mean with standard error)

Treatment	1972	1973	1974	1975
Control	141 ± 22	272 ± 39	226 ± 27	234 ± 28
Water	199 ± 35	291 ± 14	265 ± 30	179 ± 16
Nitrogen	168 ± 16	241 ± 26	228 ± 31	255 ± 21
Water + nitrogen	325 ± 34	478 ± 52	633 ± 53	556 ± 37

Soil Microarthropods

Soil organisms are surely critical components of native ecosystems, but their role is not understood as well as those of vascular plants and vertebrates. In this experiment, soil acarines showed a significant response to the water and water-plus-nitrogen treatments, where their numbers increased greatly (Leetham, unpublished data).

In spite of the fact that the producer component of the system, on which the soil acarines are directly or indirectly dependent for an energy source, was significantly altered by each of the treatments and showed a synergistic response to water and nitrogen in combination, the soil acarine fauna responded only to the two water treatments.

Based on season-long averages, microarthropod densities and biomass increased about fourfold on the water and the water-plus-nitrogen treatments and did not respond to the nitrogen treatment (Figure 3.11). The microarthropod populations remained high throughout the growing season on the two water treatments, but decreased to low levels during the latter part of the growing season on the control and on the nitrogen treatment (Figure 3.12). The effect of the water treatment on trophic composition of the microarthropod community was to decrease the proportion of both fungivores and herbivores and to increase the proportion of predators (Table 3.4).

Aboveground Macroarthropods

The aboveground macroarthropod response to the stress treatments (Kirchner 1977) was very similar to the response shown by the soil microarthropods. They increased on the water and water-plus-nitrogen treatments and did not appear to change as a result of the nitrogen application.

Small Mammals

The major species of small mammals common to the type of upland shortgrass prairie examined in this study are the deer mouse *(Peromyscus maniculatus)*, thirteen-lined ground squirrel *(Spermophilus tridecemlineatus)*, and the grasshopper mouse *(Onychomys leucogaster)*. The prairie vole *(Microtus ochrogaster)* is present in the shortgrass prairie region, but is normally restricted to wet habitats adjacent to streams, springs, roadside ditches, or other sites that have more mesic conditions than normal for the region.

Table 3.4. Soil Microarthropod Trophic Structure (% total biomass)

Soil microarthropods	Control	N	H_2O	H_2O + N
Fungivore	55	56	21	23
Herbivore	31	28	12	13
Predator	14	15	58	55
Unclassified	1	1	9	9

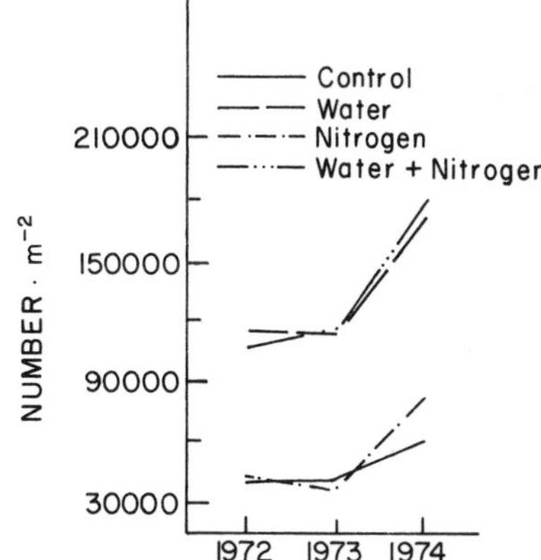

Figure 3.11. Average values for total number of microarthropods in each of three years for ecosystem stress treatments.

The effect of the water and nitrogen system stress on the small mammals was dramatic and not fully anticipated (Table 3.5; Grant et al 1977). Although small shifts in species composition occurred, total small mammal biomass was not greatly changed as a result of the separate treatments of water or nitrogen, but increased dramatically when the two factors were combined. This response is mainly attributable to a successful invasion of the water plus nitrogen treated area by *Microtus ochrogaster*. This increase is apparently due to the greatly

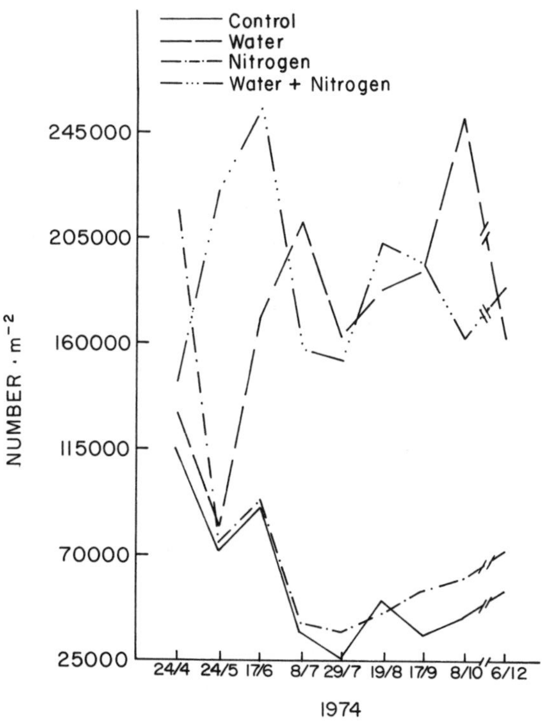

Figure 3.12. Seasonal dynamics of total microarthropod numbers for stress treatments.

Table 3.5. Peak Biomass of Small Mammals in 1974 (g · ha^{-1} live weight)

Small mammals	Control	N	H_2O	H_2O + N
Spermophilus tridecemlineatus	500	680	440	220
Onychomys leucogaster	60	+	+	+
Peromyscus maniculatus	70	50	70	150
Microtus ochrogaster	–	–	370	1900

From Grant et al 1977. Dash indicates absence, (+) indicates presence but very low biomass.

increased herbage and litter standing crop which provides much more cover for protection from predators, more food resources, and a more humid microclimate. The most important of these factors is believed to be cover (Birney et al 1976). A late immigrant to the water-and-nitrogen treatment, first appearing in 1974, was the harvest mouse *(Reithrodontomys megalotus)*. Like the prairie vole, it became numerous although the source of immigrants is uncertain (Abramsky 1976).

Diversity

Water plus nitrogen had the greatest effect on both plant and arthropod diversity (Kirchner 1977). Plant species diversity declined while aboveground arthropod diversity increased in response to this treatment. Water or nitrogen treatment alone had less effect on diversity, but both showed increases in diversity of both producer and invertebrate consumer communities.

Conclusions

It was hypothesized that the elevation of soil water level and/or the mineral nitrogen level well above those normally experienced by the system would constitute system stress and that this stress would be evidenced by fundamental changes in the structure and function of the ecosystem.

On the basis of changes that took place in ANP and standing-crop biomass, it is apparent that the combined forces of water and nitrogen clearly constitute system stress (Table 3.6). Whether or not the two forces applied separately

Table 3.6. Summary of Ecosystem Component Responses to H_2O and N Stress (standing crop)

Ecosystem component	N	H_2O	H_2O + N
Plant shoots	+	+	+
Roots	0	0	0
Litter	0	0	+
Mammals	0	0	+
Macroarthropods	0	+	+
Microarthropods	0	+	+

(+) indicates increase.

Table 3.7. Summary of Ecosystem Component Responses to H_2O and N Stress (species composition)

Ecosystem component	N	H_2O	H_2O + N
Plants	Slight	+Legumes	+Exotics
Mammals	Slight	Slight	+*Microtus*
Macroarthropods	Slight	Slight	+Predators
Microarthropods	Slight	+Predators	+Predators

constitute stress is less clear. The magnitude of change in producer and arthropod consumer standing crop brought about by the water treatment appear to be greater than changes to be expected through long-term variation under natural conditions. On the other hand, the standing-crop change brought about by the nitrogen treatment is probably similar to or less than would be experienced on a long-term basis under natural conditions.

Changes in species composition (based on biomass) also indicate that the combination of water and nitrogen alterations made in this experiment constitute system stress and that the water treatment applied separately was a system stress (Table 3.7). Changes in species composition prompted by the dryland nitrogen treatment were slight and are within the normal range of variation.

Overall, it is concluded that the water-plus-nitrogen and the water perturbations induced system stress because they resulted in alterations of structural and functional characteristics outside the range of normal variation for the shortgrass prairie. By the same criteria, the nitrogen treatment did not induce system stress.

Summary

Stress in ecological systems results from the application of any force which extends any of the system's homeostatic processes beyond their normal limits. Since the shortgrass prairie ecosystem on the western edge of the Great Plains is adapted to semiarid climate with nitrogen-deficient soils, it was hypothesized that the removal of soil water and mineral nitrogen deficiencies would create system stress which would be evidenced by fundamental changes in the structural and/or functional characteristics of the system.

A replicated two-way factorial experimental design combining water (sufficient to maintain soil matric potential between 0 and -0.8 bars during the growing season) and mineral nitrogen applications (sufficient to maintain 50 $kg \cdot ha^{-1}$ greater quantity of mineral nitrogen than on the control) was used to test the hypothesis. Each cell of the 8-cell design was one hectare in size.

The treatments were maintained and ecosystem responses were monitored for six years. Aboveground annual net primary production was increased by factors of 1.3 to 2.7 on the nitrogen, 2.0 to 4.6 on the water, and 5.0 to 13.0 on the water-plus-nitrogen treatment. Shifts in plant species composition were slight on the nitrogen, great on the water-plus-nitrogen, and intermediate on the water treatment. Similar responses were noted in the mammalian consumer portion of the system with the most dramatic change being invasion and dominance of the water-plus-nitrogen treatment by *Microtus ochrogaster,* a species that is rarely found in the shortgrass prairie. Significant, but less dramatic, changes took place on the other treatments. Interestingly, the *Microtus* population dynamics for the six years of observation were unicyclic (low in spring and high in summer) and did not exhibit the two- to four-year cycle found in other *Microtus* populations. Insect and mite populations also were found to change significantly among the treatments.

We conclude that the interactive force of combined water and mineral nitrogen applications resulted in system stress to the shortgrass prairie and that the application of the water separately also resulted in system stress but to a lesser degree. The application of nitrogen without water did not constitute stress since changes resulting from this factor did not exceed changes normally experienced by the system due to normal climatic fluctuations.

References

Abramsky, Z. 1976. Small mammal studies in natural and manipulated shortgrass prairie (Ph.D. diss.). Fort Collins: Colorado State Univ.

Birney, E. C., W. E. Grant, and D. D. Baird. 1976. Importance of vegetative cover to cycles of *Microtus* populations. *Ecology* **57**:1043–1051.

Dodd, J. L. and W. K. Lauenroth. 1975. Responses of *Opuntia polyacantha* to water and nitrogen perturbations in the shortgrass prairie. *In* M. K. Wali (ed.), *Prairie: A Multiple View,* pp. 229–40. Grand Forks: University of North Dakota Press.

Esch, G. W., J. W. Gibbons, and J. E. Bourque. 1975. An analysis of the relationship between stress and parasitism. *Am. Midl. Nat.* **93**:339–352.

Grant, W. E., N. R. French, and D. M. Swift. 1977. Response of a small mammal community to water and nitrogen treatments in a shortgrass prairie ecosystem. *J. Mammal.* **58**:637–652.

Hyder, D. N., R. E. Bement, E. E. Remmenga, and D. F. Hervey. 1975. Ecological responses of native plants and guidelines for management of shortgrass range, *Agric. Res. Serv., USDA Tech. Bull. No. 1503.* Washington, D.C.: U.S. Government Printing Office.

Kirchner, T. B. 1977. The effects of resource enrichment on the diversity of plants and arthropods in a shortgrass prairie. *Ecology* **58**:1334–1344.

Leetham, J. W. 1975. A summary of field collecting and laboratory processing equipment and procedures for sampling arthropods at Pawnee Site, *US/IBP Grassland Biome Tech. Rep. No. 284,* Fort Collins: Colorado State Univ.

Sims, P. L., J. S. Singh, and W. K. Lauenroth. 1978. The structure and function of ten western North American grasslands. I. Abiotic and vegetational characteristics. *J. Ecol.* **66**:251–285.

4. Grassland Biomass Trophic Pyramids

NORMAN R. FRENCH, R. KIRK STEINHORST, and DAVID M. SWIFT

Introduction

A trophic pyramid is essentially a static view of the distribution of biomass in a community among producers, consumers, and, at times, decomposers. This chapter focuses on the distribution of biomass at one point in time, unlike the other chapters which primarily consider average values or dynamics of the ecosystem. The existence of a pyramidal trophic structure in ecosystems has become one of the first principles of ecology. Evidence for this may be found in most general textbooks of ecology, which present trophic pyramids in terms of numbers, biomass, or energy content of organisms (e.g., Odum 1973).

Drawing upon extensive data resulting from the Grassland Biome studies of the American contribution to the International Biological Program (Van Dyne 1972), and with the help of numerous colleagues, the authors have compiled data for the purpose of constructing trophic pyramids depicting the biomass distribution among trophic levels for several grassland sites at different times during the growing season. The main objective was to determine if there exists a standard pattern of biomass distribution common to different types of grasslands. The data result from efforts of a large team of scientists who mobilized their energies and shared their data under the International Biological Program (IBP).

Each trophic pyramid is a diagram of the distribution of biomass in the ecosystem at a single point in time. This analysis is therefore not concerned with the dynamics of energy transfer or with questions related to dynamics such as ecological efficiency. Comparison of trophic pyramids representing three points during the growing season gives only suggestive evidence of the results of dynamic processes occurring within the system. Biomass distribution is, of course, only one aspect of system structure. Because rates of turnover are generally ignored in the construction of biomass pyramids, the results can sometimes be depicted as nonpyramids (i.e., the base of the pyramid appears to be smaller than the consumer levels it supports). The inclusion in the diagram of the rate of turnover of biomass (Clark 1946, LaMotte 1969) would alleviate this seeming inconsistency. To avoid this problem, the present study includes in the pyramids both dead and live material at the producer level, biophagic and saprophagic organisms at the consumer levels, and belowground as well as aboveground biomass. Therefore, the alternative method suggested by Kozlovsky (1968) is followed and decomposers are assigned to trophic levels according to the source from which energy is derived.

Methods

Data and Sampling Procedures

Quantitative data on primary producers, primary consumers, and secondary consumers were incorporated in construction of the pyramids. Primary producer data included live and dead standing plant material, litter that had fallen to the ground but was still intact so that it could be collected from the surface of the soil, and roots with the crowns of grasses included. Primary consumer data included birds, large native mammals such as antelope, deer, elk or moose, rabbits and hares, pocket gophers and other small mammals, insects and other aboveground invertebrates, belowground arthropods or their immature stages, and nematodes. Belowground measurements also considered, except as noted, the microarthropods. Secondary consumers included birds, large mammals such as coyotes and a fraction of the small mammals, reptiles, aboveground and belowground invertebrates, and arthropods. Additional details of sampling methods for consumer populations are given in Chapter 5.

Methods of data collection were similar at all sites. The sampling reported here was conducted on areas that were for the most part free from grazing by domestic cattle. The aboveground biomass of plant material was sampled in each of two replicates by clipping five to ten 0.5-m^2 circular quadrats, separating the plant material according to species, and drying, weighing, and categorizing the materials according to live, recent dead, or old dead. This was done at approximately monthly intervals during the growing season. All litter was then removed from the clipped plots, generally by the use of a vacuum cleaner. This, too, was oven dried and weighed. Belowground biomass was sampled by collection of soil cores, washing, extraction, and drying of the root material. At least one core was taken in each of the quadrat locations. All data were recorded on standard forms for ease of machine storage, retrieval, and analysis.

Aboveground invertebrates were sampled by dropping a circular, net-covered trap over a 0.5-m^2 area (Turnbull and Nicholls 1966). Up to ten such samples were taken per replicate. The collecting hose of a D-Vac vacuum apparatus was inserted into an opening in the net, and organisms were removed from the inside of the net and from the vegetation. The vegetation was then clipped at ground level, and the vegetation and litter was also sucked into the vacuum apparatus, later to be processed in a Berlese funnel. Invertebrates thus collected were identified by order and family, and by species where possible, and counted according to taxon. A sample of each taxon identified was dried and weighed for conversion of numbers to biomass. The larger organisms were collected from soil cores by washing through a series of sieves (4 mm to 1 mm in size). Microarthropods were extracted from 5-cm diameter soil cores by the use of a modified

Tullgren extractor (Merchant and Crossley 1970). Microarthropod weights were estimated in a manner similar to the other determinations described. Nematodes were extracted by a water-extraction procedure using screens and funnels to separate the animals from the soil particles (Christie and Perry 1951).

Avian populations were censused during breeding by the flush-census technique (Wiens 1973). Two 10.6-ha areas were censused by forcing the territorial male to fly repeatedly and plotting the path taken by the bird. Aggressive encounters with neighboring birds were also noted. A map of the movements of individual birds indicated the approximate territorial boundaries. The number of these was multiplied by an appropriate value which represented the average number of females per male in the breeding season for the species in question. In adjacent locations, birds were taken for determination of weights and diet composition. At the desert grassland site, it was necessary to examine and census a larger area (Raitt and Pimm 1977). Data from roadside censuses at each site were correlated with densities determined by the flush-census method, and density estimates were therby made for different seasons of the year (Rotenberry and Wiens 1976).

Small mammals were censused by live trapping on a 2.7-ha area. After five or more consecutive days of marking and releasing the animals, data were evaluated by either the Jolly (1965) stochastic method or by the Zippin (1956) regression method to estimate the density of each species. The range of movements, as indicated by live trapping, of individual animals was used to estimate the area of influence of the grid for each species, thereby converting population numbers to population-density estimates. This was verified by the limited use of an assessment-line procedure (Swift and Steinhorst 1976). In an adjacent area, sample specimens of small mammals were captured for sacrifice and examination of reproductive condition and diet composition. At the mixed-grass and the northern shortgrass prairie sites, where the ungrazed treatment was relatively small, the small mammal estimate was made on the lightly grazed pasture.

Numbers of pocket gopers were estimated by obliterating their recent mounds and counting the new mounds produced in the area of the trapping grid over a three- to five-day period. Lagomorphs and larger herbivorous mammals were estimated on the basis of transects, generally run at night along little-traveled roads. All values for vertebrates were converted to dry weight in grams per unit area, according to average recorded weights for the species if the animals were not actually collected in this study. Density estimates of large grazing herbivores were taken either from literature values or from the most experienced observer in the area. Coyotes were estimated according to an aerial census conducted by experienced personnel at the northern shortgrass prairie site, and results were compared to the index of a sand-tracking technique employed by the Bureau of Sport Fisheries and Wildlife (D. Balser, personal communication). These data allowed conversion of sand-tracking results from locations near other grassland sites to an approximation of the density in the appropriate area. Snakes and lizards were quantitatively evaluated at only one site, the northern shortgrass prairie site. Estimates were taken for the desert grassland site from reports of work conducted under the US/IBP Desert Biome studies. At only three sites, the desert grassland, the northern shortgrass, and the southern shortgrass prairie sites, was the herpetofauna considered to be a significant part of the total biomass.

Soil microflora was studied in detail only at the northern shortgrass and the tallgrass prairie sites, and these values are not included in this analysis. It should be noted that the biomass of this missing component may be great, single estimates indicating approximately 67 and 635 $g \cdot m^{-2}$ at these locations.

The collation of data for trophic pyramid analysis required that standard data be selected and treated in a standard manner. Data were collated for inclusion in the trophic pyramids by the person most familiar with the data set or most knowledgeable in the subject matter. Weights for roots with crowns were expressed on an ash-free, dry-weight basis. It is estimated that the error of sampling resulting from this is less than 20%. Sampling was generally conducted to include the depth which would include at least 90% of the total root biomass. Periodically, samples to greater depths were taken to enable estimation of the 100% biomass values. Therefore, samples at different sites were generally adjusted to an estimate of 100% root biomass. Litter was also expressed on an ash-free, dry-weight basis. Corrections were made to account for soil and mineral particles collected with the material during sampling. The standing crop of vegetation was expressed as oven-dry weight. The error is believed to be less than 20%.

Invertebrate taxa were generally assigned to trophic levels (primary or secondary consumer) by the investigator most familiar with the invertebrate fauna of the site in question. In some cases, where this was unknown, the trophic-level assignment was used which conformed to that determined for the same taxon at another site. Some of these were unknown, though generally this amounted to less than 10% of the biomass at any particular date. Literature was generally the source of such information. The biomass of omnivores was arbitrarily divided equally between the herbivore and carnivore trophic levels, and the biomass of microarthropods, primarily mites, was less than 3% of the biomass of other belowground arthropods, and was generally ignored.

Biomass of nematodes was measured from soil-core samples taken at the mixed-grass, mountain, and northern shortgrass prairie sites. Numbers were estimated from soil cores taken at the southern shortgrass prairie site. From these determinations and literature values for other ecosystems, estimates were made for the remainder of the sites. Complete comparative data are available only for the year 1972, the first year in which nematode sampling was carried out at more than one site. No values are included in this category in 1970 or in 1971 trophic pyramids.

Biomass estimates of small mammals and of birds were obtained by applying the weights of samples collected in the field to density estimates for the study area. For larger mammals, average weights were taken from literature values and applied to the density estimates. Trophic-level assignments were made according to diet studies which indicated the proportion of animal material and plant material in the diet.

For construction of the pyramid diagrams, consumer biomass in each case was further divided between biophage, those that consume living material, and saprophage, those that consume dead or decaying organic material. Invertebrates classified as scavengers were considered to be 100% saprophagic. Such biomass was apportioned to the primary or secondary consumer level according to the availability of plant biomass and animal biomass. This assumes that they are nonselective in their feeding on dead organic material and places a large portion of scavenger biomass in the primary consumer category. The mammals and birds classified as primary consumers were considered to be 100% biophagic. Birds and mammals classified as secondary consumers were considered in some cases to be partly saprophagic, that is, feeding on carrion. Raptors were considered to be 25% saprophagic, coyotes to be 15%. Carnivorous small mammals (shrews and grasshopper mice) were considered to be 100% biophagic. Among the small mammals, *Mus* and *Peromyscus* were considered to be 10% saprophagic, and ground squirrels *(Spermophilus)* were considered to be 25% saprophagic. These percentage values were applied only to that portion of the diet of these animals which was in the secondary consumer category. These divisions are similar to those used in analysis of consumer energy utilization of Chapter 5, but estimates of energy required integration over time utilizing many sample dates.

Data Analysis

For purposes of analysis, the trophic pyramid data were grouped into three separate series. The first series was the most complete in terms of the system components included. These included above- and belowground biomass with nematodes and belowground arthropods. Only the 1972 data from the bunchgrass, mixed-grass, desert grassland, tallgrass, and northern shortgrass sites were sufficiently complete to be included in this series. The second series was constructed by deleting nematodes and belowground arthropods from consideration but retaining root biomass. Adequate data for this series were available from five sites (mixed-grass, desert grassland, tallgrass, southern shortgrass, and northern shortgrass) for three years (1970–1972). The third series included data on aboveground components of the systems only. Data from the sites and years used for the second series were adequate for inclusion in this series.

The calendar date associated with each trophic pyramid was categorized as early, middle, or late, according to its position in the growing season. Growing season starting and ending dates for any year (Table 4.1) were based primarily on a 15-day moving average of temperature. When this average exceeded 40°F, the growing season was considered to start, and when it dropped below this value, the growing season was at an end. This was used only if precipitation at the site was adequate for that year. If precipitation was not adequate at the beginning of the temperature-determined growing season, then the beginning of the growing season was considered to occur when the first significant jump in the rate of increase of cumulative precipitation occurred. The end of the growing season was considered to be two weeks after the last significant rate increase of

Table 4.1. Thermal-Moisture Growing Seasons at Grassland Sites

Grassland site	Year	Julian days		Total days
		Begin	End	
Bunchgrass	1971	80	196	116
(SE Washington)	1972	62	182	116
Mountain	1970	155	258	103
(Bridger Mountains, Montana)	1972	137	277	141
Mixed-grass	1970	120	280	160
(SW South Dakota)	1971	97	309	212
	1972	103	235	132
Desert	1970	183	308	125
(New Mexico)	1971	182	349	167
	1972	155	354	199
Tallgrass	1970	87	298	211
(NE Oklahoma)	1971	69	338	269
	1972	52	327	275
Southern shortgrass	1970	95	258	163
(Texas panhandle)	1971	166	334	168
	1972	126	324	198
Northern shortgrass	1970	95	245	150
(Colorado)	1971	111	272	161
	1972	99	305	206

precipitation. For the bunch-grass site, which has a very early growing season which follows the winter supply of moisture, the beginning was temperature-determined. At this site, the end of the growing season was moisture-determined.

The calendar dates selected for these comparisons were modified to some degree to conform to the dates on which sampling was conducted at the various sites. Because an attempt was made to compare different parts of the growing season at each site, the calendar dates do not coincide (Table 4.2). In a few cases it was necessary to interpolate between two collection periods.

Multivariate analysis of variance was used to test for differences among sites, dates (early, middle, and late growing season), and years (where data from more than one year were used). Analyses were performed on four response vectors, each of which describes the pyramids in a different way. Two response vectors describe the sizes of the pyramids. The first trivariate vector contains, for each pyramid, the biomass observed at the primary producer (PP), primary consumer (PC), and secondary consumer (SC) trophic levels. The second response vector is the same as the first except that logarithmic transformations of the standing-crop data were used. This was done because of the concern that, in the untransformed case, the very large size of PP relative to PC and SC might result in an analysis in which essentially all of the information was being added by the PP component. This procedure reduced absolute differences between values for the three trophic levels.

Pyramid shape was described by two bivariate response vectors, one containing biomass ratios, the other biomass proportions. The ratio vector includes the ratio of primary consumer to primary producer biomass (PC/PP) and secondary consumer to primary consumer biomass (SC/PC). The proportion vector consists of the proportion of total biomass contributed by the primary producer (PP/Total) and primary consumer trophic levels (PC/Total). It should be noted that for each of the two shape vectors a third element could be specified, (SC/PP) and (SC/Total). These were not included because, in each case, specification of two elements in the vector uniquely defines the third, and the third element thus adds no information to the analysis.

With three series of trophic pyramids, each including data on different components of the system, and with four response vectors for each pyramid, two describing size and two describing shape, 12 multivariate analyses of variance were performed. Each analysis included information from five sites, three dates per year, for either one or three years. If any analysis revealed a significant difference among sites, years, or dates, the source of that difference was investigated using multiple comparison of means (Miller 1966). Each analysis of variance involved five sites. Ten distinct comparisons between site means were thus possible for each analysis. It was intended to make these ten comparisons simultaneously, so that the α level for significance would be associated with all ten tests taken together. This problem is approached through the application of

Table 4.2. Percentage of Growing Season Represented by Trophic Pyramid Dates

Grassland site	Year	% of growing season by trophic pyramid date		
		Early	Middle	Late
Bunchgrass	1971	1	55	98
	1972	18	72	92
Mountain	1970	25	46	85
	1972	29	50	69
Mixed-grass	1970	4	35	67
	1971	21	43	62
	1972	44	85	100
Desert	1970	10	49	100
	1971	26	47	77
	1972	0	24	57
Tallgrass	1970	31	45	67
	1971	23	45	79
	1972	30	39	71
Southern shortgrass	1970	44	52	67
	1971	4	41	86
	1972	0	33	96
Northern shortgrass	1970	6	48	86
	1971	0	35	65
	1972	36	59	85

Bonferroni's inequality (Miller 1966). This inequality states that, having established an α level for the set of simultaneous comparisons, the α level for each comparison within the set is equal to α/n, where n is the number of comparisons in the set. If this is done, then the significance level of the entire set of comparisons is equal to or less than α. An α level of 0.05 was established for each set of comparisons. Thus, to be significant, any individual comparison must have a significance level of $\alpha/10$ or 0.005. When this procedure is followed, the probability that the result of all ten comparisons considered together is correct is 95 percent or better.

Results

The biomass data which went into the construction of the pyramids appear in Tables 4.3, 4.4, and 4.5. Diagrams of the pyramids are shown in Figure 4.1a–g. These diagrams were constructed on a logarithmic scale because of the great differences in biomass between trophic levels. In these figures, primary producer biomass is broken down into live, dead, and litter components, and the two consumer trophic levels are divided vertically on a linear scale into biophagic and saprophagic components. These divisions were made so that the data might be presented as completely as possible. No such divisions existed in the data subjected to analysis of variance.

Results of the multivariate analyses of variance are presented in Tables 4.6 and 4.7. The analysis of all four series of trophic pyramids showed highly significant site differences ($\alpha < 0.01$) in all cases. In two instances, (aboveground pyramids, transformed and untransformed size response) a significant ($\alpha < 0.05$) year difference was found. The shape responses never showed significant annual variation, and neither dates within years nor any of the interaction terms showed significant differences in any of the measures of trophic structure.

A multiple comparison of means (Miller 1966) was used to determine which site or sites were responsible for the differences detected by the analyses of variance. The results are found in Tables 4.8, 4.9, 4.10, and 4.11. The entries in these tables are the α level at which each two pairs of sites can be considered different; significant differences are indicated.

The results of these comparisons do not present a clear picture of the factors responsible for site differences. The pattern of significant differences indicates that the desert grassland site is a distinct site in terms of trophic structure. Of all individual comparisons performed, 45 were found to be significant. Thirty-six of these involved the desert grassland site. Only one significant difference among sites, other than comparisons involving the desert grassland site, was found for either of the shape vectors. Still, some significant differences among the other sites are indicated, particularly with regard to size. In two cases (size response, transformed and untransformed, of aboveground biomass pyramid), the northern and southern shortgrass sites are significantly different. Both of these sites are shortgrass prairie and are similar floristically.

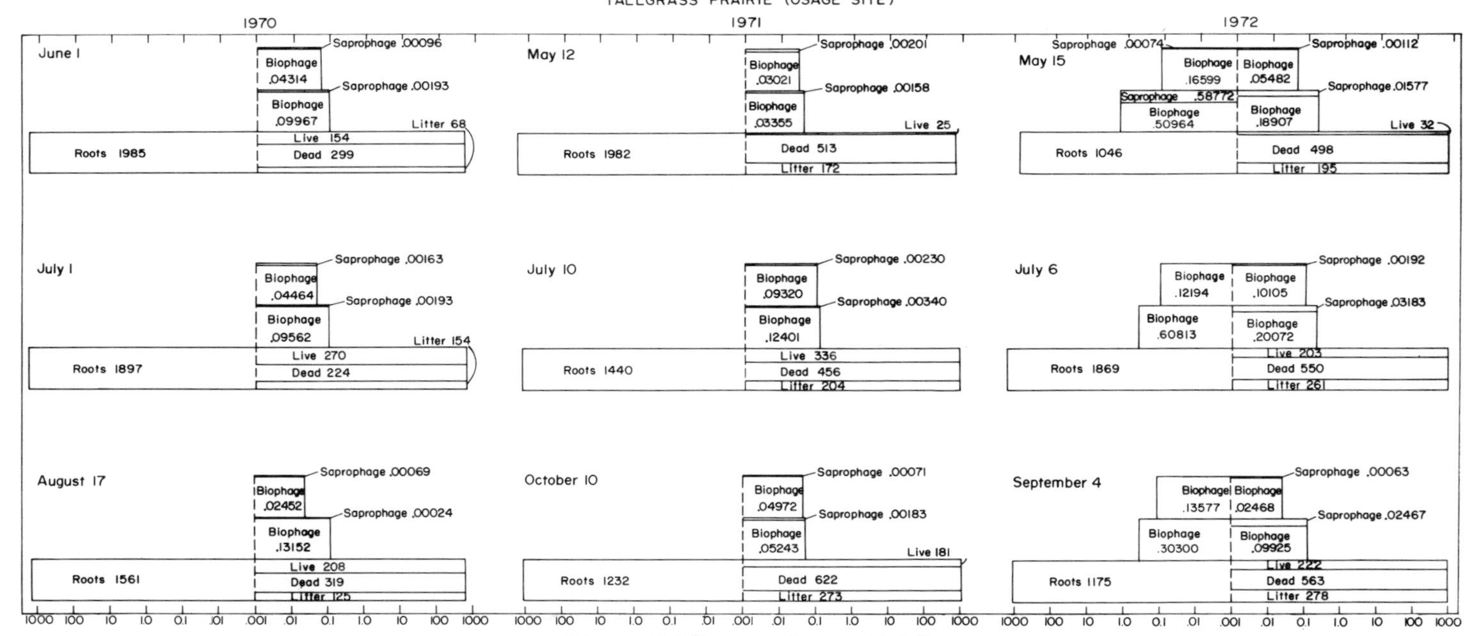

Figure 4.1a. Biomass trophic pyramids for grassland sites for three dates per year.

The base of each pyramid represents biomass (g dry weight · m^{-2}) of producers, the second (middle) level primary consumers, and the top secondary consumers. Aboveground (right) and belowground (left) biomass values are separated by a dashed vertical line. The trophic-level magnitudes are plotted on a horizontal logarithmic scale; compartments are divided on a linear vertical scale according to live, standing dead, and litter, or biophagic and saprophagic consumer biomass.

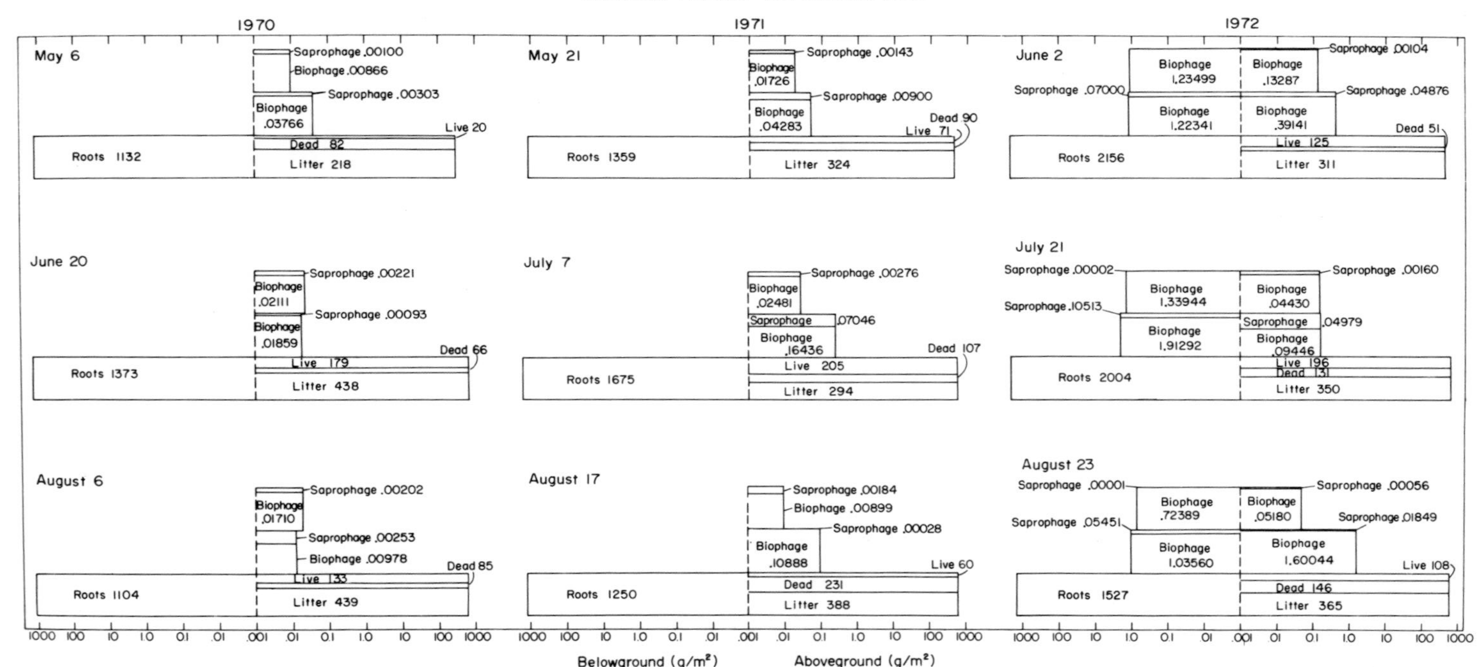
MIDGRASS PRAIRIE (COTTONWOOD SITE)
1970
1971
1972
May 6
Saprophage .00100
Biophage .00866
Saprophage .00303
Biophage .03766
Live 20
Dead 82
Roots 1132
Litter 218
May 21
Saprophage .00143
Biophage .01726
Saprophage .00900
Biophage .04283
Dead 90
Live 71
Roots 1359
Litter 324
June 2
Saprophage .00104
Biophage 1.23499
Biophage .13287
Saprophage .07000
Saprophage .04876
Biophage 1.22341
Biophage .39141
Dead 51
Live 125
Roots 2156
Litter 311
June 20
Saprophage .00221
Biophage .02111
Saprophage .00093
Biophage .01859
Dead 66
Live 179
Roots 1373
Litter 438
July 7
Saprophage .00276
Biophage .02481
Saprophage .07046
Biophage .16436
Dead 107
Live 205
Roots 1675
Litter 294
July 21
Saprophage .00002
Saprophage .00160
Biophage 1.33944
Biophage .04430
Saprophage .10513
Saprophage .04979
Biophage 1.91292
Biophage .09446
Live 196
Dead 131
Roots 2004
Litter 350
August 6
Saprophage .00202
Biophage .01710
Saprophage .00253
Biophage .00978
Dead 85
Live 133
Roots 1104
Litter 439
August 17
Saprophage .00184
Biophage .00899
Saprophage .00028
Biophage .10888
Live 60
Dead 231
Roots 1250
Litter 388
August 23
Saprophage .00001
Saprophage .00056
Biophage .72389
Biophage .05180
Saprophage .05451
Saprophage .01849
Biophage 1.03560
Biophage 1.60044
Live 108
Dead 146
Roots 1527
Litter 365
1000 100 10 1.0 0.1 .01 .001 .01 0.1 1.0 10 100 1000
Belowground (g/m²)
Aboveground (g/m²)

Figure 4.1b.

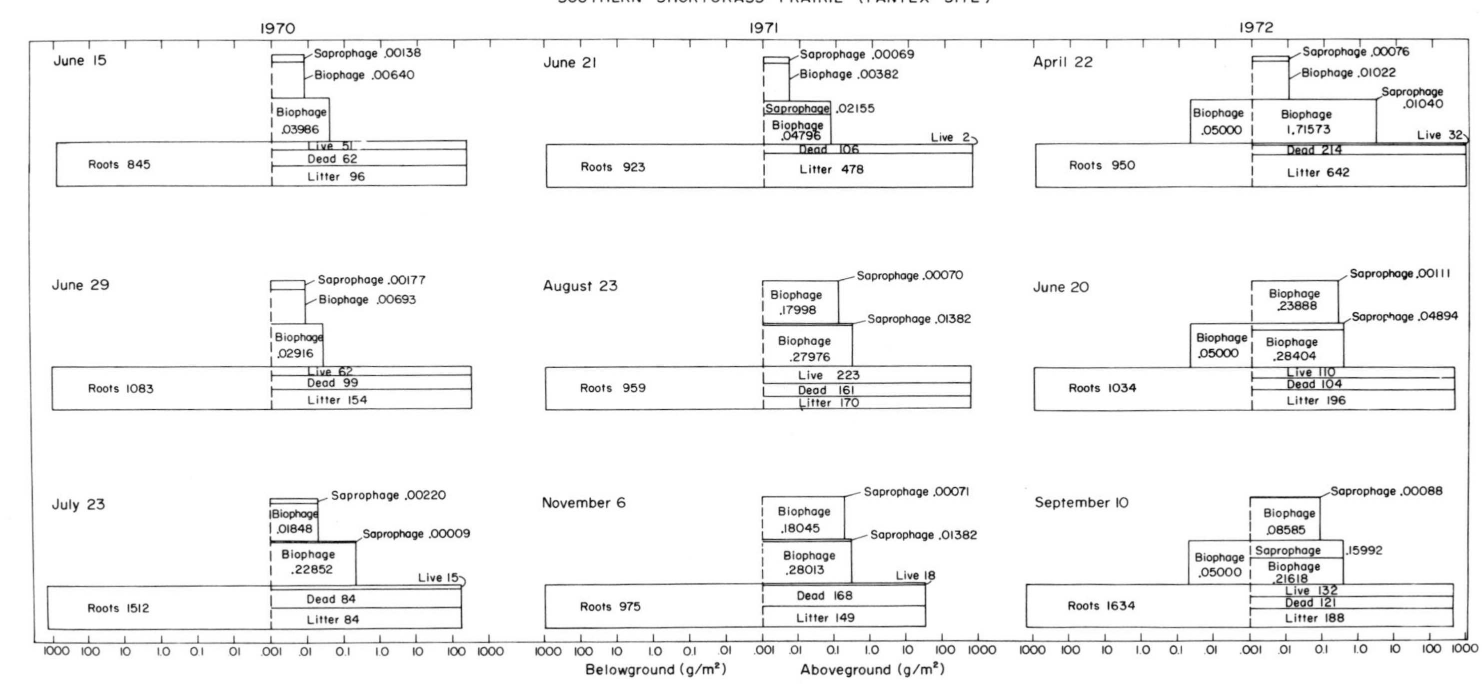
SOUTHERN SHORTGRASS PRAIRIE (PANTEX SITE)
1970
June 15
Saprophage .00138
Biophage .00640
Biophage .03986
Live 51
Dead 62
Litter 96
Roots 845
June 29
Saprophage .00177
Biophage .00693
Biophage .02916
Live 62
Dead 99
Litter 154
Roots 1083
July 23
Saprophage .00220
Saprophage .00009
Biophage .01848
Biophage .22852
Live 15
Dead 84
Litter 84
Roots 1512
1971
June 21
Saprophage .00069
Biophage .00382
Saprophage .02155
Biophage .04796
Live 2
Dead 106
Litter 478
Roots 923
August 23
Saprophage .00070
Saprophage .01382
Biophage .17998
Biophage .27976
Live 223
Dead 161
Litter 170
Roots 959
November 6
Saprophage .00071
Saprophage .01382
Biophage .18045
Biophage .28013
Live 18
Dead 168
Litter 149
Roots 975
1972
April 22
Saprophage .00076
Biophage .01022
Saprophage .01040
Biophage 1.71573
Biophage .05000
Live 32
Dead 214
Litter 642
Roots 950
June 20
Saprophage .00111
Saprophage .04894
Biophage .23888
Biophage .28404
Biophage .05000
Live 110
Dead 104
Litter 196
Roots 1034
September 10
Saprophage .00088
Saprophage .15992
Biophage .08585
Biophage .21618
Biophage .05000
Live 132
Dead 121
Litter 188
Roots 1634
Belowground (g/m²)
Aboveground (g/m²)

Figure 4.1c.

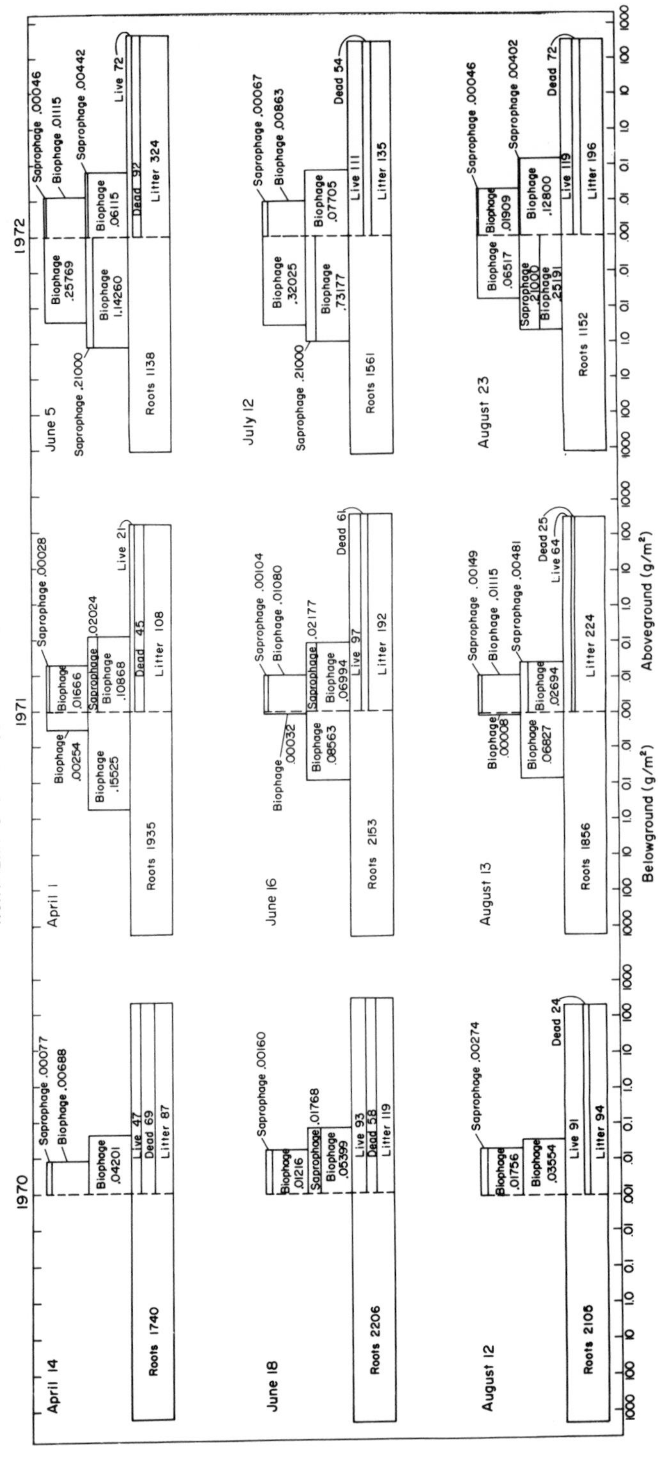
NORTHERN SHORTGRASS PRAIRIE (PAWNEE SITE)
1970
April 14
Saprophage .00077
Biophage .00688
Biophage .04201
Live 47
Dead 69
Litter 87
Roots 1740
June 18
Saprophage .00160
Biophage .01216
Saprophage .01768
Biophage .05399
Live 93
Dead 58
Litter 119
Roots 2206
August 12
Saprophage .00274
Biophage .01756
Biophage .03554
Live 91
Litter 94
Dead 24
Roots 2105
1971
April 1
Saprophage .00028
Biophage .01666
Saprophage .02024
Biophage .10868
Dead 45
Litter 108
Live 21
Biophage .00254
Biophage .15525
Roots 1935
June 16
Saprophage .00104
Biophage .01080
Saprophage .02177
Biophage .06994
Live 97
Litter 192
Dead 61
Biophage .00032
Biophage .08563
Roots 2153
August 13
Saprophage .00149
Biophage .01115
Saprophage .00481
Biophage .02694
Litter 224
Dead 25
Live 64
Biophage .00008
Biophage .06827
Roots 1856
1972
June 5
Saprophage .00046
Biophage .01115
Saprophage .00442
Biophage .06115
Dead 92
Litter 324
Live 72
Biophage .25769
Biophage 1.14260
Saprophage .21000
Roots 1138
July 12
Saprophage .00067
Biophage .00863
Biophage .07705
Live 111
Litter 135
Dead 54
Biophage .32025
Biophage .73177
Saprophage .21000
Roots 1561
August 23
Saprophage .00046
Saprophage .00402
Biophage .01909
Biophage .12800
Live 119
Litter 196
Dead 72
Biophage .06517
Saprophage .2100
Biophage .25191
Roots 1152
1000 100 10 1.0 .1 .01 .001 .01 .1 1.0 10 100 1000
Belowground (g/m²)
Aboveground (g/m²)

Figure 4.1d.

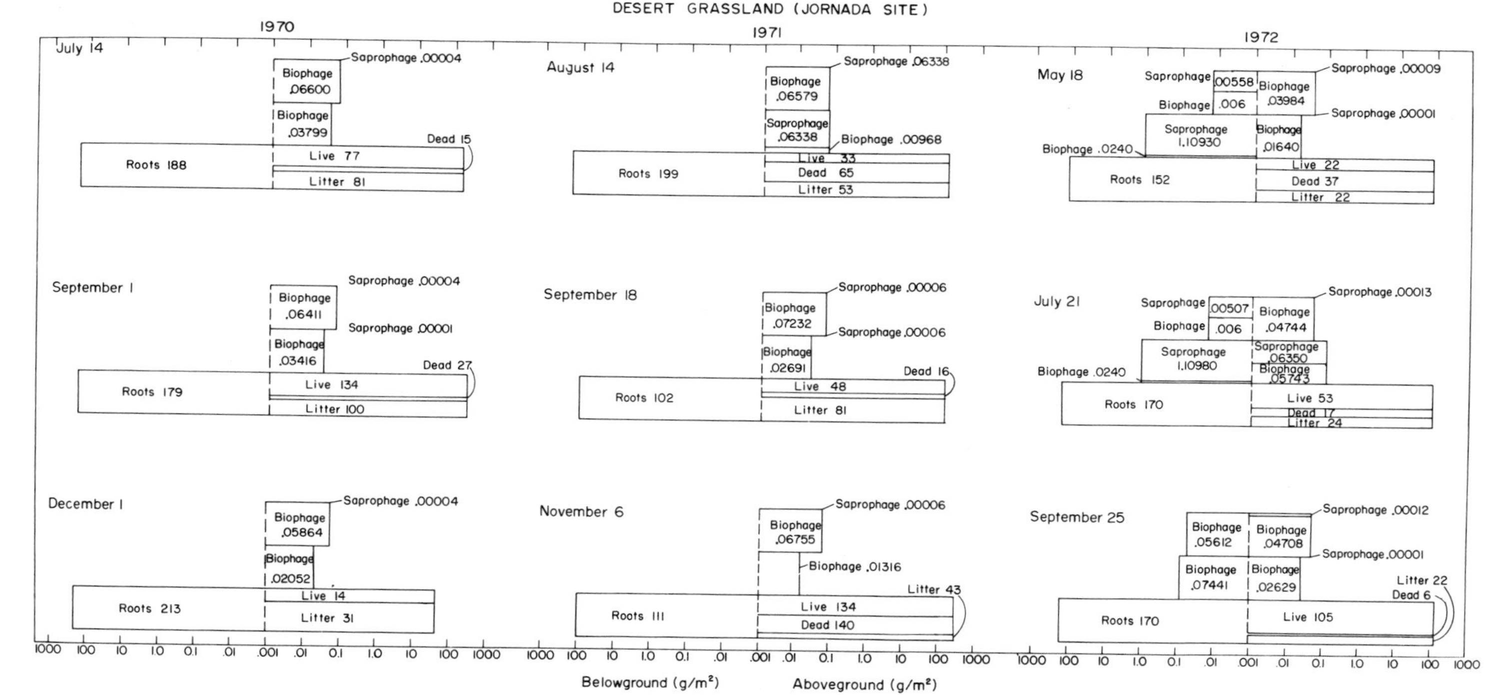
DESERT GRASSLAND (JORNADA SITE)
1970
1971
1972
July 14
Biophage .06600
Saprophage .00004
Biophage .03799
Dead 15
Roots 188
Live 77
Litter 81
August 14
Biophage .06579
Saprophage .06338
Saprophage .06338
Biophage .00968
Roots 199
Live 33
Dead 65
Litter 53
May 18
Saprophage .00558
Biophage .006
Biophage .03984
Saprophage .00009
Saprophage .00001
Saprophage 1.10930
Biophage .01640
Biophage .0240
Roots 152
Live 22
Dead 37
Litter 22
September 1
Biophage .06411
Saprophage .00004
Saprophage .00001
Biophage .03416
Dead 27
Roots 179
Live 134
Litter 100
September 18
Biophage .07232
Saprophage .00006
Saprophage .00006
Biophage .02691
Dead 16
Roots 102
Live 48
Litter 81
July 21
Saprophage .00507
Biophage .006
Biophage .04744
Saprophage .00013
Saprophage 1.10980
Saprophage .06350
Biophage .05743
Biophage .0240
Roots 170
Live 53
Dead 17
Litter 24
December 1
Biophage .05864
Saprophage .00004
Biophage .02052
Roots 213
Live 14
Litter 31
November 6
Biophage .06755
Saprophage .00006
Biophage .01316
Litter 43
Roots 111
Live 134
Dead 140
September 25
Biophage .05612
Biophage .04708
Saprophage .00012
Saprophage .00001
Biophage .07441
Biophage .02629
Litter 22
Dead 6
Roots 170
Live 105
1000 100 10 1.0 0.1 .01 .001 .01 0.1 1.0 10 100 1000
Belowground (g/m²)
Aboveground (g/m²)

Figure 4.1e.

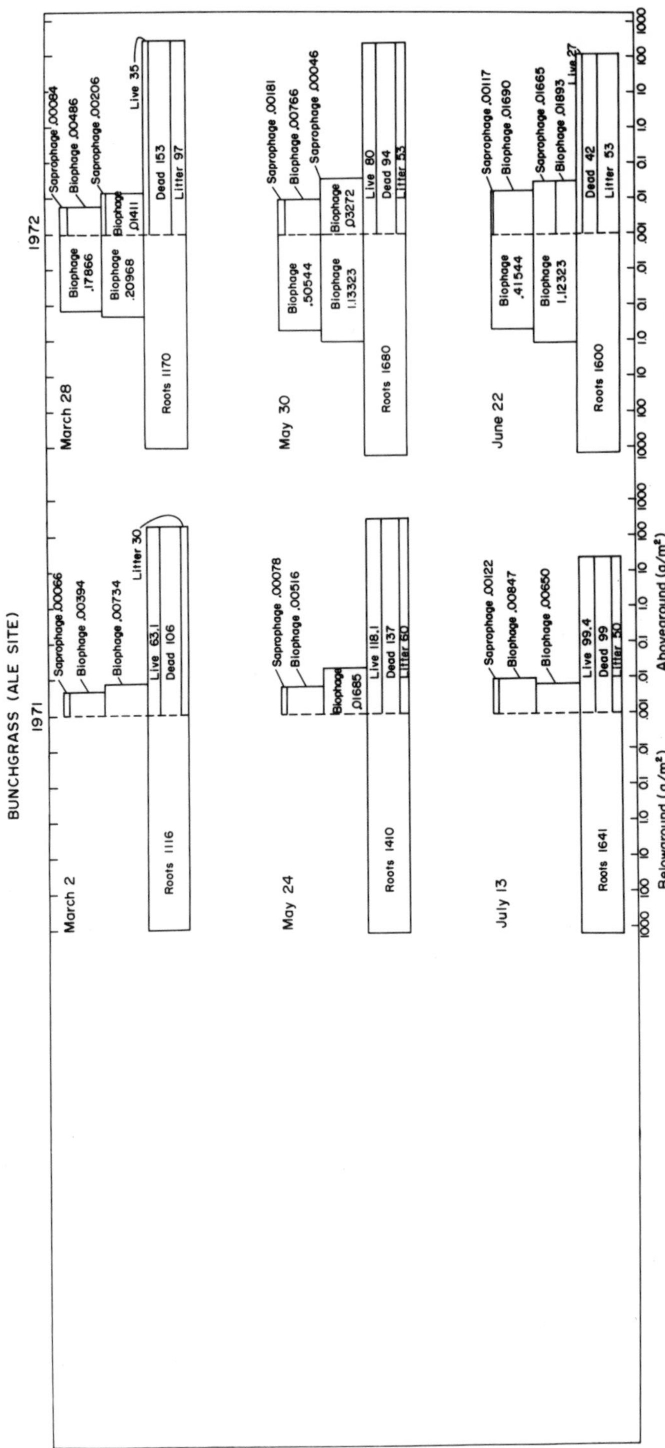

BUNCHGRASS (ALE SITE)
1971
1972
March 2
March 28
May 24
May 30
July 13
June 22
Saprophage .00066
Biophage .00394
Biophage .00734
Litter 30
Live 63.1
Dead 106
Roots 1116
Saprophage .00084
Biophage .00486
Saprophage .00206
Biophage .17866
Biophage .20968
Biophage .01411
Live 35
Dead 153
Litter 97
Roots 1170
Saprophage .00078
Biophage .00516
Biophage .01685
Live 118.1
Dead 137
Litter 60
Roots 1410
Saprophage .00181
Biophage .00766
Saprophage .00046
Biophage .50544
Biophage 1.13323
Biophage .03272
Live 80
Dead 94
Litter 53
Roots 1680
Saprophage .00122
Biophage .00847
Biophage .00650
Live 99.4
Dead 99
Litter 50
Roots 1641
Saprophage .00117
Biophage .01690
Saprophage .01665
Biophage .01893
Biophage .41544
Biophage 1.12323
Live 27
Dead 42
Litter 53
Roots 1600
1000 100 10 1.0 .1 .01 .001 .01 .1 1.0 10 100 1000
Belowground (g/m²)
Aboveground (g/m²)

Figure 4.1f.

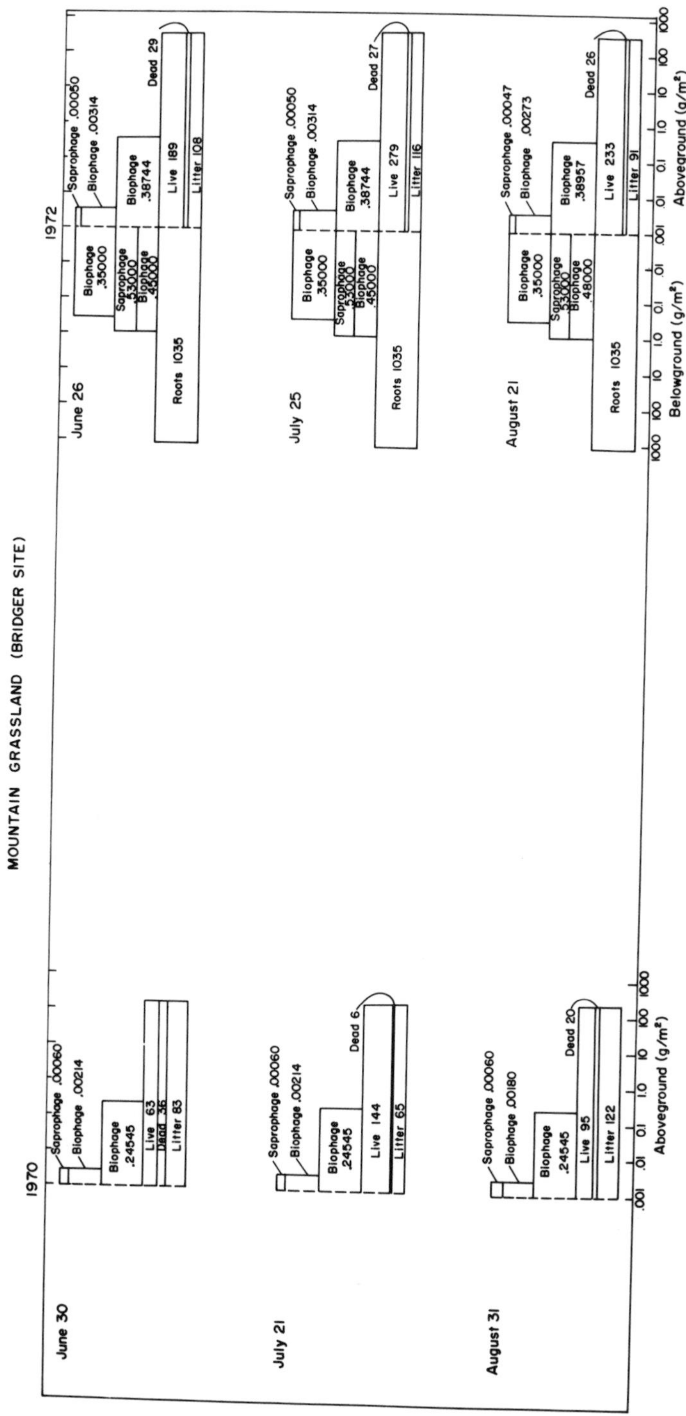

MOUNTAIN GRASSLAND (BRIDGER SITE)
1970
June 30
Saprophage .00060
Biophage .00214
Biophage .24545
Live 63
Dead 36
Litter 83
July 21
Saprophage .00060
Biophage .00214
Biophage .24545
Live 144
Dead 6
Litter 65
August 31
Saprophage .00060
Biophage .00180
Biophage .24545
Live 95
Dead 20
Litter 122
.001 .01 .01 1.0 10 100 1000
Aboveground (g/m²)
1972
June 26
Saprophage .00050
Biophage .00314
Biophage .35000
Saprophage .53000
Biophage .42000
Roots 1035
Biophage .38744
Live 189
Dead 29
Litter 108
July 25
Saprophage .00050
Biophage .00314
Biophage .35000
Saprophage .53000
Biophage .45000
Roots 1035
Biophage .38744
Live 279
Dead 27
Litter 116
August 21
Saprophage .00047
Biophage .00273
Biophage .35000
Saprophage .53000
Biophage .48000
Roots 1035
Biophage .38957
Live 233
Dead 26
Litter 91
1000 100 10 1.0 0.1 .01 .001 .01 0.1 1.0 10 100 1000
Belowground (g/m²)
Aboveground (g/m²)

Figure 4.1g.

Table 4.3. Biomass Values (g · m^{-2} dry weight) for Each Category of Organisms at Grassland Sites in 1970

		Primary producers						Primary consumers						
Grassland site	Date	Roots with crowns	Litter	Old dead	Recent dead	Live	Total	Aboveground invertebrates	Belowground arthropods	Nematodes	Small mammals	Pocket gophers	Lagomorphs	Mule deer
Mountain	6/30/70	–	83	36	0	63	182				.00863	.0100	.03409	
	7/21/70	–	65	6	0	144	215				.00863	.0100	.03409	
	8/31/70	–	122	0	20	95	237				.00862	.0100	.03409	
Mixed-grass	5/6/70	1132	218	81	1	20	1452	.03962			.00100			
	5/20/70	1373	438	56	10	179	2056	.01601			.00188			
	8/6/70	1104	439	50	35	133	1761	.08046			.00157			
Desert	7/14/70	188	81	15	0	77	361	.00106			.02971		.00169	
	9/1/70	179	100	20	7	134	440	.00198			.02383		.00283	
	12/1/70	213	31	0	0	14	258	.00052			.01333		.00114	
Tallgrass	6/1/70	1985	68	299	0	154	2506	.06950			.03179			
	7/1/70	1897	154	223	1	270	2545	.06950			.02758			
	8/17/70	1561	125	157	162	208	2213	.10708			.02462			
Southern shortgrass	6/15/70	845	96	62	0	51	1054	.03383			.00355		.00146	
	6/29/70	1083	154	99	0	62	1398	.02252			.00398		.00150	
	7/27/70	1512	84	84	0	15	1695	.22195			.00485		.00094	
Northern shortgrass	4/14/70	1740	87	69	0	47	1943	.02846			.00246	.0040		
	6/18/70	2206	119	58	0	93	2476	.05331			.00676	.0040		
	8/12/70	2105	94	4	20	91	2134	.00928			.01555	.0040		

Grassland site	Date	Primary consumers					Secondary consumers							
		Antelope	Elk	Moose	Birds	Total	Above-ground invertebrates	Below-ground arthropods	Reptiles	Nematodes	Birds	Coyotes	Small mammals	Total
Mountain	6/30/70	0	.07645	.11467	.001612	.24545					.002398		.00034	.00274
	7/21/70	0	.07645	.11467	.001612	.24545					.002398		.00034	.00274
	8/31/70	0	.07645	.11467	.001612	.24545					.002398			.00240
Mixed-grass	5/6/70	0	0	0	.000070	.04069	.00543				.003854		.00038	.00966
	5/20/70	0	0	0	.001631	.01952	.01407				.008591		.00066	.02332
	8/6/70	0	0	0	.000277	.01231	.01057				.007503		.00105	.01912
Desert	7/14/70	.0055	0	0	.000033	.03799	.00193		.042		.000143		.02197	.06604
	9/1/70	.0055	0	0	.000033	.03417	.00304		.042		.000143		.01897	.06415
	12/1/70	.0055	0	0	.000033	.02052	.00392		.052		.000143		.01262	.05868
Tallgrass	6/1/70	0	0	0	.000307	.10160	.03552				.003834		.00475	.04410
	7/1/70	0	0	0	.000466	.09755	.03552				.006532		.00422	.04627
	8/17/70	0	0	0	.000057	.13176	.01862				.002741		.00385	.02521
Southern shortgrass	6/15/70	0	0	0	.001021	.03986	.00129				.003171		.00332	.00778
	6/29/70	0	0	0	.001158	.02916	.00210				.004090		.00251	.00870
	7/27/70	0	0	0	.000932	.22867	.01065				.004502		.00553	.02068
Northern shortgrass	4/14/70	.0064	0	0	.000678	.04200	.00275		0		.001572		.00333	.00765
	6/18/70	.0064	0	0	.001193	.07167	0		.006		.002507		.00525	.01376
	8/12/70	.0064	0	0	.030302	.03554	.00140		.006		.001602		.01130	.02030

Table 4.4. Biomass Values (g · m^{-2} dry weight) for Each Category of Organisms at Grassland Sites in 1971

		Primary producers						Primary consumers						
Grassland site	Date	Roots with crowns	Litter	Old dead	Recent dead	Live	Total	Aboveground invertebrates	Belowground arthropods	Nematodes	Small mammals	Pocket gophers	Lagomorphs	Mule deer
Bunchgrass	3/22/71	1116.0	30	106	0	63	1315				.00666			
	5/24/71	1410.0	60	128	9	118	1725				.01550			
	7/13/71	1641.0	50	96	3	99	1889				.00543			
Mixed-grass	5/21/71	1359.0	324	90	0	71	1844	.05009			.00021		.00125	
	7/7/71	1675.0	294	55	52	205	2281	.22535			.00391		.00022	
	8/17/71	1250.0	388	23	208	60	1929	.10474			.00411		.00011	
Desert	8/14/71	198.5	53	30	35	33	349	.06353			.00256		.00147	
	9/18/71	102.3	81	14	2	48	247	.00563			.00571		.00219	
	11/6/71	111.0	43	91	49	134[1]	428	.00284			.00115		.00191	
Tallgrass	5/12/71	1982.0	172	513	0	25	2692	.03382			.00066			
	7/10/71	1440.0	204	456	0	336	2436	.11004			.01550		.00089	
	10/10/71	1232.0	273	248	374	181	2308	.04341			.00606		.00479	
Southern shortgrass	6/21/71	923.0	478	103	3	2	1509	.05981			.00096		.00801	
	8/23/71	959.0	170	92	69	223	1513	.29024			.00134		.00148	
	11/6/71	975.0	149	0	168	18	1310	.29024			.00155		.00164	
Northern shortgrass	4/1/71	1935.0	108	45	0	21	2109	.10897	.15525		.00094	.0040		
	6/16/71	2153.0	192	54	7	97	2503	.07017	.08563		.00202	.0040		
	8/13/71	1856.0	224	0	25	64	2169	.00762	.06827		.00523	.0040		

Grassland site	Date	Primary consumers					Secondary consumers							
		Antelope	Elk	Moose	Birds	Total	Above ground invertebrates	Below-ground arthropods	Reptiles	Nematodes	Birds	Coyotes	Small mammals	Total
Bunchgrass	3/22/71	0	0	0	.00068	.00734					.00198		.00262	.00460
	5/24/71	0	0	0	.00135	.01685					.00295		.00299	.00594
	7/13/71	0	0	0	.00107	.00650					.00322		.00647	.00969
Mixed-grass	5/21/71	0	0	0	.00028	.05183	.01279				.00554		.00036	.01869
	7/7/71	0	0	0	.00534	.23482	.01610				.00923		.00224	.02757
	8/17/71	0	0	0	.00020	.10916	.00286				.00577		.00220	.01083
Desert	8/14/71	.0055	0	0	0	.07306	.00012		.0633		0		.00267	.06582
	9/18/71	.0055	0	0	.00794	.02697	.00542		.0630		.00018		.00378	.07238
	11/6/71	.0055	0	0	.00176	.01316	.00109		.0630		.00020		.00332	.06761
Tallgrass	5/12/71	0	0	0	.00065	.03513	.02446				.00514		.00262	.03222
	7/10/71	0	0	0	.00098	.12741	.08349				.00676		.00299	.09324
	10/10/71	0	0	0	0	.05426	.04724				.00278		.00041	.05043
Southern shortgrass	6/21/71	0	0	0	.00073	.06951	.00117				.00249		.00085	.00451
	8/23/71	0	0	0	.00052	.29358	.17658				.00192		.00218	.18068
	11/6/71	0	0	0	.00052	.29395	.17658				.00182		.00876	.18716
Northern shortgrass	4/1/71	.0146	0	0	.00041	.28417	.01331	.00254	0		.00164		.00199	.01948
	6/16/71	.0146	0	0	.00092	.17734	.00294	.00032	.00354		.00305		.00225	.00856
	8/13/71	.0146	0	0	.00030	.10002	.00171	.00008	.00354		.00233		.00480	.01246

[1] Includes 112 perennial live.

Table 4.5. Biomass Values ($g \cdot m^{-2}$ dry weight) for Each Category of Organisms at Grassland Sites in 1972

		Primary producers						Primary consumers							
Grassland site	Date	Roots with crowns	Litter	Old dead	Recent dead	Live	Total	Above-ground invertebrates	Below-ground arthropods	Nematodes	Small mammals	Pocket gophers	Lagomorphs	Mule deer	Antelope
Bunchgrass	3/28/72	1170	97	153.00	0	35	1455	0.00618	0.16968	.04000	.00975				
	5/30/72	1680	53	94.00	0	80	1907	0.01827	1.09323	.04000	.01411				
	6/22/72	1600	53	42.00	0	27	1722	0.02788	1.08323	.04000	.00683				
Mountain	6/26/72	1035	108	7.20	22.10	189	1362			.98000	.01662	.01050		0.16830	
	7/25/72	1035	116	12.40	14.60	279	1457			.98000	.01662	.01050		0.16830	
	8/21/72	1035	91	9.40	17.00	233	1386			.98000	.46875	.01050		0.16830	
Mixed-grass	6/2/72	2156	311	28.00	23.00	125	2643	0.18344	0.66341	.63000	.00191			0.25464	
	7/21/72	2004	350	19.00	112.00	196	2681	0.14118	1.03805	.98000	.00276				
	8/23/72	1527	365	61.00	85.00	108	2146	0.22267	0.66011	.43000	.00230			1.39390	
Desert	5/18/72	152	22	9.34	27.88	22	234	0.00431	1.10930	.02400	.00477		.00096		.00550
	7/21/72	170	24	6.57	10.89	53	264	0.11052	1.10930	.02400	.00383		.00073		.00550
	9/24/72	170	22	6.13	0.26	105	303	0.01541	0.05041	.02400	.00325		.00114		.00550
Tallgrass	5/15/72	1046	195	98.00	0	32	1771	0.11205	0.81236	.28500	.09234				
	7/6/72	1869	261	540.00	10.00	203	2883	0.16618	0.32313	.28500	.05769		.00791		
	9/4/72	1175	278	484.00	79.00	222	2238	0.07340	0.01800	.28500	.04257		.00791		
Southern shortgrass	4/22/72	950	642	214.00	0	32	1838	1.71586		.05000	.00883		.00120		
	6/20/72	1034	196	81.00	23.00	110	1444	0.32180		.05000	.01063		.00012		
	9/10/72	1634	188	33.00	88.00	132	2075	0.36543		.05000	.00894		.00138		
Northern shortgrass	6/5/72	1138	324	71.00	21.00	72	1626	0.01507	0.98260	.37000	.00217	.00627	.03250		.00324
	7/12/72	1561	135	37.00	17.00	111	1861	0.02662	0.57177	.37000	.00218	.00627	.03250		.00324
	8/23/72	1152	196	37.00	35.00	119	1539	0.03436	0.09191	.37000	.00186	.00627	.03250		.00324

Grassland site	Date	Primary consumers				Secondary consumers								Soil microflora
		Elk	Moose	Birds	Total	Above-ground invertebrates	Below-ground arthropods	Reptiles	Nematodes	Birds	Coyotes	Small mammals	Total	
Bunchgrass	3/28/72			.00024	0.23585	.00072	.16866		.01000	.00087	.00008	.00403	0.18465	
	5/30/72			.00080	1.16641	.00162	.49544		.01000	.00116	.00008	.00661	0.51491	
	6/22/72			.00087	1.15881	.01277	.40544		.01000	.00275	.00008	.00247	0.43351	
Mountain	6/26/72	.07645	.11467	.00090	1.36744				.35000	.00120	.00006	.00238	0.35364	
	7/25/72	.07645	.11467	.00090	1.36744				.35000	.00120	.00006	.00238	0.35364	
	8/21/72	.07645	.11467	.00090	1.81957				.35000	.00120	.00006	.00194	0.35320	
Mixed-grass	6/2/72			.00018	1.73358	.12981	.66499		.57000	.00349	.00008	.00053	1.36890	
	7/21/72			.00031	2.16199	0.3909	.53946		.80000	.00626	.00008	.00047	1.38536	
	8/23/72			.00006	2.70904	.04994	.16390		.56000	.00170	.00008	.00064	0.77626	
Desert	5/18/72			.00087	1.14971	.00378	.00558	.03213	.00600	.00025	.00011	.00366	0.05152	
	7/21/72			.00030	1.25473	.01158	.00507	.03213	.00600	.00026	.00011	.00349	0.05864	
	9/25/72			.00100	0.10071	.01134	.05012	.03213	.00600	.00034	.00011	.00328	0.10332	
Tallgrass	5/15/72			.00045	2.10720	.04240	.05423		.11250	.00379	.00022	.00953	0.11017	635
	7/6/72			.00077	1.65568	.08682	.00944		.11250	.00704	.00022	.00889	0.11241	635
	9/4/72			.00004	1.24192	.01753	.02327		.11250	.00206	.00022	.00550	0.04858	635
Southern shortgrass	4/22/72			.00024	1.77613	.00474				.00207	.00013	.00404	0.01098	50
	6/20/72			.00043	0.38298	.23246				.00305	.00013	.00435	0.23999	50
	9/10/72			.00034	0.42610	.08103				.00154	.00013	.00403	0.08673	50
Northern shortgrass	6/5/72			.00632	1.41817	.00518	.19769	.00252	.06000	.00180	.00009	.00202	0.26930	67
	7/12/72			.00624	1.01882	.00200	.26025	.00252	.06000	.00265	.00009	.00204	0.32955	67
	8/23/72			.00379	0.59393	.01325	.00517	.00252	.06000	.00177	.00009	.00192	0.08472	67

Table 4.6. Significance Levels for Multivariate Analysis of Variance for Complete Biomass Pyramids

	Size (PP, PC, SC)	Log_{10} size [log_{10}(PP + 1), log_{10}(PC + 1), log_{10}(SC + 1)]	Ratio (PC/PP, SC/PC)	Proportion (PP/Total, PC/Total)
Sites[1]	.0002[2]	.0000 hr.	.0016[2]	.0035[2]
Dates[3]	.3502	.2301	.1616	.4316

[1] Bunchgrass, mixed-grass, desert grassland, tallgrass, northern shortgrass.
[2] Significant at 1% level.
[3] 1972, 3 dates per year.

In two cases, an annual difference in aboveground pyramid size was revealed by analysis of variance. These annual differences in size appear in both the transformed and untransformed cases (see Table 4.7). The multiple comparison of means shows that, in both cases, the 1970 pyramids are significantly different from the 1971 pyramids. Differences between 1970 and 1972 approach the established significance level (Table 4.12). Note that the simultaneous alpha level for each set of tests was set at 0.05. Since there are three comparisons per set, the alpha level for significance for an individual comparison is 0.05/3, or 0.0167. The pattern of results suggests that aboveground pyramids from 1971 and 1972 are very similar while those from 1970 tend to be different.

Discussion

That communities are organized into trophic levels which assume pyramidal shapes is evidenced by the fact that these have been diagramed and discussed for such divergent systems as temperate old fields, tropical forests, and coral atolls.

Table 4.7. Significance Levels for Multivariate Analysis of Variance for Partial Biomass Pyramids

	Size (PP, PC, SC)		Log_{10} size		Ratio (PC/PP, SC/PC)		Proportion (PP/Total, PC/Total)	
	1[1]	2[2]	1[1]	2[2]	1[1]	2[2]	1[1]	2[2]
Sites (S)[3]	.0000[4]	.0000[4]	.0000[4]	.0000[4]	.0000[4]	.0000[4]	.0000[4]	.0000[4]
Years (Y)[5]	.2705	.0186[6]	.2574	.0310[6]	.3406	.4385	.4184	.9512
Dates (D)	.4406	.3239	.5661	.4701	.1773	.1367	.7746	.9738
S · Y	.1756	.1320	.3770	.2688	.6920	.7341	.3898	.9393
S · D	.9460	.7061	.9755	.9455	.5067	.5141	.8653	.9520
Y · D	.7328	.6200	.6698	.4369	.6412	.7498	.5611	.6421

[1] Pyramid type: total biomass minus nematodes and belowground arthropods.
[2] Pyramid type: aboveground biomass only.
[3] Mixed-grass, desert grassland, tallgrass, northern shortgrass, southern shortgrass.
[4] Significant at 1% level.
[5] 1970, 1971, 1972; 3 dates per year.
[6] Significant at 5% level.

Table 4.8. Significance Levels for Multiple Comparisons of Means for Sites: Size (PP, PC, SC).

	Complete pyramids (1972 only)				Complete minus nematodes and belowground arthropods (3 years)				Aboveground only (3 years)			
	Northern shortgrass	Mixed-grass	Tallgrass	Bunchgrass	Northern shortgrass	Southern shortgrass	Mixed-grass	Tallgrass	Northern shortgrass	Southern shortgrass	Mixed-grass	Tallgrass
Desert grass	.0119	.0031[1]	.0011[1]	.0134	.0000[1]	.0000[1]	.0000[1]	.0000[1]	.2050	.0005[1]	.0006[1]	.0000[1]
Northern shortgrass		.0197	.0789	.05447		.0068	.1052	.0388		.0029[1]	.0054	.0000[1]
Southern shortgrass							.1263	.0006[1]			.3282	.0001[1]
Mixed-grass			0039[1]	.0136				.1290				.0058
Tallgrass				.0943								

[1] Significant such that, for all comparisons within a set, $\alpha \leq 0.05$.

Table 4.9. Significance Levels for Multiple Comparisons of Means for Sites: $\log_{10}$ size [$\log_{10}$ (PP + 1), $\log_{10}$ (PC + 1), $\log_{10}$ (SC + 1)]

	Complete pyramids (1972 only)				Complete minus nematodes and belowground arthropods (3 years)				Aboveground only (3 years)			
	Northern shortgrass	Mixed-grass	Tallgrass	Bunchgrass	Northern shortgrass	Southern shortgrass	Mixed-grass	Tallgrass	Northern shortgrass	Southern shortgrass	Mixed-grass	Tallgrass
Desert grass	.0000[1]	.0000[1]	.0000[1]	.0000[1]	.0000[1]	.0000[1]	.0000[1]	.0000[1]	.0175	.0001[1]	.0003[1]	.0000[1]
Northern shortgrass		.0255	.0526	.4203		.0041[1]	.0964	.1217		.0054	.0213	.0015[1]
Southern shortgrass							.2257	.0031[1]			.4431	.0059
Mixed-grass			.0050	.0394				.2431				.1776
Tallgrass				.0330								

[1] Significant such that, for all comparisons with a set, $\alpha \leq 0.05$.

Table 4.10. Significance Levels for Multiple Comparisons of Means for Sites: Ratios (PC/PP, SC/PC)

	Complete pyramids (1972 only)				Complete minus nematodes and belowground arthropods (3 years)				Aboveground only (3 years)			
	Northern shortgrass	Mixed-grass	Tallgrass	Bunchgrass	Northern shortgrass	Southern shortgrass	Mixed-grass	Tallgrass	Northern shortgrass	Southern shortgrass	Mixed-grass	Tallgrass
Desert grass	.0003[1]	.0625	.0004[1]	.0079	.0000[1]	.0000[1]	.0000[1]	.0000[1]	.0000[1]	.0000[1]	.0001[1]	.0000[1]
Northern shortgrass		.0093	.7970	.0466		.2298	.2309	.7891		.2355	.2569	.9439
Southern shortgrass							.7402	.2908			.7588	.1469
Mixed-grass			.0083	.2743				.2968				.1747
Tallgrass				.0517								

[1] Significant such that for all comparisons within a set, $\alpha \leqslant 0.05$.

Table 4.11. Significance Levels for Multiple Comparisons of Means for Sites: Proportions (PP/Total, PC/Total)

	Complete pyramids (1972 only)				Complete minus nematodes and belowground arthropods (3 years)				Aboveground only (3 years)			
	Northern shortgrass	Mixed-grass	Tallgrass	Bunchgrass	Northern shortgrass	Southern shortgrass	Mixed-grass	Tallgrass	Northern shortgrass	Southern shortgrass	Mixed-grass	Tallgrass
Desert grass	.0207	.0850	.0073	.0393	.0000[1]	.0002[1]	.0004[1]	.0000[1]	.0025[1]	.0200	.0292	.0038[1]
Northern shortgrass		.0075	.0139	.4913		.0157	.1095	.3605		.0734	.2421	.7281
Southern shortgrass							.7161	.0774			.8370	.0802
Mixed-grass			.0020[1]	.0139				.3058				.2192
Tallgrass				.2304								

[1] Significant such that for all comparisons within a set, $\alpha \leq 0.05$.

Table 4.12. Significance Levels for Multiple Comparisons of Means for Years, Aboveground Pyramids

	Response: size (PP, PC, SC)			Response: $\log_{10}$ size [$\log_{10}$(PP + 1), $\log_{10}$(PC + 1), $\log_{10}$(SC + 1)]		
	1970	1971	1972	1970	1971	1972
1970		.0045[1]	.0221		.0099[1]	.0472
1971			.9023			.7293

[1] Significant such that for all comparisons within a set, $\alpha \leq 0.05$.

There are two reasons for the community trophic levels assuming the shape of pyramids: (1) energy is lost at each level due to respiration of the organisms and, therefore, there is less biomass or energy available for transfer to the next higher level; and (2) the transfer of energy between trophic levels in biological systems is inefficient. The main differences between the grassland pyramids presented here and the typical pyramids presented in other works are three. We have distinguished between the biomass in two separate realms of the terrestrial community by plotting the aboveground biomass to the right of the midline and the belowground biomass to the left of the midline for each trophic level. This separation seems of importance to emphasize the magnitude of the belowground components of the grassland system. Further, we have attempted to separate the primary producer biomass into that which is live, that which is standing dead, and that which is litter. In addition, we have attempted to separate the consumer biomass into saprophage and biophage, according to their different functions in the system.

Certain qualifications of the trophic pyramids presented in the diagrams should be pointed out. There were no invertebrate data for the mountain grassland site for either year nor for the bunchgrass site in 1971, and no belowground invertebrate data for the southern shortgrass prairie. Therefore, the consumer biomass is underestimated in these cases. Reptile biomass was not measured at the desert grassland sampling site, but estimates of their biomass were derived from nearby sites of the Desert Biome study. These aboveground desert pyramids appear to be top heavy due to the high biomass of secondary consumers. The estimates of reptiles may be rather high (W. Whitford, personal communication). The midseason of 1972 at the desert grassland site showed a very high biomass of saprophagic consumers. This is primarily due to a number of large darkling beetles *(Eleodes)* in the samples at that particular date.

According to statistical analyses, trophic pyramids show a high degree of temporal stability. No significant intraseasonal variation in size or shape was revealed. Significant variation between years was shown in only one case and that involved change in size of aboveground pyramids only. 1970 was an unusually dry year on the Great Plains (Sims et al. 1978). All sites were affected, the southern sites most severely. Aboveground primary producer biomass was generally lower in 1970 than in 1971 or 1972. For the five sites included in the aboveground analysis, mean primary producer standing crop in 1970 was only 69% of that in 1972. The mean value for 1971 was 96% of that for 1972 (Table 4.13). Clearly, the lack of moisture in 1970 depressed aboveground production

Table 4.13. Aboveground Primary Producer Biomass (annual mean, g · m^{-2})

Site	1970	1971	1972
Tallgrass	607	927	934
Mixed-grass	553	590	594
Northern shortgrass	227	279	392
Southern shortgrass	236	492	580
Desert	160	203	103
Cross-site mean (% 1972)	357 (69)	498 (96)	521 (100)

enough to cause a significant difference in pyramid size. Total biomass pyramids (including belowground biomass) did not show a significant response to this dry year. This reflects the greater lability of the aboveground components of the system in response to short-term perturbations.

Pyramid shape was temporally stable throughout, both within and among years. Intraseasonal stability may result from consumer biomass response to changes in the abundance of food resources in lower trophic levels. Interseasonal stability may be conferred by the perennial nature of these communities, which could provide a buffer against annual variations in environmental conditions. It should be recalled also that the sites involved in these analyses generally share a history of light or no grazing by domestic stock and should thus be at or near the climax condition. Climax communities, by definition, should show greater temporal stability than seral communities.

These analyses reveal that North American grassland types have detectable differences in trophic structure, as expressed by their biomass pyramids. The substantial and consistent differences between the desert grassland site and the other grassland sites suggests large differences in structural organization and argues for the desert site being considered a shrub desert rather than a grassland. The sizes and shapes of trophic pyramids are apparently determined in part by some other factors. Perhaps the trophic structure reflects the successional stage of the community or is a result of relatively short-term functional responses of the community to its relatively recent environmental history.

Some generalizations become apparent from inspection of the trophic pyramids. Primary producer biomass is least in the desert grassland, and increases in the shortgrass, the mixed-grass, and the tallgrass prairies. The bunchgrass and mountain grassland sites are similar to the shortgrass prairie in primary producer biomass. The mixed-prairie is most variable, usually ranging between northern and southern shortgrass prairies. Differences in the primary consumer level are less striking. The aboveground trophic pyramids tend to be top-heavy in the desert grassland, because of the high biomass of reptiles and of birds. Aboveground primary consumer biomass is principally biophagic, whereas saprophagic consumers are more important belowground. Litter accumulation is relatively high in the Great Plains grasslands and is low in desert, mountain grassland, and bunchgrass sites, and tends to be higher at the northern Great Plains sites than at the southern sites. The aboveground, primary consumer trophic level is generally mostly biophagic biomass, while the saprophagic biomass is more important belowground.

Summary

Trophic pyramids were constructed for seven grassland sites to depict the biomass (dry weight g · m^{-2}) above- and belowground, with consumers divided according to biophage or saprophage and producers according to live, dead, and litter. Separate pyramids for three different dates during the growing season of each of three successive years are presented. In nearly all cases, with the possible exception of the desert grassland, biomass belowground greatly exceeds that aboveground. The differences in trophic pyramids between years are not great. Only aboveground biomass reflected the drought conditions of 1970. Both the sizes and shapes of grassland trophic pyramids were significantly different between sites, but not between dates within seasons at the same site. This substantiates the separate classification of different types of grasslands in North America.

References

Christie, J. R. and V. G. Perry. 1951. Removing nematodes from soil. *Proc. Helminthol. Soc. Wash.* **18**:106–108.

Clark, G. L. 1946. Dynamics of production in a marine area. *Ecol. Monogr.* **16**:321–335.

Jolly, G. M. 1965. Explicit estimates from capture-recapture data with both death and immigration—stochastic model. *Biometrika* **52**:225–247.

Kozlovsky, D. G. 1968. A critical evaluation of the trophic level concept. *Ecology* **49**:48–60.

LaMotte, M. M. 1969. Représentation synthétique des aspects statique et dynamique de la structure trophique d'un écosystème. Comptes Rendus Herbomadaires des Séances de l'Académie des Sciences, Ser. D **268**:2952–2955.

Merchant, V. A. and D. A. Crossley, Jr. 1970. An inexpensive, high-efficiency Tullgren extractor for soil microarthropods. *J. Georgia Entomol. Soc.* **5**:83–87.

Miller, R. G., Jr. 1966. *Simultaneous Statistical Inference.* New York: McGraw-Hill.

Odum, E. P. 1973. *Fundamentals of Ecology,* third ed. Philadelphia: W. B. Saunders.

Raitt, R. J. and S. L. Pimm. 1977. Dynamics of bird communities in the Chihuahuan desert, New Mexico. *Condor* **78**:427–442.

Rotenberry, J. T., and J. A. Wiens. 1976. A method for estimating species dispersion from transect data. *Am. Midl. Nat.* **95**:64–78.

Sims, P. L., J. S. Singh, and W. K. Lauenroth. 1978. The structure and function of ten western North American grasslands. I. Abiotic and vegetational characteristics. *J. Ecol.* **66**:251–285.

Swift, D. M. and R. K. Steinhorst. 1976. A technique for estimating small mammal population densities using a grid and assessment lines. *Acta Theriol.* **21**(32):471–480.

Turnbull, A. L., and C. F. Nicholls. 1966. A "quick trap" for area sampling of arthropods in grassland communities. *J. Econ. Entomol.* **59**:1100–1104.

Van Dyne, G. M. 1972. Organization and management of an integrated ecological research program—with special emphasis on systems analysis, universities and scientific cooperation. *In* J. N. R. Jeffers (ed.) *Mathematical Models in Ecology,* pp. 111–72. Oxford: Blackwell Scientific Publishers.

Wiens, J. A. 1973. Pattern and process in grassland bird communities. *Ecol. Monogr.* **43**:237–270.

Zippin, C. 1956. On evaluation of the removal method of estimating animal populations. *Biometrika* **12**:163–189.

5. Patterns of Consumption in Grasslands

James A. Scott, Norman R. French, and John W. Leetham

Introduction

Previous chapters have focused on primary production of grasslands. Chapter 4 related consumer populations to producers in terms of biomass. We now consider the functional role of consumers and their role in ecosystem function. Consumers may have various effects on ecosystems. Consumers can:

1. damage plants by direct or indirect consumption or by their activities (grasshoppers can destroy almost as much plant matter as they ingest, Mitchell 1975; aphids can transmit plant diseases);
2. increase productivity of plants by pruning (i.e., increasing the growth rate of remaining tissue, Eaton 1931, Brougham 1956, Ellison 1960, Jameson 1963, Kulman 1965, 1971, Sweet and Wareing 1966, Mueggler 1967, Skuhravý 1968, Tanskiy 1969, Harris 1973, Chew 1974); or by stimulating plant growth through consumer chemicals such as saliva (Jameson 1964, Reardon et al. 1972, 1974); or by delaying plant senescence (Jameson 1963, McNaughton 1976);
3. increase reproduction of plants in cases where consumption of flowers or immature fruits increases seed size and survival rate (Black 1958, Kaufmann and McFadden 1963, Maun and Cavers, 1971);
4. control plant or host animal population density (Huffaker 1957, DeBach 1964, Harris 1973);
5. increase or decrease plant community diversity (Harper 1969, Whittaker and Feeny 1971, Harris 1973, Chew 1974);
6. control various ecosystem processes including the regulation of primary production and the rate of turnover of matter and energy in the ecosystem (Mattson and Addy 1975);
7. cause plants and prey animals to evolve defenses against attack (Janzen 1971, Rhoades and Cates 1976); and
8. aid in pollination or dispersal of plant propagules (Faegri and van der Pijl 1971, Snow 1971, McKey 1975).

Many of these effects have been poorly studied. This chapter will examine production and consumption by consumers in several ungrazed grassland sites sampled in 1972 by investigators in the International Biological Program in North America. Productivity and consumption rates between trophic levels among four sites are compared, and evidence is presented that major consumers (such as nematodes) are important in controlling ecosystem processes such as plant productivity and animal population size. To determine the flows of matter and energy resulting from consumer activity, computer models were used to evaluate 1972 data from four sites: tallgrass prairie, mixed prairie, shortgrass prairie, and desert grassland.

Techniques involved the use of data models, which utilize field data for plant and animal biomass and density, and air and soil temperature and soil moisture, as well as data on diets, assimilation, and energetics. Data-based, rather than pure simulation, models were employed in order to obtain more realistic estimates. The effects of many species were modeled simultaneously.

Methods

Sampling Methods for Vertebrates

Sampling methods are similar to those described in Chapter 4, since some of the same data were used, but details are added here of samples required for estimation of metabolic parameters. Utilizing the flush-census technique developed by Wiens (1973), breeding densities of territorial male birds were estimated on two 10.6-ha marked study areas at each grassland site. To this was added the estimated number of females, according to the average number of females per male characteristic of the species. Different characteristics of the avifauna at the desert grassland site required different census techniques and a larger study area (see Raitt and Pimm 1977). Avian density estimates for other seasons of the year were derived from roadside census data, based on correlation in the breeding season between roadside census and flush-census results. These density estimates provided input data for the vertebrate energetics model. Additional data for the energetics model were obtained by examination of crop contents of bird specimens collected in the same region but distant from the census areas. Diet analyses indicated trophic position and energy intake of the avian populations.

Small mammals were censused at bimonthly intervals during the growing season on similar but smaller (2.7-ha) areas by the mark-release-recapture method. Density estimates were derived for each species by utilizing either the Jolly (1965) stochastic model or the Zippin (1956) regression model or direct enumeration, according to the suitability of the data, in conjunction with an estimate of the effective sample area derived from the mean distance of movement detected for each species. The effective sample area was also checked by an assessment-line procedure (Swift and Steinhorst 1976) which measured dispersion of marked animals around the sampling area. As in avian studies, specimens were collected from different areas for diet analyses. Data on density, trophic position and energy intake for each species provided input for the vertebrate energetics model.

Sampling Procedures for Arthropods

The aboveground arthropods were collected at the various sites by use of a quick-trap system in which a trap or cage of known size was dropped over randomly selected locations in such a way as to minimize disturbance of the arthropods. At the shortgrass site a portable, cart-mounted boom was used to drop the quick traps. At the other sites, the traps were suspended above the sample area by use of metal tripods, the traps being set a minimum of 24 hours prior to being dropped over the sample location. In most cases, the quick traps were constructed of metal frames and 18-mesh nylon netting. At the shortgrass and tallgrass sites, 32-mesh Saran netting was substituted for the 18-mesh material.

After trap placement, the vegetation within was clipped and bagged for later extraction and the litter material vacuumed and separately bagged for later extraction of arthropods. At the shortgrass site the vegetation was lightly vacuumed prior to clipping to retrieve as many active arthropods on the vegetation as possible without contaminating the sample with plant refuse. Tullgren or Berlese type extraction methods were used to retrieve the arthropods from the vegetation and litter material. The lightly vacuumed material at the shortgrass site was hand sorted.

Soil microarthropods were extracted from soil cores 4.8 cm diameter and 10 cm deep by temperature gradient Tullgren extraction. Soil macroarthropods were sampled by taking soil cores and sieving them through a 1-mm screen. In some cases, the sieved material was floated in magnesium sulfate ($MgSO_4$) to further separate organic from inorganic material. The arthropods were then hand sorted from the sieved material. At the shortgrass site, the soil cores used were 12.5 cm diameter and 15.0 cm deep while, at the other site, the cores were 7.5 cm diameter and varied in depth.

All arthropods were identified (at least to family), counted, and given trophic or functional classifications. Representatives of various taxonomic groups were oven dried at 60 to 70°C for 24 hours, then weighed. Leetham (1975) and Swift and French (1971) give detailed descriptions of the above procedures.

Estimation of Primary Production

Total net primary production (NPP) for the 1972 season at four sites has been evaluated by Sims and Singh (1978) for aboveground plant material by the summation of peak live weights of individual species, for crowns by summing the statistically significant positive increases in crown biomass during the growing season, and for roots by summation of the significant positive increases in root biomass by depth through the sample periods during the growing season. Since these methods ignore material lost or consumed prior to peak live weight or between sampling periods, net primary production estimated by these methods was adjusted for primary consumption and wastage by adding modeled consumption and wastage to NPP in the appropriate aboveground and belowground categories. Such adjustment for the consumers was not necessary because their production was estimated from growth and metabolic rates of the animal groups rather than by comparison of standing-crop estimates.

Solar Energy Input

Input values of solar energy were determined by comparing the value for growing season usable solar radiation (light usable for photosynthesis) with the length of the growing season in days (Sims et al, 1978). Growing season usable radiation was estimated to be 45% of the total incoming radiation. Total kcal going into primary production was calculated from the growing season usable radiation for each site by multiplying with the value for efficiency of energy capture, as estimated by Sims et al. This takes into account percent of plant cover. Efficiency of energy capture was used as in Botkins and Malone (1968).

Vertebrate Energetics

Energetics of avian and mammalian populations were estimated by use of bioenergetics models. The small-mammal model (French et al 1976) utilizes density, age-class distribution, and age-class weights for each species determined at various times during the season and interpolates between sample dates according to rates of development of different age classes, and estimates individual energy requirements by literature-derived metabolism-weight relationships. Production is estimated as a proportion (approximately 2.3% for rodents and approximately 1% for insectivores) of maintenance metabolism. Application of diet information and assimilation efficiency for the species allowed the estimation of energy consumption.

Wastage by mammalian primary consumers was estimated from data on clipping (Petryszyn and Fleharty 1972) and on consumption (Fleharty and Choate 1973) by the cotton rat, *Sigmodon hispidus*. They estimated that less than 1.0% of the net primary production of their study area was consumed, and 0.4% was clipped by the herbivorous rodents. A factor of 33% was applied to estimated consumption as wastage.

The bird model (Wiens and Innis 1974) utilizes density estimates of the different species populations, and data on weights, migrations, and breeding periods to estimate population energy requirements, from which consumption can be evaluated on the basis of diet analysis. Production is estimated by summing the biomass of additions of young to the population and their growth.

Invertebrate Energetics

Grassland field data were used to drive a literature-based invertebrate bioenergetics model to determine consumption, respiration, production, and other rates for invertebrate consumers. The invertebrate model, described in detail in Chapter 6, computes respiration as a function of weight and temperature. Growth per day is a function of life-cycle characteristics, weight, and degree-days.

Consumption of each food type is a function of respiration, growth, assimilation, diet selection, biomass of each food available, and density of the consumers. Consumers may waste food in addition to that ingested.

Aboveground categories assigned for food and for consumers were live and dead biomass of five plant groups (grass, forbs, shrubs, cactus, and other plants), litter, and arthropods of seven trophic groups (plant-tissue feeders, plant-sap feeders, pollinators, omnivores, scavengers, predators, and parasitoids). Belowground categories used were crowns, roots, fungi, bacteria, protozoa, five trophic groups of macroarthropods (plant-tissue feeders, plant-sap feeders, omnivores, scavengers, predators), three trophic groups of microarthropods (fungivores, plant-sap feeders, predators), and three trophic groups of nematodes (plant-sap-feeders, saprophages, and predators). Field data included both biomass and density for arthropods and nematodes, biomass only for plants, litter, fungi, bacteria, and protozoa. For the mixed prairie site, belowground arthropod biomass data were multiplied by 1.5 because only 0 to 10 cm soil depth was sampled and the sampling methods perhaps missed some larger macroarthropods. The model was run with a daily time step. Linearly interpolated data values were used for days between sample data points.

Air and soil temperatures were used for calculation of degree days (the heat budget) above and belowground to drive growth and respiration processes. Aboveground temperature data used were daily maxima and minima 2 m above ground. Soil-temperature data used were maxima and minima at 15 cm depth. Soil-moisture data used were soil water tension (bars) at the midpoint depth of nematode numbers (12 cm at the shortgrass and tallgrass sites, 13 cm at the mixed grassland site). Soil moisture was applied to nematodes only because nematodes were assumed to reduce growth and respiration under conditions of soil drought and extreme soil saturation.

Conversion Factors

Grams dry weight were converted to kilocalories using the following conversion factors (kcal/gram dry weight): aboveground plants and litter, 4.0; crowns, 4.4; roots, 4.7; plant sap, 4.5; pollen nectar and seeds, 4.4; fungi, 3.6; mammals and birds, 5.5; all arthropods, 5.8; nematodes, bacteria, and protozoa, 4.9; dead animals, 5.6; feces, 4.0.

Results

The consumption and production data according to trophic groups shown in Figure 5.1 are presented for four grassland sites in Figures 5.2 to 5.5. The data on consumer production, consumption, and wastage of Tables 5.1 to 5.3 are summed according to trophic groups in Figures 5.2 to 5.5.

Ecological efficiencies were calculated as season-long energy production divided by the season-long energy input (input values are usable solar energy for producers and total energy consumed for consumers). Producer efficiency was

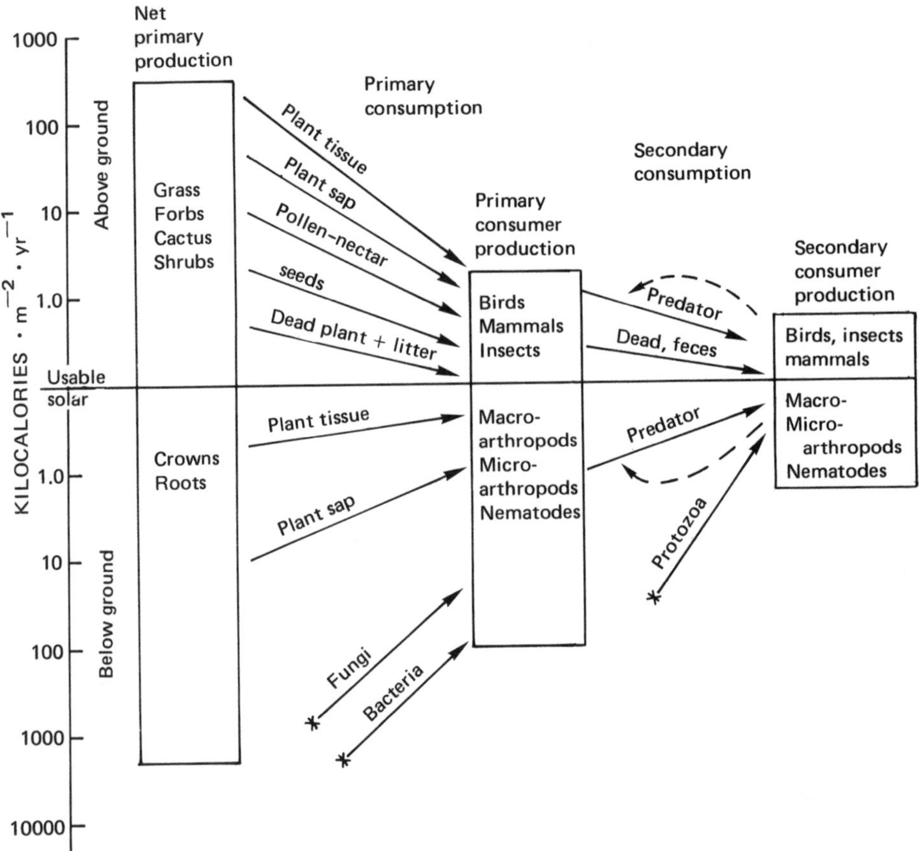

Figure 5.1. Key to production values and to quantities of consumption by trophic groups in Figures 5.2, 5.3, 5.4, and 5.5. (---) indicates that predators also eat predators, (*) indicates food consumed from the saprophagic system.

0.8 to 0.9% at the three sites for which complete belowground data were available (Table 5.4). Consumer efficiencies ranged from about 11 to 24% at the three sites.

Table 5.5 gives production and consumption figures for the major taxa. The most conspicuous animals are the least important energetically. Birds contribute almost nothing to production and very little to consumption (Figures 5.2–5.5) Their relatively high consumption in the desert grassland is due largely to the influx of migrants during the nongrowing season. Mammals contribute a small amount to total production and total consumption. The aboveground arthropods contribute a greater amount, but the energetically most important consumers are the soil animals, especially nematodes. Aboveground consumption represents only 3 to 8% of total consumption, and aboveground production represents only 4 to 7% of total production (Table 5.6).

Nematodes seem to be the key consumers in grasslands (Table 5.7). Forty-six to 67% of root and crown consumption is due to nematodes, 23 to 85% of fungal

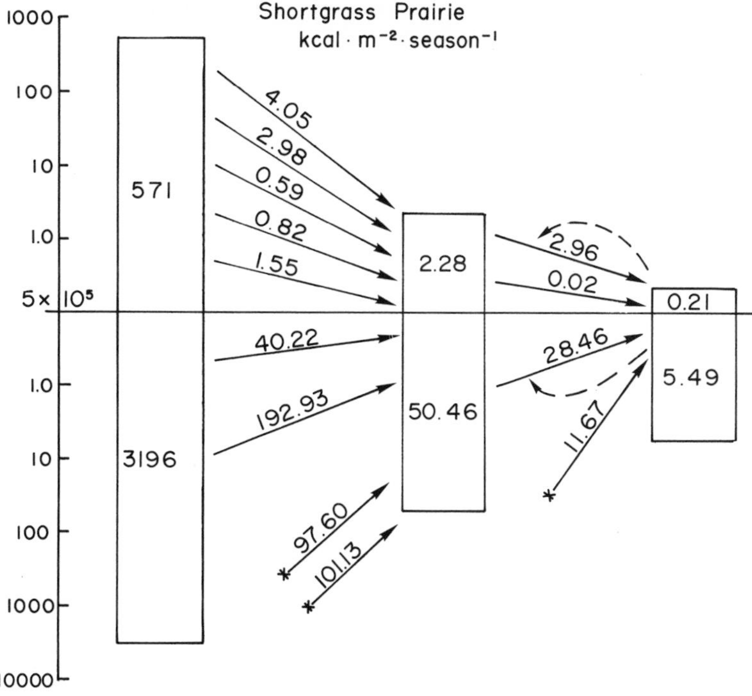

Figure 5.2. Solar energy input, primary production, and consumer consumption and production for the shortgrass prairie (kcal/m² season).

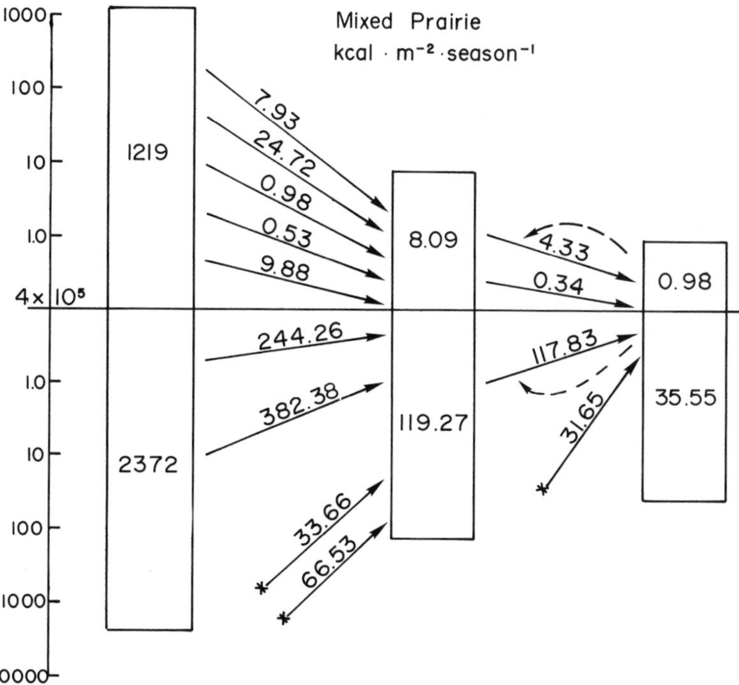

Figure 5.3. Solar energy input, primary production, and consumer consumption and production for the mixed prairie (kcal/m² season).

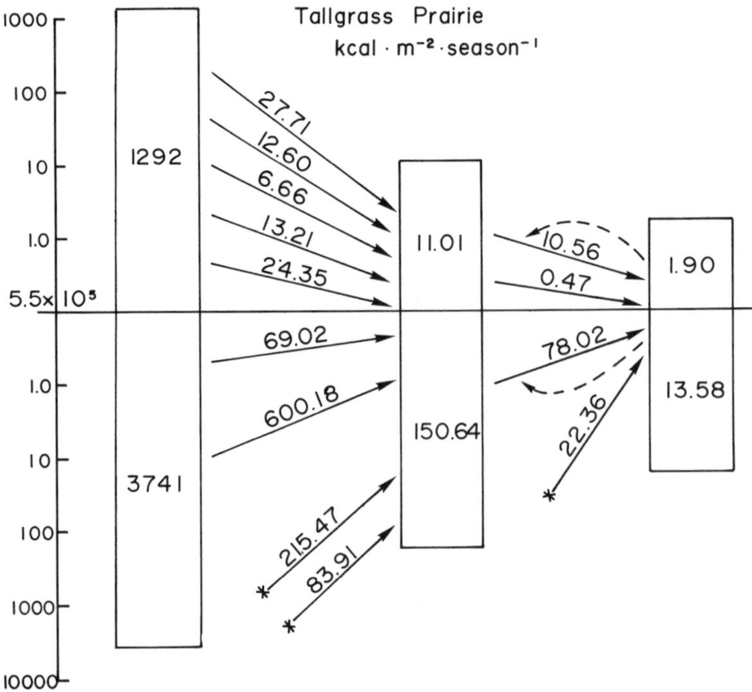

Figure 5.4. Solar energy input, primary production, and consumer consumption and production for the tallgrass prairie (kcal/m² season).

consumption, and 43 to 88% of belowground predation is due to nematodes. Nematodes may in fact control total grassland primary production. Smolik (1974) treated plots at the mixed prairie site with nematicide and found that "the nematicide significantly reduced nematode populations, increased aboveground herbage weight by as much as 59%, and further, provided a demonstration of the importance of nematodes as controllers of productivity in range."

Turnover rates indicate rates of energy processing and nutrient utilization, and

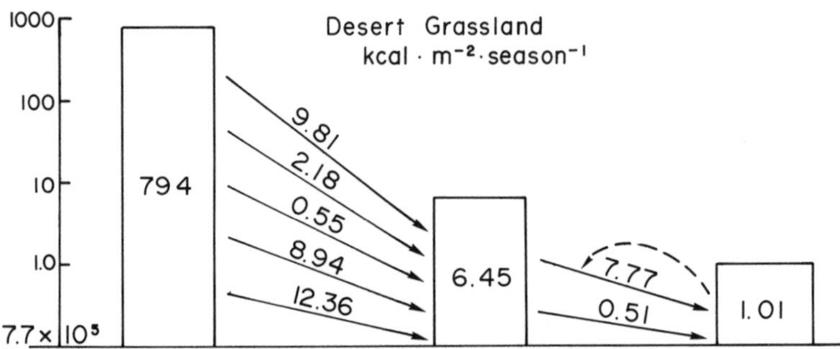

Figure 5.5. Solar energy input, primary production, and consumer consumption and production for the desert grassland (kcal/m² season).

Table 5.1. Production (kcal · m^{-2} season $^{-1}$) by Consumers at Four Grassland Sites

Consumers	Desert grassland	Shortgrass	Mixed	Tallgrass
Aboveground				
Primary consumers				
Plant-tissue feeders				
Mammals	.027	.008	.018	.348
Arthropods	2.05	.86	1.13	1.38
Plant-sap feeding arthropods	.57	.76	5.16	2.65
Pollen-nectar feeding arthropods	.17	.20	.26	1.54
Seed feeders				
Birds	$.41 \times 10^{-8}$	2.65×10^{-8}	$.505 \times 10^{-8}$	1.02×10^{-8}
Mammals	.011	.002	.002	.191
Arthropods	.44	.03	.04	.30
Dead plant-litter feeding arthropods	3.18	.42	1.48	4.60
Secondary consumers				
Predators				
Birds	19.9×10^{-8}	4.93×10^{-8}	5.66×10^{-8}	5.45×10^{-8}
Mammals	.023	.015	.003	.041
Arthropods	.88	.19	.94	1.80
Scavenger arthropods	.11	.004	.04	.06
Belowground invertebrates				
Primary consumers				
Plant-tissue feeders	–	7.41	34.39	7.94
Plant-sap feeders	–	21.46	64.74	94.20
Fungal feeders	–	11.59	5.51	39.42
Bacteria feeders	–	10.00	14.63	9.08
Secondary consumers				
Predators	–	3.86	27.63	10.43
Protozoa feeders	–	1.63	7.92	3.15

are probably roughly proportional to the number of generations per year at the sites. Table 5.8 lists the seasonal production divided by average biomass for the different consumer groups. The soil microarthropods and nematodes have the highest turnover rates among the consumers, birds have the lowest rates, and mammals have the next lowest rates.

Table 5.9 lists the percentage of plant and animal production eaten by consumers. Above ground only 2 to 7% of primary production is consumed, and 3 to 10% is eaten and wasted, but below ground the proportion consumed is larger (7–26%) and proportion consumed and wasted is still larger (13–41%). This again emphasizes the importance of belowground processes.

The yearly consumption by secondary consumers was compared to the yearly production of their primary consumer prey and found to be almost as great as or equal to production in most cases, especially above ground (Table 5.9). For the desert grassland and shortgrass sites where aboveground consumption is slightly greater than production, the consumption estimates may be slightly high.

The greater percentage of animals consumed by predators than of plants by herbivores seems to indicate that predator consumption may have a significant effect in regulating the population densities of consumers. Predators appear to control primary consumer populations, leaving the plant populations to be limited by competition for resources such as soil, water, or space.

Table 5.2. Consumption (kcal · m^{-2} $season^{-1}$) by Consumers at Four Grassland Sites

Consumers	Desert grassland	Shortgrass	Mixed	Tallgrass
Aboveground				
Primary consumers				
Plant-tissue feeders				
Mammals	1.69	.51	1.60	20.90
Arthropods	8.12	3.54	6.33	6.91
Plant-sap feeding arthropods	2.18	2.98	24.72	12.60
Pollen-nectar feeding arthropods	.55	.59	.98	6.66
Seed feeders				
Birds	6.51	.62	.16	.59
Mammals	.70	.08	.20	11.28
Arthropods	1.73	.12	.17	1.34
Dead plant-litter feeding arthropods	12.36	1.55	9.88	24.35
Secondary consumers				
Predators				
Birds	3.98	1.13	.88	1.65
Mammals	1.49	1.28	.20	2.48
Arthropods	2.30	.55	3.25	6.43
Scavenger arthropods	.51	.02	.34	.47
Belowground invertebrates				
Primary consumers				
Plant-tissue feeders	–	40.22	244.26	69.02
Plant-sap feeders	–	192.93	382.38	369.64
Fungal feeders	–	97.60	33.66	215.47
Bacteria feeders	–	101.13	66.53	83.91
Secondary consumers				
Predators	–	28.46	117.83	78.02
Protozoa feeders	–	11.67	31.65	22.36

Predator control of consumers is most striking above ground. Below ground, predators consume a smaller proportion of animal production but, as it is shown below, animals consume a greater proportion of plant production. One can hypothesize that aboveground animal populations are kept in check mainly by predators, whereas soil animals are kept in check both by predation and—for primary consumers—by the scarcity of plant food or its availability constricted by movement through the soil, and perhaps by other factors such as soil moisture.

Certain trends among sites were noted. Production and consumption of consumers generally increase from the shortgrass to the tallgrass sites, and production and consumption for the desert grassland consumers are a little greater than for the shortgrass site (Tables 5.1 and 5.2). The ratio of aboveground to belowground consumption and production increases from shortgrass to tallgrass prairie; aboveground consumers are most important at the tallgrass site (Table 5.6). The proportion of plant production consumed by herbivores is larger at the tallgrass than at the shortgrass site (Table 5.9). Aboveground, the proportion of primary production which is eaten generally increases with increasing

Table 5.3. Wastage (kcal · m^{-2} $season^{-1}$) by Consumers at Four Grassland Sites

Consumers	Desert grassland	Shortgrass	Mixed	Tallgrass
Aboveground				
Primary consumers				
Plant-tissue feeders				
Mammals	.56	.17	.53	6.93
Arthropods	4.20	2.47	4.35	4.67
Plant-sap feeding arthropods	4.35	5.96	49.44	25.20
Pollen-nectar feeding arthropods	.11	.12	.20	1.33
Seed feeders				
Birds	0.00	0.00	0.00	0.00
Mammals	0.00	0.00	0.00	0.00
Arthropods	.86	.02	.03	.27
Dead plant-litter feeding arthropods	6.14	.46	4.26	9.30
Secondary consumers				
Predators				
Birds	0.00	0.00	0.00	0.00
Mammals	0.00	0.00	0.00	0.00
Arthropods	.46	.11	.65	1.29
Scavenger arthropods	.25	.01	.17	.23
Belowground invertebrates				
Primary consumers				
Plant-tissue feeders	–	58.70	107.05	42.38
Plant-sap feeders	–	122.07	240.10	369.64
Fungal feeders	–	44.68	18.55	332.73
Bacteria feeders	–	20.23	13.31	16.78
Secondary consumers				
Predators	–	5.69	23.57	15.60
Protozoa feeders	–	2.33	6.33	4.47

Table 5.4. Total Production (season-long kcal · m^{-2}) and Ecological Efficiency (%) by Trophic Level at Three Grassland Sites[1]

	Shortgrass	Mixed	Tallgrass
Growing season (days)	206	200	275
Primary producers	3767	3591	5033
	(0.8)	(0.9)	(0.9)
Primary consumers	53	127	162
	(11.9)	(16.5)	(5.3)
Secondary consumers	6	37	15
	(13.2)	(23.7)	(13.9)

[1] Producer and consumer efficiencies are calculated differently: producer efficiency is primary production/photosynthetic solar energy striking the plant canopy; consumer efficiency is secondary production/secondary consumption.

Table 5.5. Production and Consumption by Major Taxa (kcal · yr^{-1}) at Four Grassland Sites

Taxa	Desert grassland	Shortgrass	Mixed	Tallgrass
		Production		
Birds	20.3×10^{-8}	7.6×10^{-8}	6.2×10^{-8}	6.5×10^{-8}
Mammals	0.061	0.025	0.023	0.58
Aboveground arthropods	7.40	2.46	9.04	12.33
Belowground				
macroarthropods	–	14.95	60.27	54.87
microarthropods	–	3.81		44.79
nematodes	–	37.19	94.57	64.56
		Consumption		
Birds	10.49	1.75	1.04	2.24
Mammals	3.88	1.87	2.00	34.66
Aboveground arthropods	31.35	9.35	45.67	58.76
Belowground				
macroarthropods	–	64.15		217.34
microarthropods	–	37.46	358.02	232.00
nematodes	–	358.73	518.29	619.62

primary production. The proportion is 3% at a bunchgrass site in Washington (primary production 480g·m^{-2}; Sims and Singh, 1978), and increases gradually (except for the mixed prairie site) to about 7% at the tallgrass site (primary production 1274g·m^{-2}; Table 5.9). This increasing proportion may involve increasing niche diversification in the more productive habitats. It may also serve as a density-dependent control on plant growth. As plants produce more, the consumers eat an increasing proportion until a balance is reached. We are studying ecosystems that are presumed to approximate a state of equilibrium.

Table 5.10 shows that plant-tissue feeders (such as Orthoptera, Chrysomelidae, Scarabaeidae, Curculionidae, Tenebrionidae, Carabidae, Lepidoptera larvae) usually dominate the herbivorous consumption aboveground, whereas below ground the plant-sap feeders—mainly Homoptera (Pseudococcidae and Margarodidae), mites, and nematodes—predominate. The predominance of sap

Table 5.6. Aboveground Production and Consumption by Birds, Mammals, Arthropods, and Nematodes as a Percentage of Total Production or Consumption

	Shortgrass	Mixed	Tallgrass
Producers			
Production	15	34	26
Consumers			
Consumption	3	5	8
Production	4	6	7

[1] Producer production figures are given for comparison.

Table 5.7. Nematode Impact (percentage of total consumption of each soil food item by all consumers that is eaten by nematodes)

Food items	Shortgrass	Mixed	Tallgrass
Roots and crowns	67	46	59
Fungi	85	51	23
Arthropods and nematodes	43	88	82

Table 5.8. Production/Average Season-Long Biomass[1]

	Desert grassland	Shortgrass	Mixed	Tallgrass
Plants				
Aboveground	1.9	0.4	0.5	0.4
Belowground	0.8	0.7	0.3	0.8
Mammals	1.5	1.3	1.8	2.4
Birds	0.4	0.8	0.7	0.7
Invertebrates				
Aboveground	11.2	6.6	7.6	13.2
Belowground				
Macroarthropods	–	6.7	} = 4.2	7.2
Microarthropods	–	10.3		20.4
Nematodes	–	17.3	13.4	12.0

[1] Plant biomass used was live, dead, and litter above ground, crowns and roots below ground.

Table 5.9. Percentage of Plant and Consumer (excluding microbes) Production Eaten, and Wasted, by Consumers

	Desert grassland	Shortgrass	Mixed	Tallgrass
Plant production eaten				
Aboveground	4.3	1.7	3.6	6.5
Belowground	–	7.3	26.4	17.9
Plant production eaten and wasted				
Aboveground	6.3	3.4	8.4	10.2
Belowground	–	13.0	41.1	28.9
Consumer production eaten				
Aboveground	110.9[1]	119.7[1]	51.5	85.4
Belowground	–	50.9	76.1	47.5
Consumer production eaten and wasted				
Aboveground	120.5[1]	124.5[1]	60.5	97.2
Belowground	–	61.0	91.3	57.0

[1] Consumption may be slightly overestimated or production underestimated, or part of consumption may be by belowground animals.

Table 5.10. Plant Tissue/Plant Sap Consumption Ratio Compared (aboveground versus belowground)

	Desert grassland	Shortgrass	Mixed	Tallgrass
Aboveground	4.5	1.36	.33	2.20
Belowground	–	.21	.64	.11

feeders below ground probably saves the plants from the greater damage that would occur if plant-tissue feeders predominated; a hunk bitten out of a plant is likely to sever a root but may be only a small part of the size of a leaf.

Table 5.11 compares the energy budget estimates for the shortgrass prairie derived by Coleman et al (1977) and by the present study. They used a lightly grazed pasture, whereas ours was ungrazed. The figures for macroarthropod production are very similar, but this study's figures for microarthropods and nematodes are much greater and can be argued to be more realistic because Coleman et al. did not model microarthropod or nematode processes. According to Coleman et al. the total production budget is dominated by microbes. They gave a rough estimate of 700 kcal · m^{-2} for microbe production.

Summary

Data models, involving use of computer models with field data as input, were used on birds, mammals, above- and belowground arthropods, and soil nematodes to obtain estimates of consumption, production, and other ecosystem processes at shortgrass, mixed-grass, tallgrass, and desert grassland sites. Field data included above and belowground temperatures, soil moisture, solar energy input, and censuses of animal and plant species' biomass and densities. The data

Table 5.11. Production of a Shortgrass Prairie (results of Coleman et al (1977) are compared with results of the present study)

	Coleman et al (1977)	Present
Aboveground		
Herbivores		
arthropods	2.6	2.3
cattle	3.2	ungrazed
Carnivores	0.2	0.2
Belowground		
Herbivores		
arthropods	15.8	15.1
nematodes	1.9	13.7
Carnivores	1.1	5.5
Saprophages		
arthropods	0.6	2.2
nematodes	2.8	19.4

models use respiration equations, growth equations (based on life-cycle characteristics and other developmental traits), assimilation rates, and diet preferences, which are specific to each taxon, to determine production and consumption. Ecological efficiencies (production/consumption) were 0.8–0.9% for producers, and 11–24% for consumers at all sites. The major grassland consumers are the minute soil fauna, especially nematodes; previous papers have underestimated their importance. Aboveground animal consumption and production is only 3–8% of the total. Nematodes may act as important constraints to primary production. The minute soil organisms have high population turnover rates while birds have the lowest turnover rates. Only 2–7% of primary production is consumed above ground, but below ground 7–26% is consumed. Predators consume most of the production of primary consumers, however.

It is hypothesized that grassland plants may be limited by nematode consumption of roots, by soil water, and by competition for space, whereas consumer populations are controlled by predators. Consumer production and consumption increase from the shortgrass to the tallgrass sites, and aboveground consumption and production become slightly greater. As primary production aboveground becomes greater between sites, consumers eat a greater proportion of this production, indicating a density-dependent mechanism of plant growth control. Plant-tissue feeders are more important than plant-sap feeders above ground, but the reverse is true below ground. There may, therefore, be less damage to underground parts by consumers. Results suggest that primary consumers may contribute to control of primary production above ground in a density-dependent fashion, that nematodes may greatly reduce plant production, that the predominant form of herbivory may be selected for minimizing damage to the plants, and that secondary consumption controls primary consumers.

References

Black, J. N. 1958. Competition between plants of different initial seed sizes in swards of subterranean clover (*Trifolium subterraneum* L.) with particular reference to leaf area and light microclimate. *Aust. J. Agric. Res.* **9**:299–318.

Botkin, D. B., and C. R. Malone. 1968. Efficiency of net primary production based on light intercepted during the growing season. *Ecology* **49**:438–444.

Brougham, R. W. 1956. Effect of intensity of defoliation on regrowth of pasture. *Aust. J. Agric. Res.* **7**:377–387.

Chew, R. M. 1974. Consumers as regulators of ecosystems: An alternative to energetics. *Ohio J. Sci.* **74**:359–370.

Coleman, D. C., R. Andrews, J. E. Ellis, and J. S. Singh. 1977. Energy flow and partitioning in selected man-managed and natural ecosystems. *Agro-Ecosystems* **3**:45–54.

DeBach, P. (ed.). 1964. *Biological Control of Insect Pests and Weeds*. London: Chapman and Hall.

Eaton, F. M. 1931. Early defloration as a method of increasing cotton yields of fruitfulness to fiber and boll characters. *J. Agric. Res.* **42**:447–462.

Ellison, L. 1960. Influence of grazing on plant succession of rangelands. *Bot. Rev.* **26**:1–78.

Faegri, K., and van der Pijl, L. 1971. *The Principles of Pollination Ecology*. Oxford: Pergamon Press.

Fleharty, E. D., and J. R. Choate. 1973. Bioenergetic strategies of the cotton rat, *Sigmodon hispidus*. *J. Mammal.* **54**:680–692.

French, N. R., W. E. Grant, W. Grodzinski, and D. M. Swift. 1976. Small mammal energetics in grassland ecosystems. *Ecol. Monogr.* **46**:201–220.

Harper, J. L. 1969. The role of predation in vegetational diversity. *Brookhaven Symp. Biol.* **22**:48–62.

Harris, P. 1973. Insects in the population dynamics of plants. *In* H. F. Van Emden (ed.), *Insect/Plant Relationships,* Royal Entomol. Soc. London Symp. No. 6. Oxford: Blackwell Scientific Publishers.

Huffaker, C. B. 1957. Fundamentals of biological control of weeds. *Hilgardia* **27**:101–157.

Jameson, D. A. 1963. Responses of individual plants to harvesting. *Bot. Rev.* **29**:532–594.

Jameson, D. A. 1964. Forage plant physiology and soil-range relationships. Effect of defoliation of forage plant physiology. *Am. Soc. Agron.,* Special Publ. **5**:67–80.

Janzen, D. H. 1971. Seed predation by animals. *Annu. Rev. Ecol. Syst.* **2**:465–492.

Jolly, G. M. 1965. Explicit estimates from capture-recapture data with both death and immigration—stochastic model. *Biometrics* **52**:225–247.

Kaufmann, M. L., and A. D. McFadden. 1963. The influence of seed size on the results of barley yield trials. *Can. J. Plant Sci.* **43**:51–58.

Kulman, H. M. 1965. Effects of disbudding on the shoot mortality, growth, and bud production in red and sugar maples. *J. Econ. Entomol.* **58**:23–26.

Kulman, H. M. 1971. Effects of insect defoliation on growth and mortality of trees. *Annu. Rev. Entomol.* **16**:289–324.

Leetham, J. W. 1975. A summary of field collecting and laboratory processing equipment and procedures for sampling arthropods at Pawnee Site, *US/IBP Grassland Biome Tech. Rep. No. 284*. Fort Collins: Colorado State Univ.

Mattson, W. J. and N. A. Addy. 1975. Phytophagous insects as regulators of forest primary production. *Science* **190**:515–522.

Maun, M. A. and P. B. Cavers. 1971. Seed production and dormancy in *Rumex crispus*. II. The effects of removal of various proportions of flowers at anthesis. *Can. J. Bot.* **49**:1841–1848.

McKey, D. 1975. The ecology of coevolved seed dispersal systems. *In* L. E. Gilbert and P. H. Raven (eds.), *Coevolution of Animals and Plants,* pp. 159–91. Austin: University of Texas Press.

McNaughton, S. J. 1976. Serengeti migratory wildebeest: Facilitation of energy flow by grazing. *Science* **191**:92–94.

Mitchell, J. E. 1975. Variation in food preferences of three grasshopper species (Acrididae: Orthoptera) as a function of food availability. *Am. Midl. Nat.* **94**:267–283.

Mueggler, W. F. 1967. Response of mountain grassland vegetation to clipping in southwestern Montana. *Ecology* **48**:942–949.

Petryszyn, Y. and E. D. Fleharty. 1972. Mass and energy of detritus clipped from grassland vegetation by the cotton rat *(Sigmodon hispidus)*. *J. Mammal.* **53**:168–175.

Raitt, R. J. and S. L. Pimm. 1977. Dynamics of bird communities in the Chihuahuan Desert, New Mexico. *Condor* **78**:427–442.

Reardon, P. Q., C. L. Leinweber, and L. B. Merrill. 1972. The effect of bovine saliva on grasses. *J. Anim. Sci.* **34**:897–898.

Reardon, P. Q., C. L. Leinweber, and L. B. Merrill. 1974. Response of sideoats grama to animal saliva and thiamine. *J. Range Manag.* **27**:400–401.

Rhoades, D. F. and R. G. Cates. 1976. Toward a general theory of plant antiherbivore chemistry. *Recent Adv. Phytochem.* **10**:168–213.

Sims, P. L. and J. S. Singh. 1978. The structure and function of ten western North American grasslands. III. Net primary production, turnover, and efficiencies of energy capture and water use. *J. Ecol.* **66**:573–597.

Sims, P. L., J. S. Singh, and W. K. Lauenroth. 1978. The structure and function of ten western North American grasslands. I. Abiotic and vegetational characteristics. *J. Ecol.* **66**:251–285.

Skuhravý, V. 1968. Einfluss der Entblatterund und des Kartoffelkäferfrasses auf die Kartoffelernte. *Anz. Schädlingskd.* **41**:180–188.

Smolik, J. D. 1974. Nematode studies on the cottonwood Site, *US/IBP Grassland Biome Tech. Rep. No. 251*. Fort Collins: Colorado State Univ.

Snow, D. W. 1971. Evolutionary aspects of fruit-eating by birds. *Ibis* **113**:194–202.

Sweet, G. B., and P. F. Wareing. 1966. Role of plant growth in regulating photosynthesis. *Nature* **210**:77–79.

Swift, D. M. and N. R. French. 1971. Basic field data collection procedures for the Grassland Biome 1972 season, *US/IBP Grassland Biome Tech. Rep. No. 145*. Fort Collins: Colorado State Univ.

Swift, D. M. and R. K. Steinhorst. 1976. A technique for estimating small mammal population densities using a grid and assessment lines. *Acta Theriol.* **21**:471–480.

Tanskiy, V. I. 1969. The harmfulness of the cotton bollworm, *Heliothis obsoleta* F. (Lepidoptera, Noctuidae), in southern Tadzhikistan. *Entomol. Obozr.* **48**:44–56; *Entomol. Rev.* (Engl. Transl.) **48**:23–29.

Whittaker, R. H. and P. P. Feeny. 1971. Allelochemics: Chemical interactions between species. *Science* **171**:757–770.

Wiens, J. A. 1973. Pattern and process in grassland bird communities. *Ecol. Monogr.* **43**:237–270.

Wiens, J. A., and G. S. Innis. 1974. Estimation of energy flow in bird communities: A population bioenergetics model. *Ecology* **55**:730–746.

Zippin, C. 1956. An evaluation of the removal method of estimating animal populations. *Biometrics* **12**:163–189.

6. An Ecosystem-Level Trophic-Group Arthropod and Nematode Bioenergetics Model

JAMES A. SCOTT

Introduction

The purpose of this chapter is to describe a systems model which uses data on arthropods, nematodes, plants, other organisms, and weather to simulate energy flow involving invertebrates in the ecosystem. This model was used for the invertebrate computations included in Chapter 5.

Modeling of invertebrates has usually been conducted for single species of insect or nematode pests of agricultural crops. These models are often quite detailed; they usually monitor the growth, weight, and numbers of each animal stage, the damage produced on the crop, and the effect of numerous abiotic and biotic factors on the animal population. The goal of modeling the dynamics of agricultural pests is to precisely simulate plant damage as a function of many factors so that the effect of artificially manipulating these factors or the animal population on plant production can be determined.

The goals of an ecosystem-level trophic-group model are somewhat different. It is also desirable to determine the effect of changing abiotic and biotic factors or of changing the animal populations on production and consumption by invertebrates. However, ecosystem processes such as consumption are emphasized rather than damage to the economically important part of the plant. The entire invertebrate fauna is modeled rather than a single species. These different goals require an altered approach. At some grassland sites, more than 800 invertebrate species are present. There is an incredible diversity in bionomics among these species. This necessitates rather simple and general equations rather than the complex specific equations which can be developed for a single agricultural pest.

Because of these differing goals and limitations, trophic groups are modeled rather than particular species. A trophic group model can be easily adapted to other sites and applications, whereas a specific model of particular species cannot. The present model can be easily adapted to a small community of individual species or, with the addition of a few more trophic groups, it could be applied to more complex ecosystems. Each trophic group is modeled by a hypothetical composite animal rather than by one particular species. Feeding strategies are kept simple in order to represent the different individual species' strategies that occur in a trophic group.

The Model

Field Data Input to the Model

Aboveground categories were live and dead biomass of five plant groups (grass, forbs, shrubs, cactus, and other plants), litter, and arthropods of seven trophic groups (plant-tissue feeder, plant-sap feeder, pollinator, omnivore, scavenger, predator, and parasitoid). Belowground categories used were crowns, roots, fungi, bacteria, protozoa, five trophic groups of macroarthropods (plant-tissue feeder, plant-sap feeder, omnivore, scavenger, predator), three trophic groups of microarthropods (fungivore, plant-sap feeder, predator), and three trophic groups of nematodes (plant-sap feeder, saprophage, and predator). Field data include both biomass and density for arthropods and nematodes, biomass only for plants, litter, fungi, bacteria, and protozoa. The model was run with a daily time step. For days between sample data points, linear interpolation between data values was used.

Temperature was used to calculate degree days above- and belowground to drive growth and respiration processes. Aboveground temperature data used were daily maxima and minima 2 m above the ground surface. Soil temperature used were maxima and minima at 15-cm depth. Soil water data used were soil water tension (bars) at the midpoint depth of nematode numbers.

Daily Temperature Simulation

Temperature was simulated throughout the day from recorded daily maximum (T_{max}) and minimum (T_{min}) temperatures. Daily maxima and minima were obtained from weather-station data measured at the site. One sine wave was used to simulate the eight-hour rise in temperature from minimum to maximum, and another sine wave with equal amplitude but twice the period was used to simulate the fall from maximum to minimum (Figure 6.1). For both rising and falling sine waves, the same values of T_{max} and T_{min} are used. The two sine wave simulation method is a good approximation for grassland temperatures (Parton, 1978).

For calculation of daily respiration, temperature was computed for twelve points (i = 1, 2 . . . , 12) during this cycle:

$$T = \frac{(T_{max} - T_{min})(\sin 2\pi X)}{2} + \frac{(T_{max} + T_{min})}{2}$$

where

$$X = \begin{cases} \dfrac{i-3}{8} \text{ for } (i = 1, \ldots, 5) \\ \dfrac{i-1}{16} \text{ for } (i = 6, \ldots, 12) \end{cases}$$

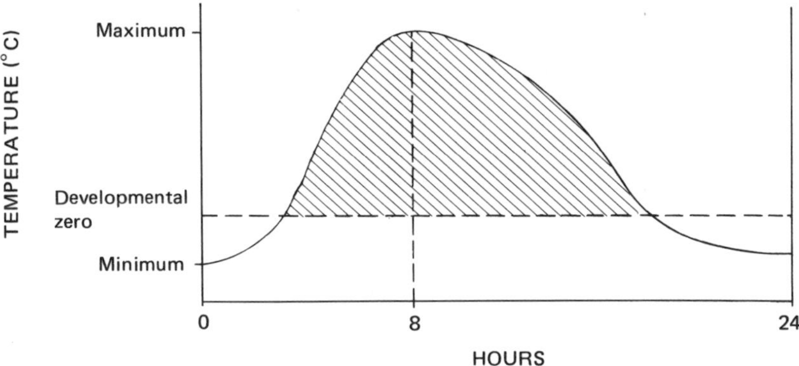

Figure 6.1. Temperature as simulated from daily values of maximum and minimum temperature, and calculation of degree days per day (shaded area).

Respiration

Respiration is a function of individual weight and of temperature. Respiration was calculated for two-hour intervals at each of the twelve daily temperature points using the following equation:

$$R_t = .00214\ W^{.79}\ e^{.0833(T-20)}$$

where W is weight (grams dry weight per individual) and T is expressed in °C. Respiration was summed for the 12 points to give the daily respiration R (grams dry body weight respired per individual per day).

Respiration equation parameters were based on Hemmingsen (1960), Van Hook (1971), and Keister and Buck (1974). The literature on respiration of mites and nematodes was consulted but discarded because the yearly respiration estimates were often impossibly high; the respiration of minute soil organisms on a population and yearly basis needs to be reexamined. Average weight per individual (W) for use in respiration and growth equations is calculated as the biomass divided by the density of the organisms considered. Respiration of diapausing animals was set at 10 percent of those of nondiapausing animals (Keister and Buck 1974), and the parameter c takes diapause into account. A proportion c has the normal respiration rate given above, and a proportion (1-c) respires at a rate 10% of normal.

Degree Days Per Day

Temperature effects on growth were incorporated using the degree-day concept. Daily temperature was simulated as above (Figure 6.1) and the number of degree days was defined as the area between the temperature curve and the line for 10°C, the developmental zero (Danilevski 1965). If the daily maximum (T_{max}) is less than or equal to 10° the number of degree days is zero.

Degree days (D) is calculated from daily maximum (T_{max}) and daily minimum (T_{min}), by integration of the first sine wave from 0 to 1/3 day, and the second from 1/3 to 1 day:

$$D = \left[\left(\frac{(T_{max} + T_{min})}{2} - 10.\right)(X2 - X1)\right] + \frac{1}{2\pi}\left[\frac{2}{3}\left(\cos\left(3\pi\left(\frac{1}{6} - X1\right)\right) - \cos\frac{\pi}{2}\right) + \frac{4}{3}\left(\cos\left(\frac{3\pi}{2}\left(X2 - \frac{2}{3}\right)\right) - \cos\frac{\pi}{2}\right)\right]\left[\frac{(T_{max} - T_{min})}{2}\right]$$

Where $X1$ and $X2$ are defined as follows: If T_{min} is less than 10°C, but T_{max} is greater than 10°C, then

$$Y = \frac{1}{2\pi}\operatorname{Arcsin}\left(\frac{2(10 - T_{min})}{T_{max} - T_{min}} - 1\right)$$

$$X1 = \frac{2Y}{3} + \frac{1}{6}$$

$$X2 = \frac{2}{3} - \frac{4Y}{3}$$

If T_{min} and T_{max} are greater than or equal to 10°C, then $X1 = 0$ and $X2 = 1$. If T_{max} is $\leqslant$ 10°C, $D = 0$.

Growth-Rate Function

Growth in the model is a function of individual weight and of temperature. Arthropods and nematodes grow in a roughly geometric manner, and the duration of growing stages in the life cycle is roughly in an inverse proportion to temperature (Rockstein 1964, Sohlenius 1968, Chapman, 1969, Ferris 1976), leading to the following general equation for weight at any time during a life stage:

$$W_t = W_0 K^t$$

$$T = \frac{b}{D}$$

Here W_t = weight at time t, W_0 = weight at the start, T = duration of a stage, D = degree days per day, and K and b are constants. Now, if T_s = duration from egg to adult, W_a = weight of adults, W_e = weight of eggs, then the following specific equations apply:

$$W_a = W_e K^{Ts}$$

$$T_s = \frac{b}{D}$$

Solving for K:

$$\frac{W_a}{W_e} = K^{b/D}$$

$$K = \left(\frac{W_a}{W_e}\right)^{D/b} \qquad (6.1)$$

Growth G (grams dry weight per individual per day) is

$$G = W_{t+1} - W_t$$

$$G = KW_t - W_t = W_t(K - 1) \qquad (6.2)$$

Substituting equation (6.1) into equation (6.2) gives

$$G = cW_t(a^{D/b} - 1.) \qquad (6.3)$$

where

$$a = \frac{W_a}{W_e}$$

Parameter b in equation (6.3) now equals the degree-day duration from eggs to adults. Parameter a is the ratio of adult weight to egg weight. Parameter c takes into account diapause (nondevelopment); it is the average proportion of the individuals of a trophic group that is active (feeding and actively respiring) at any given point during the growing season. Values for parameters a, b, and c are based on the literature, cited above, used to derive the equations and on the taxonomic literature which gives rough estimates of life cycles and developmental rates for arthropod and nematode taxa (Table 6.1). Equation (6.3) correctly simulates the greater number of generations in warmer habitats that is well known for arthropods.

Food Demand and Consumption

To calculate the amount of each food consumed by each consumer, four things were considered: (1) the "absolute" preference for each food by each consumer; (2) the biomass of each food available; (3) the density of consumers; and (4) the food demand per individual consumer.

Food demand (F), in grams dry weight per individual per day, is equal to growth (G) plus respiration (R) both divided by assimilation efficiency (A):

$$F = \frac{G + R}{A}$$

Based on a conceptual model of diet selection by Ellis et al. (1976), relative feeding preferences for each consumer are assumed to be

$$\frac{\text{Relative preference}}{\text{for each food}} = \frac{\text{absolute preference}}{\text{for each food}} \times \frac{\text{biomass of}}{\text{food available}}$$

These relative preferences are then normalized (divided by the sum of the relative preferences for all foods eaten), so that the sum of relative preferences for all the available foods eaten by a consumer equals 1. Therefore, the amount consumed of each food by each consumer per m^2 is

$$\text{Amount consumed of each food} = \text{Density of consumers} \times \text{Food demand per individual} \times \text{Relative preference for each food}$$

In summary, the feeding process in the model uses growth and respiration for each consumer calculated above, assimilation values for each, absolute preferences for each food by each consumer, the biomass of each food, and the density of each consumer type. Biomass and density are obtained from field data. Assimilation parameters (Table 6.1) were based on Smalley (1960), Wiegert (1964, 1965), Waldbauer (1968), McNeill (1971), Van Hook (1971), Moulder and Reichle (1972), Grimm (1973), Mercer and Cairns (1973), Schroeder (1973), Marchant and Nicholas (1974), Van Hook and Dodson (1974), Nicholas and Viswanathan (1975), and Wasilewska and Paplinska (1975).

Table 6.1. Parameter Values Used in the Model for Invertebrate Consumers

Invertebrate consumers	Wastage factors	Assimilation efficiency (A)	Growth parameter *a*	Growth parameter *b*	Growth parameter *c*
Aboveground arthropods					
plant tissue	0.7	0.4	75	500	0.4
plant sap	2.0	0.5	75	500	0.7
pollinator	0.2	0.8	75	500	0.4
omnivore	0.2	0.5	75	500	0.7
scavenger	0.5	0.3	75	500	0.4
predator	0.2	0.8	75	500	0.4
parasitoid	0.2	0.8	75	500	0.4
Soil macroarthropods					
plant tissue	2.0	0.4	75	700	0.4
plant sap	1.0	0.5	75	500	0.7
omnivore	0.2	0.5	75	500	0.7
scavenger	0.5	0.3	75	700	0.4
predator	0.2	0.8	75	700	0.4
Soil microarthropods					
fungivore	2.0	0.5	75	500	0.7
plant sap	0.5	0.6	75	500	0.7
predator	0.2	0.7	75	500	0.7
Soil nematodes					
plant sap	0.5	0.5	75	300	0.7
saprophagous	0.2	0.5	75	300	0.7
predator	0.2	0.7	75	300	0.7

Absolute Feeding-Preference Parameters

Feeding-preference parameters were constrained partly by definition of the consumer trophic groups, and were based largely on the feeding preferences for the component taxa as reported in the taxonomic literature. Predator and omnivore types of invertebrates could consume all invertebrates. Other invertebrates could consume aboveground live or dead herbage of grass, forbs, shrubs, cactus, or other plants, aboveground litter, dead animals, and feces, or soil crowns, roots, soil fungi, soil bacteria, and soil protozoa.

Aboveground Arthropods. Plant-tissue feeders consume all live plants with equal preference. Plant-sap feeders consume live grass, cactus, and other plants (relative preference, 1) and live forbs and shrubs (2). Pollinators consume all live plants except grasses with a preference of 1. Omnivores (mostly ants) consume live plants, litter, and other arthropods with a preference of 1. Scavengers consume live and dead plants (relative preference 1), litter (5), dead animals (10), and feces (10). Predators and parasitoids consume all arthropods with a preference of 1.

Soil Macroarthropods. Plant-tissue and sap feeders consume crowns (1), but prefer roots (5) because of their greater availability for consumption. Omnivores consume crowns (0.4), roots (2), soil fungi (1), other macroarthropods (2), and soil microarthropods (1). Scavengers consume crowns (1), roots (5), and fungi (5). Predators prefer macroarthropods (2) to microarthropods (1) due to the size difference.

Soil Microarthropods. Fungivores consume only fungus. Plant-sap feeders consume crowns (1) and roots (5). Predators prefer microarthropods (5) and nematodes (5) to macroarthropods (1) due to the size difference.

Soil Nematodes. Plant-sap feeders consume crowns (1) and roots (5). Saprophagous nematodes consume fungi (2), bacteria (2), and protozoa (1). Predators consume macroarthropods (2), microarthropods (20), nematodes (20), protozoa (5), and bacteria (0.2).

Wastage

Wastage is defined as part of the plant or animal destroyed but not consumed by feeding, or as future reduction in growth caused by feeding. For example, grasshoppers may eat part of a leaf (consumption) and the remainder of the leaf may fall to the ground (wastage); or aphids may suck out sap (consumption) and reduce plant growth due to feeding (wastage). Amount of wastage is calculated as:

$$\text{Wastage of a food by a consumer} = \text{Consumption of same food by same consumer} \times \text{Wastage parameter for the consumer}$$

Wastage parameters (Table 6.1) were from Mittler (1958) Mitchell and Pfadt (1974), Mitchell (1975), and other sources.

Moisture Effects on Nematodes

Nematodes have been found to become inactive under soil drought conditions. In the model, nematodes were assumed to reduce growth and respiration under soil drought and extreme soil saturation conditions. Quantitative effects of soil moisture on nematodes (Figure 6.2) were based on Nielsen (1961), Robbins and Barker (1974), and an unpublished nematode model of R. Andrews and J. Anway (personal communication). Soil water data used were soil water tension (bars) at the midpoint depth of nematode numbers (12 cm at the shortgrass and tallgrass sites, 13 cm at the mixed-grass site).

Model Output

Daily values for the above processes are calculated. Ecologically important items are then summed during each growing season: total amount eaten of each food by all consumers, total amount wasted of each food by consumers, population production, population respiration, population feces production, and population consumption of each consumer group, and the total amount of each food eaten by each consumer group.

Table 6.2 gives a sample of the output from the model and illustrates, among other things, the dominance of nematodes. These findings and others are presented in an ecosystem context in Chapter 5.

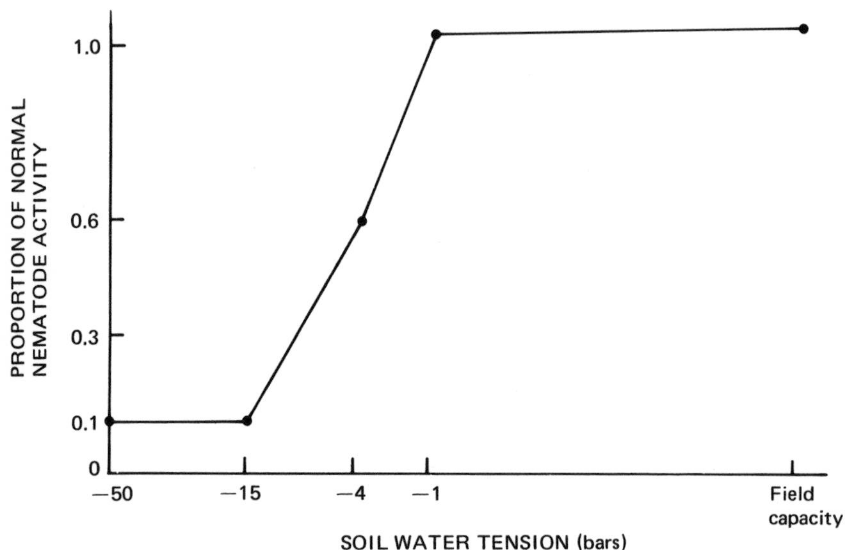

Figure 6.2. Effect of soil water on nematode growth and respiration.

Table 6.2. Sample Model Output, Consumption of Food Items (g dry weight · m^{-2} yr^{-1}) by Invertebrates at the Pawnee Shortgrass Site during 1972

Invertebrates	Aboveground arthropods	Soil Macroarthropods	Soil Microarthropods	Soil Nematodes
Plant-tissue feeders	.87	6.09		
Fungivores			3.88	
Plant-sap feeders	.66	6.08	1.97	34.83
Pollinator	.02			
Omnivores	.40	2.70		
Scavengers	.14	.17		
Predators	.09	.22	2.97	7.90
Parasitoids	.0004			
Saprophagous (microbivorous)				40.51

Summary

A bioenergetics model for invertebrates is described. The model uses field data on trophic groups of aboveground arthropods, soil macroarthropods, soil microarthropods, soil nematodes, above- and belowground plants, and temperature and soil water data to drive a literature-based simulation model. Interpolation is used to provide daily values between field data points. Trophic groups modeled are 7 for aboveground arthropods, 5 for soil macroarthropods, 3 for soil microarthropods, and 3 for soil nematodes. Respiration is calculated from average weight of the trophic groups and from temperature. Growth is calculated from the ratio of weight of adults to weight of eggs, from the proportion of animals in diapause, from the degree-days required for growth from eggs to adults, from the degree days per day, and from average weight. Food demand is calculated from growth, respiration, and assimilation values for each trophic group. Consumption of each food is a function of food demand, diet selection, the density of consumers, and the biomass available of each food. Consumers may waste a proportion of the food they contact. Nematode processes are curtailed by soil drought. Model output includes daily values of the above variables, yearly estimates of population respiration, consumption, wastage, production, and feces production, and yearly amount eaten of each food item by each consumer group.

References

Chapman, R. F. 1969. *The Insects: Structure and Function.* London: English University Press.

Danilevski, A. S. 1965. *Photoperiodism and Seasonal Development of Insects.* Edinburgh: Oliver and Boyd.

Ellis, J. E., J. A. Wiens, C. F. Rodell, and J. C. Anway. 1976. A conceptual model of diet selection as an ecosystem process. *J. Theor. Biol.* **60**:93–108.

Ferris, H. 1976. Development of a computer simulation model for a plant-nematode system. *J. Nematol.* **8**:255–263.

Grimm, R. 1973. Zum Energieumsatz phytophager Insekten. Untersuchungen an Populationender Rüsselkäfer *Rhynchaenus fagi, Strophosomus,* und *Otiorrhynchus singularis. Oecologia* **11**:187–262.

Hemmingsen, A. M. 1960. Energy metabolism as related to body size and respiratory surface, and its evolution, p. 7–110. *In Steno Memorial Hospital and Nordisk Insulin Laboratorium Report,* Vol. 9, Part 2.

Keister, M. and J. Buck. 1974. Respiration: Some exogenous and endogenous effects on rate of respiration. *In* M. Rockstein (ed.), *The physiology of Insecta.* 2nd ed. Vol. 6, pp. 469–509.

Marchant, R. and W. L. Nicholas. 1974. An energy budget for the free-living nematode *Pelodera* (Rhabditidae). *Oecologia* **16**:237–252.

McNeill, S. 1971. The energetics of a population of *Leptoptera dolabrata* (Heteroptera: Miridae). *J. Anim. Ecol.* **40**:127–140.

Mercer, E. K., and E. J. Cairns. 1973. Food consumption of the free-living aquatic nematode *Pelodera chitwoodi. J. Nematol.* **5**:201–208.

Mitchell, J. E., 1975. Variation in food preferences of three grasshopper species (Acrididae: Orthoptera) as a function of food availability. *Am. Midl. Nat.* **94**:267–283.

Mitchell, J. E. and R. F. Pfadt. 1974. A role of grasshoppers in a shortgrass prairie ecosystem. *Environ. Entomol.* **3**:358–360.

Mittler, T. E. 1958. Studies on the feeding and nutrition of *Tuberolachnus salignus* (Gmelin) (Homoptera, Aphididae). II. The nitrogen and sugar composition of ingested phloem sap and excreted honeydew. *J. Exp. Biol.* **35**:74–84.

Moulder, B. C. and D. E. Reichle. 1972. Significance of spider predation in the energy dynamics of forest floor arthropod communities. *Ecol. Monogr.* **42**:473–498.

Nicholas, W. L. and S. Viswanathan. 1975. A study of the nutrition of *Caenorhabditis briggsae* (Rhabditidae) fed on ^{14}C and ^{32}P-labeled bacteria. *Nematologica* **21**:385–400.

Nielsen, C. O. 1961. Respiratory metabolism of some populations of enchytraeidae worms and free-living nematodes. Oikos **12**:17–35.

Parton, W. J. 1978. Abiotic section of ELM. In G. S. Innis (ed.), *Grassland Simulation Model.* Ecological Studies, 26, pp. 31–53. New York: Springer-Verlag.

Robbins, R. T. and K. R. Barker. 1974. The effects of soil type, particle size, temperature, and moisture on reproduction of *Belonolaimus longicaudatus. J. Nematol.* **6**:1–6.

Rockstein, M. (ed.) 1964. *The Physiology of Insecta* (3 vols.). New York: Academic Press, Inc.

Schroeder, L. A. 1973. Energy budget of the larvae of the moth *Pachysphinx modesta. Oikos* **24**:278–281.

Smalley, A. E. 1960. Energy flow of a salt marsh grasshopper population. *Ecology* **41**:672–677.

Sohlenius, B. 1968. Influence of microorganisms and temperature upon some Rhabditid nematodes. *Pedobiologia* **8**:137–145.

Van Hook, R. I., Jr. 1971. Energy and nutrient dynamics of spider and orthopteran populations in a grassland ecosystem. *Ecol. Monogr.* **41**:1–26.

Van Hook, R. I. and G. J. Dodson. 1974. Food energy budget for the yellow poplar weevil, *Odontopus calceatus* (Say). *Ecology* **55**:205–207.

Waldbauer, G. P. 1968. The consumption and utilization of food by insects. *Adv. Insect Physiol.* **5**:229–288.

Wasilewska, L., and E. Paplinska. 1975. Energy flow through the nematode community in a rye crop in the region of Poznan. *Polish Ecological Studies* **1**(3):75–82.

Wiegert, R. G. 1964. Population energetics of meadow spittlebugs (*Philaenus spumarius* L.) as affected by migration and habitat. *Ecol. Monogr.* **34**:217–241.

Wiegert, R. G. 1965. Energy dynamics of the grasshopper populations in old field and alfalfa field ecosystems. *Oikos* **16**:161–176.

7. Factors Influencing Input and Output of Nitrogen in Grasslands

ROBERT G. WOODMANSEE

Introduction

The influence of nitrogen (N) on grassland production was demonstrated by the dramatic results presented in Chapter 3, and some mechanisms of its action were discussed in Chapter 2. Most information pertinent to N cycling in grassland ecosystems relates primarily to flows of N within biological pathways. Kline (1969), Whitehead (1970), Henzell and Ross (1973), Porter (1975), Charley (1977), and Frissel (1977) reviewed literature relating to N cycling in grasslands. Their publications illustrate that our greatest knowledge is of transfers within plant-dominated pathways. Reference is made by various authors to biological and chemical processes and to input and loss of N, but few quantitative data are presented. Henzell and Norris (1961) reviewed pathways of N input into tropical grasslands, but their values were not specific, being averages drawn from the literature. Bazilevich (1958), Rodin and Bazilevich (1967), and Bazilevich and Rodin (1971) reviewed world literature and presented data on transfers in plant parts within ecosystems. Reuss (1971) and Reuss and Innis (1977) discussed specific grassland sites and presented estimates of N additions based on results of Eriksson (1952). No estimates of total losses were given. Clark (1977) studied transfers of ^{15}N in miniswards of blue grama *(Bouteloua gracilis)*. His research focused on living and dead grass material and soil organic matter. He concluded that, following a small initial loss of ^{15}N (which was probably a function of fertilization), no perceptible loss from the system was noted in five years; atmospheric input of N to the miniswards was not monitored.

A review of literature concerning additions and losses of N in areas of existing or potential semiarid to subhumid grasslands of western United States will clarify the problem. The N budget for one of those grasslands was discussed in detail by Woodmansee et al (1978). Some of the concepts that are currently prevalent in ecology were questioned and discussed. The concepts questioned were: (1) "The input-output budget depends above all on the hydrologic cycle" (Duvigneaud and Denaeyer-DeSmet 1975); (2) Consumers play an insignificant role in the cycling of N (Bormann and Likens 1967, Sturges et al 1974, Burton and Likens 1975); and (3) As ecosystems mature or approach climax, nutrient input-output ratios approach unity and come to a state of dynamic stability (Odum 1969, Vitousek and Reiners 1975). The conclusions presented suggest that input-output budgets depend also on meteorological cycles (wind and fire) and on animals. Large consumers (ungulates) were shown to be significant as loss vectors. Further, the validity of the concept that N input equals output in climax ecosystems was challenged.

Additions of N to Grassland Ecosystems

The principal external source of N to many unfertilized midcontinent grasslands is NH_3, NH_4^+, NO_3^-, and R-NH_2 from the atmosphere. Copley and Reuss (1972) and Reuss and Innis (1977) estimated symbiotic or nonsymbiotic fixation of N_2 to be insigificant under typical prairie conditions. Fixation of N_2 by legumes has been estimated to be 2.5 g N $\cdot$ m^{-2} $\cdot$ yr^{-1} during one year of study in the annual grassland of California, while for two years fixation via this pathway was near zero (R. G. Woodmansee and D. A. Duncan, unpublished data).

NH_4^+ and NO_3^- from Atmospheric Deposition

Ammonium, NO_3^-, and some quantities of organic N are introduced to vegetation, soils, and water by rain, snow and dry deposition. Table 7.1 shows estimates of additions of N from the atmosphere as NH_4^+ and NO_3^-. Organic N compounds are assumed to be small compared to NH_4^+ and NO_3^-.

The Arid Lands Ecology Reserve (ALE) data are similar to those from other sites near seacoasts (Eriksson 1952, Junge 1958, 1963). The San Joaquin Experimental Range (SJER) is located in the Central Valley of California, a basin which is characterized by high levels of atmospheric pollution from urban and agricultural areas. Junge (1958) attributes the high N levels noted in the Central Valley to pollution. We have no data other than those of Junge with which to compare the Jornada input values. Thus, these estimates based largely on adjusted data of Junge appear to be compatible with other existing data.

Actual amounts of mineral N that can be expected from the atmosphere at the other study sites have not been directly determined. Reuss (1971) and Reuss and Innis (1977), based on data of Eriksson (1942), estimated input at 0.4 g N $\cdot$ m^{-2} $\cdot$ yr^{-1} for the Pawnee site. This estimate is comparable to what might be expected using the data of Junge (1958) from Scottsbluff, Nebraska (160 km northeast of the Pawnee site). However, Junge's data were collected for only one year and they did not include the contribution from dry deposition. More recent data of Olson et al (1973) for Scottsbluff and for North Platte, Nebraska, showed the atmospheric input of mineral N ranged from 0.6 to 0.8 g N $\cdot$ m^{-2} $\cdot$ yr^{-1} during September 1969 to March 1972. Precise descriptions of collection techniques were not given, but presumably samples contained both liquid precipitation and dry deposition. Also, it is likely their rain collection vessels were treated to prevent the loss of N by microbial activity or chemical volatilization. The credibility of Olson et al is enhanced by comparing their work in eastern

Table 7.1. Estimated Annual Input and Output of N ($g \cdot m^{-2} \cdot yr^{-1}$) in Various Grasslands of Western United States

Input and output	ALE[1]	Jornada[2]	Pawnee[3]	Cottonwood[4]	Pantex[5]	SJER[6]	Osage[7]
				Annual Input			
Wet deposition[8] ($NH_4^+ + NO_3^-$)	0.15	0.20	0.45	0.65	0.45	0.75	0.75
Dry depoisition ($NH_4^+ + NO_3^-$)	0.05	0.10	0.15	0.25	0.15	0.25	0.25
Symbiotic fixation	<0.05	<0.05	<0.05	<0.05	<0.05	as large as 2.5	<0.05
Nonsymbiotic fixation	may be significant	<0.05	<0.05	<0.05	<0.05	<0.05	<0.05
Direct absorption by plants and soil (NH_3)	Unknown	Unknown	Unknown	Unknown	Unknown	Unknown	Unknown
Total input	0.20+[9,10]	0.30	0.60	0.90	0.60	1.00+[9,10]	1.00
				Annual Output			
Animal tissue[11]	0.10	0.10	0.10	0.30	0.20	0.40	0.40
Waste products of ungulates (NH_3 volatilization)[11]	0.20	0.30	0.20	0.60	0.40	1.10	1.00
Via redistribution[11]	0.10	0.10	0.10	0.20	0.15	0.30	0.20
Volatilization from plant and animal residues (NH_3)	<0.05	<0.05	<0.05	0.10	0.05	0.25+[10]	0.20
Denitrification	0	0	0	0	0	0	0
Leaching	0	0	0	0	0	+[10]	<0.1
Runoff	0	0	0	0	0	0	0
Total output	0.40	0.50	0.40	1.20	0.80	2.05	1.80
Net	−0.20[9]	−0.20	+0.20	−0.30	−0.20	−1.05[9]	−0.80

From Woodmansee (1978).

[1] Shrub-steppe in southeastern Washington.

[2] Desert grassland in southern New Mexico.

[3] Shortgrass prairie in northeastern Colorado.

[4] Mixed prairie of western South Dakota.

[5] Shortgrass prairie in northern Texas.

[6] Annual grassland in foothills of Central Valley of California.

[7] Tallgrass prairie in central Oklahoma.

[8] Based on annual precipitation amounts of 18, 20, 30, 37, 48, 56 and 84 (cm) for ALE, Jornada, Pawnee, Cottonwood, Pantex, SJER and Osage, respectively.

[9] Cannot be accurately estimated due to fixation or leaching.

[10] Minimum estimate.

[11] Based on ingested forage amounts of 60, 80, 60, 190, 120, 350, and 300 biomass ($g \cdot m^{-2} \cdot yr^{-1}$) for ALE, Jornada, Pawnee, Cottonwood, Pantex, SJER, and Osage, respectively.

Nebraska to data of Tabatabai and Laflen (1976) in Iowa, of Hoeft et al. (1972) in Wisconsin, and of Taylor et al (1971) in Ohio. All indicate input of mineral N to the landscape of the northeastern Great Plains to be on the order of 1.3 to 1.8 g N $\cdot$ m^{-1} $\cdot$ yr^{-1}. Precipitation amounts in the eastern Great Plains are about twice those in the west. Dahlman and Kucera (1968) estimated input from precipitation in Missouri to be about 1.0 g N $\cdot$ m^{-2} $\cdot$ yr^{-1}. For comparison, the data of Zakharchenko (1974) for a rainfall zone in USSR grassland similar to western Nebraska show a range of 0.6 to 0.9 g N $\cdot$ m^{-2} $\cdot$ yr^{-1} added from the atmosphere.

Feth (1966), Granat (1976), Galloway (1976), and Söderlund and Svensson (1976) have emphasized the importance of dry deposition to total deposition values. Based on the data of Eriksson (1952), Robinson and Robbins (1968) used 25% as an estimate of the relative contribution of dryfall of NH_4^+ and NO_3^- to total atmospheric input of N on landscape surfaces. An indication that a greater relative contribution of N by dryfall can be expected in arid regions is given by estimating the addition of NH_4^+ and NO_3^- (0.3 to 0.4 g N $\cdot$ m^{-2} $\cdot$ yr^{-1}) in liquid precipitation alone from the studies of Junge (1958) at Scottsbluff, Nebraska, and by comparing these data to those of Olson et al (1973) from the same location. The difference is about twofold, the Junge estimates being lower. Certainly, the years and techniques used were different, but the contribution by dryfall could be as great as 50% of the total N_4^+ and NO_3^- from the atmosphere. Schuman and Burwell (1974) and Tabatabai and Laflen (1976) sampled N in precipitation at different sites in Iowa during the years 1971–1973. Schuman and Burwell sampled precipitation only during storms, and Tabatabai and Laflen apparently left the sampling gauges open between storms which allowed collection of dryfall. Nitrogen input estimates from the latter technique are nearly twice those of the former. McConnell (1973) used estimates of this magnitude for dryfall.

To estimate adequately the addition of mineral N from atmospheric sources, it is clear that both liquid precipitation and dryfall must be evaluated, and separate collection procedures must be used to avoid microbiological or chemical contamination and transformation (Junge and Gustafson 1956a,b).

Absorption of NH_3 by Foliage and Soils

Direct absorption of NH_3 from the atmosphere by foliage agricultural crops has been studied by Hutchinson et al (1972) and Porter et al (1972). Denmead et al (1976) found large losses of NH_3 from soils of highly productive grasslands of Australia (and large input of N via *Trifolium subterraneum*), but most of it was absorbed by foliage as the gas diffused through the plant canopy. These studies suggest that plants may be a natural sink for atmospheric NH_3 and, furthermore, amounts of N received via this pathway may constitute a significant portion of plant N intake. This pathway, though not quantified in grasslands of North America, is potentially significant because fertilization is not extensively practiced, and nonsymbiotic and symbiotic N fixation are not important in these systems (Copley and Reuss 1972).

Malo and Purvis (1964) and Hanawalt (1969) found that soils are capable of absorbing NH_3 from the atmosphere. Studies conducted in cultivated fields in New Jersey showed that absorption was dependent on the N content of the atmosphere, soil type, temperature, and the velocity of air movement across the surface of the soil. The potential exists for organic matter at or near the surface to fix NH_3 from the atmosphere (Mortland 1958). Whether or not this process is of consequence in grasslands is unknown.

Losses of N from Grassland Ecosystems

The chemical composition of nitrogen is important to the discussion of losses of N from ecosystems. Emphasis here is on NH_3 loss from large animal (ungulate) excrement and from natural plant and animal residues because in most grasslands (with the possible exception of SJER) leaching of NO_3^- from the soil is trivial or nonexistent (Stewart et al 1967, Power et al 1973, Kilmer 1974, Rogler and Lorenz 1974, Viets 1975). Runoff from grasslands is an infrequent event, but may occasionally be important (Woodmansee 1978). Denitrification has not been shown to be important in semiarid or subhumid grasslands.

Losses of NH_3 from Animal Wastes

Doak (1952) found 12% of the N in urine was lost through volatilization while Watson and Lapins (1969) and Stewart (1970) found 84% and 90% loss, respectively. J. O. Reuss (personal communication) in an exploratory study found >50% loss of N from urine over a period of four spring and summer months in northeastern Colorado. It can be assumed that the losses noted by Reuss were minimal because he applied urine early in the year when temperatures were low and soil water more available.

Gillard (1967), studying tropical and subtropical pastures, suggested that 80% of the N in feces could be lost because of the absence of dung beetles. In systems where dung beetles are active, losses of 15% were noted. Dung beetles mix the feces into soils where the contained N is less vulnerable to loss as NH_3. Floate and Torrance (1970) and Floate (1970a,b,c) studied decomposition of sheep feces under controlled laboratory conditions and found that a maximum of 8% of the total N evolved in 12 weeks as NH_3. They found that the loss was greatly affected by N content of the feces, by temperature and moisture, as with any decomposing organic material (Alexander 1961). However, no estimate can be made from their studies of the total loss of NH_3 because the samples were collected, frozen, and then air dried and milled before incubation. Losses during preparation may have been significant (Lauer et al 1976). Barrow (1961) studied mineralization of N from sheep feces and made calculations concerning the availability of N for plants and microorganisms, assuming no loss of N. He considered the N not accounted for to be experimental error. Undoubtedly, had NH_3 been monitored, he would have found some loss. Rashid (1977) found large losses (35 to 85%) of N from various mixes of urea and organic matter, including cow dung. Much of this loss was attributed to the loss of NH_3. Thus, it seems that the potential loss of feces nitrogen ranges between 8 and 80%. A compromise estimate for N loss via this pathway is 20%.

Thus, in Table 7.1, losses of N are calculated to be directly proportional to the amount of forage consumed. A great many environmental factors can influence these losses, and these values are presented as reasonable estimates.

Amphibians and mammals excrete urinary N as urea (Whitehead 1970). Other animals excrete various nitrogen-containing compounds as waste products. Birds, snakes, lizards, insects, and snails excrete uric acid; spiders (mites) excrete guanine; and protozoans excrete NH_3 (Henzell and Ross 1973). Earthworms excrete protein-N, uric acid, urea, and NH_3 (Lofty 1974). Millipedes apparently excrete NH_3 (Edwards 1974). None of these reports contained quantitative estimates of waste products that would permit estimating NH_3 loss from ecosystems.

Presumably, all NH_3 generated below several centimeters of the soil surface remains in the system. Ammonia which is excreted or produced from excreta at or near the soil surface is more vulnerable to loss. Since many soil organisms are active near the soil surface and in the litter at the surface, it is conceivable that losses from these sources may be significant in extensively grazed ecosystems.

Losses of NH_3 from Other Forms of Dead Organic Matter

Alexander (1961) states that up to 25% of the ammonium mineralized from decomposition processes can be lost from the system above pH 7.0 as NH_3. Barrow (1960a) showed that as plant material decomposed during incubation studies, production of NH_4^+ caused an increase in the pH of the incubation solution, resulting in volatilization of NH_3. Barrow (1960b) studied N mineralization from a variety of plant residues, excluding roots. In his experiments he recognized the loss of NH_3, but treated it as an error in his calculations of results. No quantification of NH_3 loss was made. Floate and Torrance (1970) and Floate (1970a,b,c) studied NH_3 loss from residues of pasture plants under controlled laboratory conditions. They found a maximum loss of 20% of the total N in the substrate during 12 weeks of incubation at 30°C, with water at 100% water-holding capacity, when N content of grass was 2.46%. As temperature, water, and N content were reduced, mineralization and consequent NH_3 evolution was less. Up to 40% loss of NH_3 from coniferous forest litter has been found (Voigt 1965, Millar 1974). Martin and Chapman (1951) showed losses of NH_3 from orange leaves with N content of 2.2% to be about 25% at 100°F and at water-holding capacity of 75 to 100%.

Loss of NH_3 from decomposing bodies of invertebrates near the soil surface could contribute to total community N loss, even though the N of the standing crop of invertebrates is small at any one time (Woodmansee et al, 1978; see also Chapter 4). Their turnover rate may be large (see Chapter 5) and their N concentration principally protein (Edwards 1974, Lofty 1974). Thus, loss from this source could be significant.

Losses of NH_3 from Senescing Plant Parts

Loss of ammonia or other volatile N compounds from the aerial parts of perennial species of grassland plants has received little study. Henzell and Ross (1973) state that no significant quantities of N are lost via this mechanism before senescence. Certain studies (Richardson et al 1931, Pearsall and Billimoria 1937, Frank 1954, Gasser 1964, Lapins and Watson 1970) have shown that N losses can be appreciable from senescing foliage of annual plants under controlled conditions. Lapins and Watson studied dominance in annual grassland species and found that *Trifolium subterraneum,* the principal clover species, lost significant amounts (up to 43%) of its N under conditions simulating field situations. They found little loss of N from the foliage of *Bromus mollis* (the dominant grass).

Clark (1977) in a five-year study of *Bouteloua gracilis* found that after an initial 12% loss of added ^{15}N (Clark 1975), little if any loss occurred from the entire plant recycling system. It was assumed that the loss of volatile N from the foliage of principal perennial species under normal conditions in grassland plants, if it occurs, is a small percentage of the total plant N, however, this assumption needs testing. Table 7.1 does not include losses via this pathway, but Jones and Woodmansee (in press) have discussed its potential importance in annual grasslands.

Environmental Factors Controlling Loss of NH_3 by Volatilization

Since the principal pathway of N loss from grassland seems to be volatilization of NH_3 from animal excrement, the environmental factors that influence these losses will be emphasized in this section.

Factors Promoting NH_3 Losses

Information from the literature on chemical fertilizers is useful in understanding the factors controlling losses of NH_3 from natural sources. Fenn and Kissel (1973, 1974, 1975), Fenn (1975), Fenn and Escarzoga (1976a,b), Hargrove et al (1977), and Kissel et al (1977) have studied environmental variables that affect losses of NH_3 from calcareous soils in Texas. This research presents a basic set of principles for studying NH_3 volatilization from soil-plant systems.

Lauer et al (1976) postulated three steps in the loss of NH_3 from ungulate (bovine) excrement. The first step, occurring within 24 hours after deposition, is rapid hydrolysis of urea with concomitant increase in pH, total inorganic N, and pNH_3. Doak (1952) and Chin and Kroontje (1963) found the half-life of urea to be less than four hours. The second step, lasting from one to four days, involves loss of NH_3 upon drying. As NH_3 is volatilized, pH decreases, as does total inorganic N. Upon drying, the concentration of inorganic N increases, maintaining the gradient of pNH_3 of the substrate solution compared to the atmosphere. Losses may be enhanced by wetting and drying cycles. The third step is decomposition of organic material. Presumably these steps occur under conditions of free grazing, where feces and urine are not necessarily mixed as they were in the Lauer et al (1976) study.

Conrad (1942), Chin and Kroontje (1963), and Overrein and Moe (1967) have reviewed the factors that control hydrolysis of urea fertilizer, factors which should apply to urea in animal excrement. They concluded that the chemical hydrolysis of urea is slow and insignificant at low temperatures. Biochemical hydrolysis was shown to be of greater importance, acting through the catabolic enzyme urease, with losses of NH_3 exceeding 90% (Watson and Lapins 1969, Stewart 1970, Lauer et al 1976). Urease is produced by many microorganisms and higher plants. It is greatest in the surface one cm of soil (Simpson 1968). Overrein and Moe (1967) showed the rate of urea hydrolysis to be linearly related to application rate under the range of concentrations they studied. The presence of glycine, allantoin, creatinine, and hippuric acid can cause hydrolysis rates to be three times greater (Doak 1952). Quantification of the evolution of NH_3 from fertilizer urea applied to cultivated soils shows losses generally range between 10 and 20%, but up to 50% depending on environmental factors (Martin and Chapman 1951, Volk 1959, Ernst and Massey 1960, Meyer et al 1961, Chin and Kroontje 1963, Gasser 1964, Overrein and Moe 1967, Simpson 1968). These studies indicate that the hydrolysis of urea under field conditions is rapid, except at low temperatures. In native pastures NH_3 losses from urine are suspected to be very high due to the combination of high concentrations of urease and the apparent synergistic effects shown by Doak (1952).

In general, NH_3 losses vary with soil water content, being greatest at intermediate levels of moisture (Jackson and Chang 1947, Martin and Chapman 1951, Parr and Papendick 1966, Fenn and Escarzaga 1976a,b). NH_3 can be lost from soil solution, especially when the pH is greater than 7.0 (Mortland 1958), and depending on the partial pressure of NH_3. An equilibrium is established between the solution NH_3 and atmospheric NH_3. This is volatilized during drying, at rates proportional to H_2O vapor losses (Wahhab et al 1957, Ernst and Massey 1960, Chin and Kroontje 1963, Harmsen and Kolenbrander 1965, Overrein and Moe 1967, Lauer et al 1976). The rewetting of dry soil increases NH_3 loss.

The potential for loss of NH_3 decreases sharply with depth. Losses are always greatest from the surface. Except in very porous sands of low organic matter, loss from below a few centimeters of the surface from native grasslands should be negligible (Jackson and Chang 1947, Mortland 1958, Ernst and Massey 1960, Gasser 1964, Harmsen and Kolenbrander 1965, Overrein and Moe 1967, Simpson 1968, Whitehead 1970).

Temperature influences NH_3 losses by affecting the activity of plants and microorganisms (Wakesman et al 1939, Martin and Chapman 1951, Doak 1952, Volk 1959, Ernst and Massey 1960, Gasser 1964, Overrein and Moe 1967, Simpson 1968, Watson and Lapins 1969). When hydrolysis reactions are complete, temperature (including diurnal fluctuations) affects the chemical activity of NH_3 and indirectly affects volatilization through evaporative processes (Beauchamp et al 1978, McGarity and Rajaratnam 1973, Denmead et al 1974, Lauer et al 1976).

Watson and Lapins (1969) found 50 to 60% greater loss of NH_3 from sandy soils than from sandy loams. Gasser (1964) stated that soils showed losses of 20% of the N in urea when the base exchange capacity (BEC) was less than 10 meq/100 g soil but at a BEC of 20 meq/100 g soil losses were 10%. Increasing clay content, which infers greater cation exchange capacity, generally indicates decreased potential for the loss of NH_3 from soil systems, especially if the exchange sites are occupied by H^+ ions (Jackson and Chang 1947, Wahhab et al 1957, Mortland 1958, Meyer et al 1961, Brown and Bartholomew 1963, Chao and Kroontje 1964, Mortland and Wolcott 1965, Simpson 1968, Faurie et al 1975). Martin and Chapman (1951) showed that K- and Na-saturated colloids yield more NH_3 than do Ca- or Mg-saturated clays.

Soils containing the 2:1 lattice-type clays are capable of fixing substantial amounts of N (Nommik 1965), probably by NH_4^+ being chemically sorbed in clay lattices. Vermiculites have the greatest capacity to fix NH_4^+ followed by the illites and the montmorillonites. Clays with 1:1 lattice structure show little tendency to fix N. Chemical sorption is considered to be irreversible while physical sorption is reversible, provided subsequent chemical reactions do not occur while the NH_4^+ is temporarily detained (Mortland 1958, Harmsen and Kolenbrander 1965). The clay particles also serve as sites for physical sorption of the highly polar NH_3 tetrahedron (Mortland 1958, Mortland and Wolcott 1965).

Increasing organic matter decreases the potential for loss of NH_3 by physical sorption and by reactions with H^+ on exchange sites forming exchangeable NH_4^+ (Mortland 1958, Mortland and Wolcott 1965). NH_3 can react irreversibly with components of soil organic matter (such as lignin, carboxyl, phenol, aldehydes, and ketone and alcohol groups) which may be favored by alkaline pH (Mortland 1958, Mortland and Wolcott 1965). However, increased organic matter at the surface may improve soil water relationships, thereby favoring urease activity and the loss of NH_3 (Simpson 1968).

The soil reaction (pH) is important in determining the potential for soils to yield NH_3 to the atmosphere. In acid soils, H^+ ions will likely be available to react with NH_3 to form NH_4^+. However, even in acid soils, NH_3 can be volatilized, the important variable being the pNH_3 in solution relative to the pNH_3 of the atmosphere. In alkaline soils, the predominance of OH^- ions can force the reaction

$$NH_4^+ + OH^- \longleftrightarrow NH_3 \uparrow + H_2O \tag{7.1}$$

to the right. When certain nitrogenous compounds containing amides (urea) and amines (protein) are added to the soil, the pH can rise significantly due to the hydrolysis reaction

$$R\text{-}NH_2 + 2H_2O \rightarrow ROH + NH_4^+ + OH^- \tag{7.2}$$

Rates of loss for NH_3 resulting from pH effects can be high (Jackson and Chang 1947, Martin and Chapman 1951, Doak 1952, Mortland 1958, Wahhab et al

1957, Meyer et al 1961, Overrein and Moe 1967, Hargrove et al 1977). Mills et al (1973) found losses of NH_3 from urea increased sharply as the pH increased to 8.5, with about 67% of the applied NH_4Cl being lost. Simpson (1968) found losses of up to 60% from urea, and Watson and Lapins (1969) found losses of 84% from urine at high pH, with pH declining as NH_3 is lost from the soil solution.

Nitrite and nitrate formation can influence losses of NH_3 by removing NH_4^+ from the soil solution and forcing Equation (7.1) to the left (Doak 1952, Chin and Kroontje 1963, Watson and Lapins 1969, Khengre and Savant 1977). The removal is dependent upon factors that regulate nitrification (Alexander 1961). In native grasslands, nitrification appears to be of less importance than in cultivated systems (Soulides and Clark 1958, Clark and Paul 1970, Porter 1975).

Living plants can reduce losses of NH_3 from the soil-plant system (Meyer et al 1961, Simpson 1968, Mills et al 1973). The mechanisms involved include absorption of NH_4^+ from solution, thus forcing Equation (7.1) to the left. Gaseous NH_3 has been shown to be absorbed by living foliage through open stomates (Hutchinson et al 1972, Porter et al 1972, Denmead et al 1976). The living canopies of plants as well as standing dead plants act also to reduce temperatures at the soil surface, thus reducing the rates of chemical and biological processes that increase the activity of NH_3. Watson and Lapins (1969) found 50 to 100% greater losses of NH_3 from urine applied to bare soils than from soils with vegetative cover. Similar reductions in loss (Meyer et al 1961, Mills et al 1973) can be inferred from an increased yield of corn, which suggests increased availability to the roots of NH_4^+ and NO_3^- in soil solution. Perhaps some volatilization is offset by foliar resorbtion of NH_3. Reduction of surface temperatures could also be effective.

Plant Residues

Plant residues (litter) at the soil surface considerably enhance NH_3 loss from the soil system (Meyer et al 1961). The N source used was urea in solution. If litter occurs at the surface of the soil and urine is applied to that litter, the volatile losses of NH_3 would be considerably enhanced because the N in the urine would be held at the soil surface.

Calculations of Additions and Losses of N from Western Grasslands

Deposition rates of N via precipitation (wet deposition) were calculated using adjusted NH_4^+ and NO_3^- concentration data from Junge (1958) and rain and snowfall data from the Grassland Biome US/IBP Data Bank (Table 7.1). Because Junge's values for NH_4^+ concentrations are not consistent with other published data (Taylor et al 1971, Hoeft et al 1972, Olson et al 1973, Tabatabai and Laflen 1976), they were adjusted by assuming that N concentration of NH_4^+ in precipitation is equal to N concentration in NO_3^-. Junge's collection procedures apparently did not account for relatively high pH values (above 7.0) of rainwater in the west (Likens 1976) and consequently for the probable loss of NH_4^+ via volatilization of NH_3. The adjusted concentration data were then multiplied by quarterly precipitation totals (months of year corresponding to Junge's reported values). Precipitation values used in the calculations were 17.8, 20.3, 30.0, 37.3, 47.5, 55.5, and 84.3 mm for the Arid Land Ecology (ALE) Reserve, Jornada, Pawnee, Cottonwood, Pantex, San Joaquin Experimental Range (SJER), and Osage sites, respectively. Dry deposition rates of aerosols and particulates were calculated by assuming them to be 25% of wet deposition (Robinson and Robbins 1968).

Fixation of N through symbiotic and nonsymbiotic pathways was estimated to be small, except at ALE and SJER, based on the data of Copley and Reuss (1972). An algal crust occurs on the soil surface at ALE. Skujins (1975) has shown such crust to be capable of fixing large amounts of N_2, but the magnitude of fixation at ALE could not be estimated. Jones and Woodmansee (in press) have estimated fixation rates of N_2 by legumes to be on the order of 2.5 g N $\cdot$ m^{-2} $\cdot$ yr^{-1} in the annual grassland ecosystem in some years.

Ingested forage was calculated to be 50% of the grazable forage production. Grazable forage is defined as that remaining available after utilization by small grazers and after trampling. It excludes plant material that is unpalatable or spatially unavailable to cattle (material from 0 to 2 cm above the soil surface). The actual amount of forage consumption under light grazing by cattle has been estimated to be 15% of the aboveground net primary production of *Bouteloua gracilis*, the dominant forage in the shortgrass prairie (Coleman et al 1977). From the data of Sims and Singh (1971) and R. G. Woodmansee and D. A. Duncan (unpublished) grazable forage is estimated to be 60, 80, 60, 190, 120, 350, and 300 g biomass $\cdot$ m^{-2} $\cdot$ yr^{-1} for the ALE, Jornada, Pawnee, Cottonwood, Pantex, SJER, and Osage sites, respectively. For purposes of calculation, the grazing season is assumed to correspond with the growing season. An average herbage N concentration is assumed to be 1.5%.

Nitrogen removed in cattle tissue was estimated to be 17% of the N ingested by cattle (Dean and Rice 1974). To calculate the N loss from animal wastes it was assumed that the 83% of the ingested N remaining after the subtraction of the quantity stored in tissues was apportioned 50% to urine and 50% to feces (Whitehead 1970, Henzell and Ross 1973). Eighty percent of the urinary N and 20% of the fecal N was assumed lost to volatilization of NH_3 (Gillard 1967, Watson and Lapins 1969, Stewart 1970; Floate and Torrance 1970, Floate 1970a,b,c, J. O. Reuss, personal communication).

Plant residues not consumed by cattle were assumed to contain 1.0% N upon death of the plant tissue (R. G. Woodmansee and C. E. Dickinson, unpublished data) and 10% of that was assumed lost as NH_3 (Martin and Chapman, 1951, Alexander 1961, Floate and Torrance 1970, Floate 1970a,b,c). Denitrification and leaching losses were assumed to be small. Runoff occurs infrequently in the grasslands and is assumed not to have occurred during the years for which calculations were made. Thirty-five percent of the excreta deposited by ungulates is assumed to have fallen in 10% of the pasture (near stock tanks, fences, and bedding areas) and its N was essentially removed from circulation (Hilder 1964, Lotero et al 1966).

Conclusions

Results in Table 7.1 show that input of N to grassland ecosystems in the western United States varies considerably, depending not only on the amount of precipitation but also on geographic location (Junge 1963). The trends suggest that N input increases with increasing precipitation, and that the concentration of N in precipitation increases along the paths of air-mass movement. Thus, the northeastern Great Plains receives the greatest input of N. The sites in more arid areas and those closer to the seacoast receive less. The exception to this is SJER where input of N may be influenced by pollution. Denitrogen fixation apparently is not significant in many native grasslands. The role of foliar absorption is unknown.

Values shown in Table 7.1 for losses of N from native western grasslands clearly indicate the importance of large domestic ungulates as vectors of N loss. Even if some assumptions used to calculate these loss values are high by as much as 200% (because of loss of N from urine by volatilization, amount of forage consumed, or its N concentration), ungulates still are the dominant vector of loss. Management practices which control the intensity of grazing can therefore influence the loss of N from grassland ecosystems. These data suggest that under light or no grazing, N accumulates. At moderate grazing levels a balance may occur, except at the Pawnee site and at higher grazing intensities where an actual loss of N might occur. In the event of prolonged N depletion, the soil organic nitrogen pool could act as a buffer to the supply of N, but that pool is finite.

Summary

The development of N budgets for extensively managed, unfertilized grasslands of the western United States requires estimating the magnitudes of various pathways of additions and losses. No direct measurements of inputs and losses exist for western grassland; thus, literature was reviewed to determine probable amounts of N added and lost. The review yielded estimates of inputs as wet and dry deposition and as symbiotic and nonsymbiotic fixation. Direct absorption of NH_3 by plants was considered probable but the process could not be quantified. Input processes were dominated by wet and dry deposition. The range of total inputs was 0.2 g N $\cdot$ m^2 $\cdot$ yr^{-1} in southeastern Washington to 1.0 g N $\cdot$ m^2 $\cdot$ yr^{-1} in Oklahoma and central California during most year.

Losses of N from moderately to heavily grazed pastures were estimated to range from 0.4 g N $\cdot$ m^2 $\cdot$ yr^{-1} in southeastern Washington and southern New Mexico to about 2.0 g N $\cdot$ m^2 $\cdot$ yr^{-1} in Oklahoma and central California. The pathways for losses were dominated by volatilization of NH_3, especially from animal excrement. Because of the apparent importance of NH_3 loss from grasslands, an extensive review of environmental factors controlling such losses was presented.

References

Alexander, M. 1961. *Introduction to Soil Microbiology*. New York: John Wiley and Sons, Inc.

Barrow, N. J. 1960a. A comparison of the mineralization of nitrogen and of sulphur from decomposing organic materials. *Aust. J. Agric. Res.* **11**:960–969.

Barrow, N. J. 1960b. Simulated decomposition of soil organic matter during the decomposition of added organic materials. *Aust. J. Agric. Res.* **11**:331–338.

Barrow, N. J. 1961. Mineralization of nitrogen and sulphur from sheep faeces. *Aust. J. Agric. Res.* **12**:644–650.

Bazilevich, N. I. 1958. The minor biological cycle of ash elements and nitrogen in the processes of meadow-steppe and steppe soil development. *Soviet Soil Sci.* **1958**:1314–1330.

Bazilevich, N. I. and L. E. Rodin. 1971. Geographical regularities in productivity and the circulation of chemical elements in the earth's main vegetation types. *Soviet Geogr. Rev. Trans.* **12**:293–317.

Beauchamp, E. G., G. E. Kidd, and G. Thurtell. 1978. Ammonia volatilization from sewage sludge applied in the field. *J. Environ. Qual.* **7**:141–146.

Bormann, F. H. and G. E. Likens. 1967. Nutrient cycling. *Science* **155**:424–429.

Brown, J. M. and W. B. Bartholomew. 1963. Sorption of gaseous ammonia by clay minerals as influenced by sorbed aqueous vapor and exchangeable cations. *Soil Sci. Soc. Am. Proc.* **27**:160–164.

Burton, T. M. and G. E. Likens. 1975. Energy flow and nutrient cycling in salamander populations in the Hubbard Brook Experimental Forest, New Hampshire. *Ecology* **56**:1068–1080.

Chao, T. T. and W. Kroontje. 1964. Relationships between ammonia volatilization, ammonia concentration, and water evaporation. *Soil Sci. Soc. Am. Proc.* **28**(3):393–395.

Charley, J. L. 1977. Mineral cycling in rangeland ecosystems. *In* R. F. Sosebee (ed.), *Rangeland Plant Physiology*, Range Sci. Ser. No. 4, Society for Range Management, Denver, CO. pp. 215–256.

Chin, W., and W. Kroontje. 1963. Urea hydrolysis and subsequent loss of ammonia. *Soil Sci. Soc. Am. Proc.* **27**(3):316–318.

Clark, F. E. 1975. Viewing the invisible prairie. *In* M. K. Wali (ed.), *Prairie: A Multiple View*, pp. 181–197. Grand Forks: University of North Dakota Press.

Clark, F. E. 1977. Internal cycling of ^{15}nitrogen in shortgrass prairie. *Ecology* **58**:1322–1333.

Clark, F. E. and E. A. Paul. 1970. The microflora of grassland. *Adv. Agron.* **22**:375–435.

Coleman, D. C., R. Andrews, J. E. Ellis, and J. S. Singh. 1977. Energy flow and partitioning in selected man-managed and natural ecosystems. *Agro-Ecosystems* **3**:45–54.

Conrad, J. P. 1942. The occurrence and origin of urease like activities in soils. *Soil Sci.* **54**:367–380.

Copley, P. W. and J. O Reuss. 1972. Evaluation of biological N_2 fixation in a grassland ecosystem, *US/IBP Grassland Biome Tech. Rep. No. 152*. Fort Collins: Colorado State Univ.

Dahlman, R. C. and C. L. Kucera. 1968. Tagging native grassland vegetation with carbon-14. *Ecology* **49**:1199–1203.

Dean, R. E. and R. W. Rice. 1974. Effects of fences and corrals on grazing behavior. Proc. Western Sect. *Am. Soc. Anim. Sci.* **25**:56–58.
Denmead, O. T., J. R. Simpson, and J. R. Freney. 1974. Ammonia flux into the atmosphere from a grazed pasture. *Science* **185**:609–610.
Denmead, O. T., J. R. Freney, and J. R. Simpson. 1976. A closed ammonia cycle within a plant canopy. *Soil Biol. Biochem.* **8**:161–164.
Doak, B. W. 1952. Some chemical changes in the nitrogenous constituents of urine when voided on pasture. *J. Agric. Sci.* **42**:162–171.
Duvigneaud, P. and S. Denaeyer-DeSmet. 1975. Mineral cycling in terrestrial ecosystems. *In* D. E. Reichle, J. F. Franklin, and D. W. Goodall (eds.), *Productivity of World Ecosystems,* pp. 133–154. Washington, D.C.: National Academy of Science.
Edwards, C. A. 1974. Macroarthropods. *In* C. H. Dickinson and G. J. F. Pugh (eds.), *Biology of Plant Litter Decomposition,* pp. 533–554. New York: Academic Press, Inc.
Eriksson, E. 1952. Composition of atmospheric precipitation. 1. Nitrogen compounds. *Tellus* **4**:215–232.
Ernst, J. W. and H. F. Massey. 1960. The effects of several factors on volatilization of ammonia formed from urea in the soil. *Soil Sci. Soc. Am. Proc.* **24**(2):87–90.
Faurie, G., A. Josserand, and R. Bardin. 1975. Influence des colloides argileux sur la retention d'ammonium et la nitrification. *Rev. Ecol. Biol. Sol.* **12**:201–210.
Fenn, L. B. 1975. Ammonium volatilization from surface applications of ammonium compounds on calcareous soils. III. Effects of mixing low and high loss ammonium compounds. *Soil Sci. Soc. Am. Proc.* **39**:366–369.
Fenn, L. B. and R. Escarzaga. 1976a. Ammonium volatilization from surface applications of ammonium compounds on calcareous soils: V. Soil water content and method of nitrogen application. *Soil Sci. Soc. Am. Proc.* **40**:537–541.
Fenn, L. B. and R. Escarzaga. 1976b. Ammonia volatilization from surface applications of ammonium compounds to calcareous soils as affected by initial soil water content and quantity of applied water. *Agron. Abstr.* **1976**:127–128.
Fenn, L. B. and D. E. Kissel. 1973. Ammonia volatilization from surface applications of ammonium compounds on calcareous soils: I. General theory. *Soil Sci. Soc. Am. Proc.* **37**:855–859.
Fenn, L. B. and D. E. Kissel. 1974. Ammohium volatilization from surface applications of ammonium compounds on calcareous soils: II. Effect of temperature and rate of NH_4^+ = N application. *Soil Sci. Soc. Am. Proc.* **38**:606–610.
Fenn, L. B. and D. E. Kissel. 1975. Ammonium volatilization from surface applications of ammonium compounds on calcareous soils: IV. Effect of calcium carbonate content. *Soil Sci. Soc. Am. Proc.* **39**:631–633.
Feth, J. H. 1966. Nitrogen compounds in natural water—a review. *Water Resour. Res.* **2**:41–58.
Floate, M. J. S. 1970a. Decomposition of organic materials from hill soils and pastures. 2. Comparative studies on the mineralization of carbon, nitrogen and phosphorus from plant materials and sheep faeces. *Soil Biol. Biochem.* **2**:173–185.
Floate, M. J. S. 1970b. Decomposition of organic materials from hill soils and pastures. 3. The effect of temperature on the mineralization of carbon, nitrogen and phosphorus from plant materials and sheep feces. *Soil Biol. Biochem.* **2**:187–196.
Floate, M. J. S. 1970c. Decomposition of organic materials from hill soils and pastures. 4. The effects of moisture content on the mineralization of carbon, nitrogen and phosphorus from plant materials and sheep faeces. *Soil Biol. Biochem.* **2**:275–283.
Floate, M. J. S. and C. J. W. Torrance. 1970. Decomposition of the organic materials from hill soils and pastures. 1. Incubation method for studying the mineralization of carbon, nitrogen and phosphorus. *J. Sci. Food Agric.* **21**:116–120.
Frank, H. 1954. On the nitrogen loss in aging plants (Trans. No. 3968 from "Über den Stickstoffverlust bei alternden Pflanzen"). *Planta* **44**:319.
Frissel, M. J. (ed.). 1977. Cycling of mineral nutrients in agricultural ecosystems. *Agro-Ecosystems* **4**:1–254.

Galloway, J. N. 1976. Critical factors in the collection of precipitation for chemical analysis. *In* D. H. Matheson and F. C. Elder (eds.) (Proc. First Specialty Symp. on *Atmospheric Contribution to the Chemistry of Lake Waters* Int. Assoc. Great Lakes Res.) pp. 65–81. Vol. 2, Supplement 1, Buffalo: State University College

Gasser, J. K. R. 1964. Urea as a fertilizer. Soils Fert. **27**(3):175–180.

Gillard, P. 1967. Coprophagous beetles in pasture ecosystems. *J. Aust. Inst. Agric. Sci.* **33**:30–34.

Granat, L. 1976. Principles in network design for precipitation chemistry measurements. *In* D. H. Matheson and F. C. Elder (eds.) (Proc. First Specialty Symp. on *Atmospheric Contribution to the Chemistry of Lake Waters* Int. Assoc. Great Lakes Res.), pp. 42–55. Vol. 2, Supplement 1, Buffalo: State University College

Hanawalt, R. B. 1969. Environmental factors influencing the sorption of atmospheric ammonia by soils. *Soil Sci. Soc. Am. Proc.* **33**:231–234.

Hargrove, W. L., D. E. Kissel, and L. B. Fenn. 1977. Field measurements of ammonia volatilization from surface applications of ammonium salts to a calcareous soil. *Agron. J.* **69**:473–476.

Harmsen, G. W. and G. J. Kolenbrander. 1965. Soil inorganic nitrogen. *In* W. V. Bartholomew and F. E. Clark (eds.) *Soil Nitrogen, Agronomy* 10, pp. 43–92. Madison, Wisc.: American Society of Agronomy.

Henzell, E. F. and D. O. Norris. 1961. Processes by which nitrogen is added to the soil/plant system. *Commonw. Bur. Pastures Field Crops Bull.* **46**:1–18.

Henzell, E. F. and P. J. Ross. 1973. The nitrogen cycles of pasture ecosystems. *In* G. W. Butler and R. W. Bailey (eds.), *Chemistry and Biochemistry of Herbage,* Vol. 2, pp. 227–246. New York: Academic Press, Inc.

Hilder, E. J. 1964. The distribution of plant nutrients by sheep at pasture. *Proc. Aust. Soc. Anim. Prod.* **5**:241–248.

Hoeft, R. G., D. R. Keeney, and L. M. Walsh. 1972. Nitrogen and sulfur in precipitation and sulfur dioxide in the atmosphere in Wisconsin. *J. Environ. Qual.* **1**:203–208.

Hutchinson, G. L., R. J. Millington, and D. B. Peters. 1972. Atmospheric ammonia: Absorption by plant leaves. *Science* **175**:771–772.

Jackson, M. L., and S. C. Chang. 1947. Anhydrous ammonic retention by soils as influenced by depth of application soil texture, moisture content, pH value, and tilth. *Agron. J.* **39**:623–633.

Jones, M. B., and R. G. Woodmansee. In press. Nitrogen cycling in annual grassland ecosystems. *In* L. T. Burcham and R. G. Woodmansee (eds.), *Annual Grassland Ecosystems of California*. Stroudsburg, Pa.: Dowden, Hutchinson and Ross, Inc.

Junge, C. E. 1958. The distribution of ammonia and nitrate in rain water over the United States. *Trans. Am. Geophys. Union* **39**:248.

Junge, C. E. 1963. *Air Chemistry and Radioactivity*. New York: Academic Press, Inc.

Junge, C. E. and P. E. Gustafson. 1956a. On the distribution of sea salt over the United States and its removal by precipitation. *Tellus* **9**:164–173.

Junge, C. E. and P. E. Gustafson. 1956b. Precipitation sampling for chemical analysis. *Bull. Am. Meteorol. Soc.* **37**:244.

Khengre, S. T. and N. K. Savant. 1977. Distribution pattern of inorganic nitrogen following anhydrous ammonia injection into a vertisol. *Soil Soc. Sci. Am. J.* **41**:1139–1141.

Kilmer, V. J. 1974. Nutrient losses from grasslands through leaching and runoff. *In* D. A. Mays (ed.) *Forage Fertilization,* pp. 341–362. Madison, Wisc.: American Society of Agronomy, Crop Science Society of America, and Soil Science Society of America.

Kissel, D. E., H. L. Brewer, and G. F. Arkin. 1977. Design and test of a field sampler for ammonia volatilization. *Soil Sci. Soc. Am. J.* **41**:1133–1138.

Kline, J. R. 1969. Soil chemistry as a factor in the function of grassland ecosystems. *In* R. L. Dix and R. G. Beidleman (eds.), *The Grassland Ecosystem* (Range Sci. Dep. Sci. Ser. No. 2.) pp. 71–88. Fort Collins: Colorado State Univ.

Lapins, P. and E. R. Watson. 1970. Loss of nitrogen from maturing plants. *Aust. J. Exp. Agric. Anim. Husb.* **10**:599–603.

Lauer, D. A., D. R. Bouldin, and S. D. Klausner. 1976. Ammonia volatilization from dairy manure spread on the soil surface. *J. Environ. Qual.* **5**(2):134–141.

Likens, G. E. 1976. Acid precipitation. Chem. Eng. News 1976:29–44.

Lofty, J. R. 1974. Oligochaetes. *In* C. H. Dickinson and G. J. F. Pugh (eds.), *Biology of Plant Litter Decomposition.* Vol. 2, pp. 467–488. New York: Academic Press, Inc.

Lotero, J., W. W. Woodhouse, Jr., and R. G. Petersen. 1966. Local effect on fertility of urine voided by grazing cattle. *Agron. J.* **58**:262–265.

Malo, B. A., and E. R. Purvis. 1964. Soil absorption of atmospheric ammonia. *Soil Sci.* **97**:242–247.

Martin, J. P., and H. D. Chapman. 1951. Volatilization of ammonia from surface-fertilized soils. *Soil Sci.* **71**(1):25–34.

McConnell, J. C. 1973. Atmospheric ammonia. *J. Geophy. Res.* **78**:7812–7820.

McGarity, J. W., and J. A. Rajaratnam. 1973. Apparatus for the measurement of losses of nitrogen as gas from the field and simulated field environments. *Soil Biol. Biochem.* **5**:121–131.

Meyer, R. D., R. A. Olson, and H. F. Rhoades. 1961. Ammonia losses from fertilized Nebraska soils. *Agron. J.* **53**(4):241–244.

Millar, C. S. 1974. Decomposition of coniferous leaf litter. *In* C. H. Dickinson and G. J. F. Pugh (eds.), *Biology of Plant Litter Decomposition.* Vol. 1, pp. 105–128. New York: Academic Press, Inc.

Mills, H. A., A. V. Barker, and D. N. Maynard. 1973. Ammonia volatilization from soils. *Agron. J.* **66**(3):355–358.

Mortland, M. M. 1958. Reactions of ammonia in soils. *Adv. Agron.* **10**:325–348.

Mortland, M. M. and A. R. Wolcott. 1965. Sorption of inorganic nitrogen compounds by soil materials. *In* W. V. Bartholomew and F. E. Clark (eds.), *Soil Nitrogen,* Agronomy 10, pp. 151–197. Madison, Wisc.: American Society of Agronomy.

Nommik, H. 1965. Ammonium fixation and other reactions involving a nonenzymatic immobilization of mineral nitrogen in soil. *In* W. V. Bartholomew and F. E. Clark (eds.), *Soil Nitrogen,* Agronomy 10, pp. 198–258. Madison, Wisc.: American Society of Agronomy.

Odum, E. P. 1969. The strategy of ecosystems development. *Science* **164**:262–270.

Olson, R. A., E. C. Seim, and J. Muir. 1973. Influence of agricultural practices on water quality in Nebraska: A survey of streams, groundwater, and precipitation. *Water Resour. Bull.* **9**:301–311.

Overrein, L. N. and P. G. Moe. 1967. Factors affecting urea hydrolysis and ammonia volatilization in soil. *Soil Sci. Am. Proc.* **31**(1):57–61.

Parr, J. F. and R. I. Papendick. 1966. Retention of anhydrous ammonia by soil: II. Effect of ammonia concentration and soil moisture. *Soil Sci.* **101**:109–119.

Pearsall, W. H. and M. C. Billimoria. 1937. Loss of nitrogen from green plants. *Biochem. J.* **31**:1734.

Porter, L. K. 1975. Nitrogen transfer in ecosystems. *Soil Biochem.* **4**:1–30.

Porter, L. K., F. G. Viets, Jr., and G. L. Hutchinson. 1972. Air containing nitrogen-15 ammonia: Foliar absorption by corn seedlings. *Science* **174**:759–761.

Power, J. F., J. A. Lessi, G. A. Reichman, and D. L. Grunes. 1973. Recovery, residual effects, and fate of nitrogen fertilizer sources in a semiarid region. *Agron. J.* **65**:765–768.

Rashid, G. H. 1977. The volatilization losses of nitrogen from added urea in some soils of Bangladesh. *Plant Soil* **48**:549–556.

Reuss, J. O. 1971. Decomposer and nitrogen cycling investigations in the Grassland Biome. *In* N. R. French (ed.) *Preliminary Analysis of Structure and Function in Grasslands* (Range Sci. Dep. Sci. Ser. No. 10), pp. 133–146. Fort Collins: Colorado State Univ.

Reuss, J. O. and G. S. Innis. 1977. A grassland nitrogen-flow simulation model. *In* G. S. Innes (ed.) *Grassland Simulation Model.* Ecological Studies, 26, pp. 186–203. New York: Springer-Verlag.

Richardson, A. E. V., H. C. Trumble, and R. E. Shapter. 1931. Factors affecting the mineral contents of pasture (Bull. No. 49). *Council for Sci. Ind. Res.*

Robinson, E. and R. C. Robbins. 1968. Sources, abundance, and fate of gaseous atmospheric pollutants (Report prepared for the American Petroleum Institute, SR1 Proj. PR-6755). Menlo Park, Calif. Stanford Research Institute.

Rodin, L. E. and N. I. Bazilevich. 1967. *Production and Mineral Cycling in Terrestrial Vegetation.* (Transl.). London: Oliver and Boyd Ltd.

Rogler, G. A. and R. J. Lorenz. 1974. Fertilization of mid-continent range plants. *In* D. A. Mays (ed.), *Forage Fertilization,* pp. 231–254. Madison, Wisc.: Agronomic Society of America, Crop Science Society of America, Soil Science Society of America.

Schuman, G. E. and R. E. Burwell. 1974. Precipitation nitrogen contribution to surface runoff discharges. *J. Environ. Qual.* **3**:366–369.

Simpson, J. R. 1968. Losses of urea nitrogen from the surface of pasture soils. *Int. Congr. Soil Sci. Trans.* **9**(2):459–466.

Sims, P. L. and J. S. Singh. 1971. Herbage dynamics and net primary production in certain ungrazed and grazed grasslands in North America. *In* N. R. French (ed.), *Preliminary Analysis of Structure and Function in Grasslands* (Range Sci. Dep. Sci. Ser. No. 10) pp. 56–124. Fort Collins: Colorado State Univ.

Skujins, J. 1975. Nitrogen dynamics in stands dominated by some major cool desert shrubs, *US/IBP Research Memorandum 75-33.* Logan: Utah State Univ.

Söderlund, R. and B. H. Svensson. 1976. The global nitrogen cycle. *In* B. H. Svensson and R. Söderlund (eds.), *Nitrogen, Phosphorus, and Sulfur-Global Cycles* SCOPE Rep. 7, Ecol. Res. Comm. Bull. No. 22, pp. 23–75. Stockholm: Statens naturvetenskapliga forskningsråd.

Soulides, D. A. and F. E. Clark. 1958. Nitrification in grassland soils. *Soil Sci. Soc. Am. Proc.* **22**:308–311.

Stewart, B. A. 1970. Volatilization and nitrification of nitrogen from urine under simulated cattle feedlot conditions. *Environ. Sci. Technol.* **4**:479–582.

Stewart, B. A., F. G. Viets, Jr., G. L. Hutchinson, and W. A. Kemper. 1967. Nitrate and other water pollutants under fields and feed lots. *Environ. Sci. Technol.* **1**:763.

Sturges, F. W., R. T. Holmes, and G. E. Likens. 1974. The role of birds in nutrient cycling in a northern hardwoods ecosystem. *Ecology* **55**:149–155.

Tabatabai, M. A. and J. M. Laflen. 1976. Nitrogen and sulfur content and pH of precipitation in Iowa. *J. Environ. Qual.* **5**:108–112.

Taylor, A. W., W. M. Edwards, and E. C. Simpson. 1971. Nutrients in streams draining woodland and farmland near Coshocton, Ohio. *Water Resour. Res.* **7**:81–89.

Viets, F. G., Jr. 1975. The environmental impact of fertilizers. *CRC Critical Rev. Environ. Control* **5**:423–453.

Vitousek, P. M., and W. A. Reiners. 1975. Ecosystem succession and nutrient retention: A hypothesis. *BioScience* **25**:376–381.

Voigt, G. H. 1965. Nitrogen recovery from decomposing tree leaf tissue and forest humus. *Soil Sci. Soc. Am. Proc.* **29**:756–759.

Volk, G. M. 1959. Volatile loss of ammonia following surface application of urea to turf or bare soils. *Agron. J.* **51**(12):746–749.

Wahhab, A., M. S. Randhawa, and S. Q. Alam. 1957. Loss of ammonia from ammonium sulphate under different conditions when applied to soils. *Soil Sci.* **84**(3):249–255.

Wakesman, S. A., T. C. Cordon, and N. Hulpoi. 1939. Influence of temperature upon the microbiological population and decomposition processes in composts of stable manure. *Soil Sci.* **47**(2):83–113.

Watson, E. R. and P. Lapins. 1969. Losses of nitrogen from urine on soils from southwestern Australia. *Aust. J. Exp. Agric. Anim. Husb.* **9**:85–91.

Whitehead, D. C. 1970. The role of nitrogen in grassland productivity. Commonw. *Agric. Bur. Bull. No. 48.* Farnham Royal, Bucks, England.

Woodmansee, R. G. 1978. Additions and losses of nitrogen in grassland ecosystems. *BioScience* **28**:448–453.

Woodmansee, R. G., J. L. Dodd, R. A. Bowman, F. E. Clark, and C. E. Dickinson. 1978. Nitrogen budget for a shortgrass prairie ecosystem. *Oecologia* **34**:363–376.

Zakharchenko, I. G. 1974. Supply of nitrogen with atmospheric precipitation and its losses during soil leaching in the Ukranian poless'ye and forest-steppe. *Soviet Soil Sci.* 1974:63–67.

8. Simulated Impact of Management Practices upon the Tallgrass Prairie

William J. Parton and Paul G. Risser

Introduction

The ELM grassland model (Innis 1978) was used to simulate the impact of different management practices upon a tallgrass prairie. The ELM grassland model is a total ecosystem model of a grassland that was developed by the US/IBP Grassland Biome program. It incorporates subsystem models similar in level of resolution and mechanism to those described for primary producers in Chapter 2 and for vertebrate and invertebrate consumers in Chapters 5 and 6. It was designed to be a generalized model that could be applied to the different US/IBP grassland sites. The experimental sites range from a desert grassland in New Mexico to a tallgrass prairie in Oklahoma. The Osage site is the tallgrass prairie site located in northeastern Oklahoma.

The ELM model simulates the flow of water, heat, nitrogen, and phosphorus through the ecosystem and the biomass dynamics of up to five plant categories, ten consumers, and the decomposers. The model also simulates decomposition of aboveground and belowground plant and animal biomass. The driving variables for the model include daily rainfall, maximum and minimum air temperature, soil temperature at 180 cm, cloud cover, relative humidity, and wind speed. The model was developed to study the effects of the levels and types of herbivory, of variation of rainfall and temperature, and of the addition of nitrogen and phosphorus on grassland ecosystems.

The complete flow diagram (Figure 8.1) shows that the major components of the model include eight submodels: the abiotic, producer, mammalian consumer, grasshopper, plant phenology, decomposer, nitrogen, and phosphorus submodels. A complete description of the submodels is found in a series of summary papers (Rodell 1977, Reuss and Innis 1977, Hunt 1977, Cole et al 1977, and Innis 1978).

The three major steps in development of the Osage site version of the ELM model were: (1) determining the model structure (plant species, consumer species, etc.); (2) determining the values for the site specific parameters required by the ELM model; and (3) comparing output from the model with observed data from the grazed and ungrazed treatments at the Osage site. A list of the data collected at Osage and a description of the sampling techniques are presented by

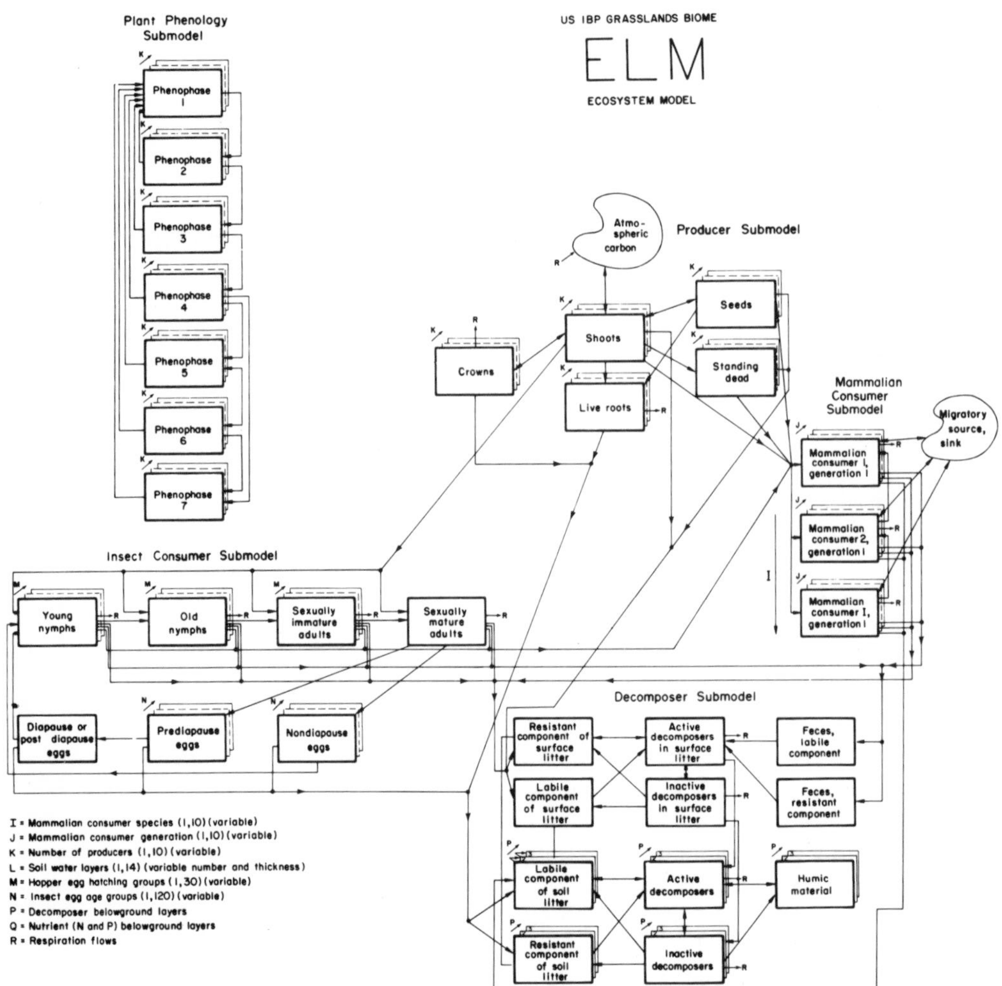

Figure 8.1. Flow diagram of the total ecosystem model ELM (Innis 1978).

Swift and French (1972) while results of data analysis are presented in reports by Blocker and Reed (1971), Risser (1971), Risser and Kennedy (1972, 1975), May and Risser (1973), Birney (1974), French et al (1976), and Chapters 1, 4, 5, and 10 of this volume. Data collected at the Osage site include state variable information about the abiotic, producer, consumer, and decomposer components of Osage from 1970 through 1972.

The structural components of the ELM model that are site-specific include specification of the producer plant types, the consumer species, the number and depth of soil water layers, and the depth of the soil layers used in the decomposer, nitrogen, and phosphorus submodels. The five plant types simulated by the producer submodel included a warm-season perennial grass, a cool-season perennial grass, warm-season forb, cool-season forb, and a cool-season annual grass. The mammalian consumer species simulated for the grazed site included

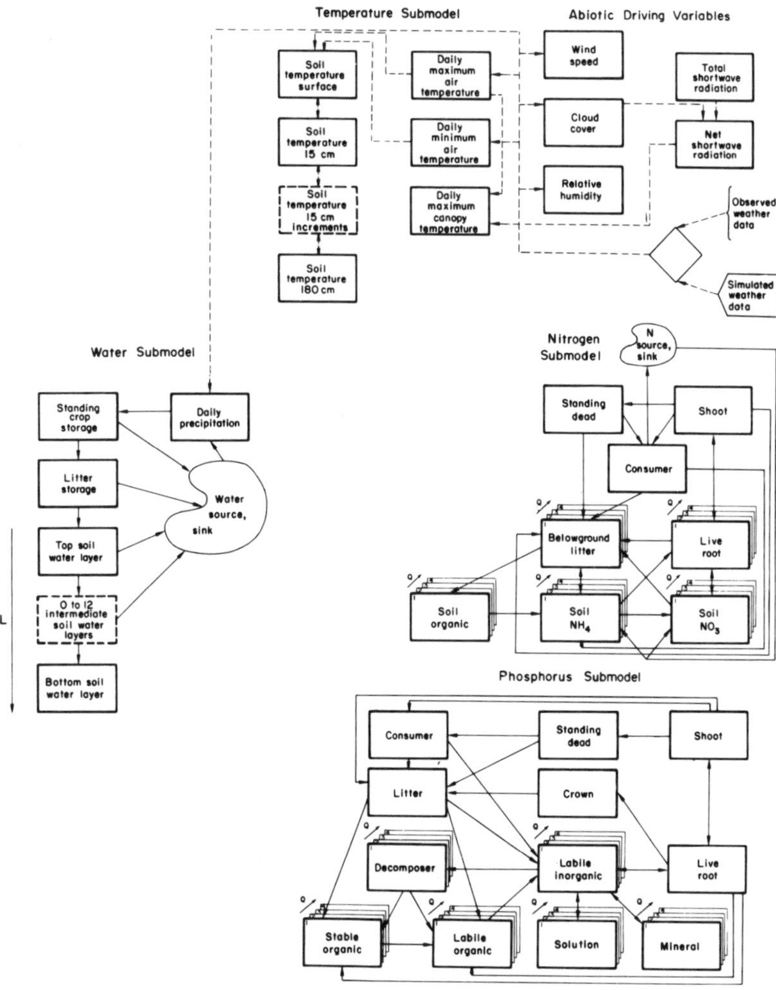

Figure 8.1. (cont'd.)

the cow *(Bos taurus)*, coyote *(Canis latrans)*, jackrabbit *(Lepus californicus)*, cottontail *(Sylvilagus floridanus)*, cotton rat *(Sigmodon hispidus)*, prairie vole *(Microtus ochrogaster)*, deer mouse *(Peromyscus maniculatus)*, Montana harvest mouse *(Reithrodontomys montanus)*, thirteen-lined ground squirrel *(Spermophilus tridecemlineatus)*, and hispid pocket mouse *(Perognathus hispidus)*, and short-tailed shrew *(Blarina brevicauda)*. The Osage site version of the ELM model did not use the grasshopper submodel because of low grasshopper biomass (Blocker and Reed 1971). The water-flow submodel had eight soil water layers (0–5 cm, 5–10 cm, 10–15 cm, 15–30 cm, 30–60 cm, 60–75 cm, and 75–90 cm), the phosphorus and nitrogen submodels four soil layers (0–5 cm, 5–15 cm, 15–30 cm, and 30–90 cm), and the decomposer model three soil layers (0–5 cm, 5–15 cm, and 15–90 cm). The temperature-profile submodel used the layer structure shown in the flow diagram (Figure 8.1).

Values for the site-specific parameters required by the ELM model were determined by using information derived from other grassland sites, by using Osage site data, and by an iterative model-tuning process in which the parameter values were determined by comparing model output with observed data and then modifying the parameter value until the difference between model output and observed data was minimized. The iterative model-tuning process was used to determine a fairly large number of site-specific parameters because many of the site-specific parameters could not be determined directly from the present data base.

In the process of developing the Osage site version of the ELM model, it became apparent that the ELM model structure was inadequate for representing the impact of a plant canopy on light interception and water loss. The ELM model was modified slightly to include these impacts. Comparison of the simulated model output with observed data is presented by Parton and Risser (1976).

Simulation of Management Practice

Many of the factors controlling production of a tallgrass prairie are manipulated with management practices. The ELM grassland model was specifically set up to simulate the impact of range management practices upon grassland systems and considers the different management practices as driving variables for the model. The range management manipulations simulated by the model include: (1) altering the grazing intensity, the grazing regimes, and the grazing time period, (2) changing the species composition, (3) adding nitrogen and phosphorus to the grassland, (4) adding water during the growing season, and (5) spring burning of the prairie.

Twenty-three different three-year computer simulations of the Osage model (two-day time step) were used to estimate results of these management practices. The important characteristics of experimental model runs are presented in Table 8.1. Each of the computer runs started with identical initial conditions. The abiotic driving variables included daily air temperature data from Pawhuska, Oklahoma, daily rainfall data from Foraker, Oklahoma, and long-term monthly average values of relative humidity, cloud cover, and wind speed from Tulsa, Oklahoma. The effects of the various management practices upon tallgrass prairie were summarized by comparing three-year average values for selected output variables. The output variables were selected from over 200 variables simulated by the model because they summarize the state of the system. These included primary and secondary production variables, standing crop variables, abiotic variables, and nitrogen and phosphorus variables.

ELM Grazing Simulations

The simulated grazing regimes include year-round cow-calf grazing and seasonal steer grazing, and the grazing intensities ranged from light to extra heavy. In the cow-calf grazing simulation the calves were born in February and were removed from the range on October 1, while the cows remained on the range throughout

Table 8.1. Characteristics of the Experimental Model Runs

Osage model run	Initial grazing intensity (acres/animal unit)	Inital weight of cattle (kg/head)	Grazing time period
Cow-calf grazing			
Light	16.0	447	Jan.–Dec.
Moderate	10.0	447	Jan.–Dec.
Heavy	8.0	447	Jan.–Dec.
Extra heavy	5.0	447	Jan.–Dec.
Early steer grazing			
Light	10.0	250	Apr. 15–Oct. 30
Moderate	6.0	250	Apr. 15–Oct. 30
Heavy	4.7	250	Apr. 15–Oct. 30
Extra heavy	3.0	250	Apr. 15–Oct. 30
Late steer grazing			
Light	10.0	250	May 1–Oct. 30
Moderate	6.0	250	May 1–Oct. 30
Heavy	4.7	250	May 1–Oct. 30
Species manipulation			
Moderate steer grazing—remove cool-season animals	6.0	250	Apr. 15–Oct. 30
Moderate steer grazing—remove warm-season forbs	6.0	250	Apr. 15–Oct. 30
Spring burning[1]			
Moderate steer grazing plus fire the first spring	6.0	250	Apr. 15–Oct. 30
Moderate steer grazing plus yearly fire	6.0	250	Apr. 15–Oct. 30
Fertilization[2]			
Moderate steer	6.0	250	Apr. 15–Oct. 30
Moderate cow-calf	10.0	447	Jan.–Dec.
Irrigation[3]			
Moderate steer grazing	6.0	250	Apr. 15–Oct. 30
Moderate cow-calf grazing	10.0	447	Jan.–Dec.
Irrigation plus fertilization			
Moderate steer	6.0	250	Apr. 15–Oct. 30
Moderate cow-calf	10.0	447	Jan.–Dec.

[1] Spring fire in April removes 68% of aboveground N.
[2] Nitrogen (20 g · m^{-2}) and phosphorus (3 g · m^{-2}) on March 31 of first year.
[3] Irrigation water applied May through September if soil water tension at −10 cm lower than −5 bars.

the year. The seasonal steer-grazing pattern included grazing of yearling steers (150 kg initial weight) from April 15 through October 30 (early grazing), or from May 1 through October 30 (late grazing). The stocking rates represented those characteristic for the southern true prairie grassland (Harlan 1960). The grazing simulations included small-mammal grazing typical of a grazed pasture while the ungrazed includes small-mammal grazing typical of an ungrazed pasture.

The results for the cow-calf grazing (Table 8.2) show that increasing the grazing intensity from light (16 acres per animal) to extra heavy (5 acres per animal) causes above- and belowground production to increase, while cattle weight gain per head and the average nitrogen content of forage consumed by cattle decreases. A more detailed analysis of the data shows that aboveground production was greater with light grazing in the first year, and in the last two years maximum production occurred with extra heavy grazing. Rainfall during the first year was 30% below normal, while the last two years were just above and slightly below normal, respectively. Herbel and Anderson (1959) found that increasing the grazing level from moderate to heavy during years with below-normal rainfall caused a decrease in aboveground production. The general increase in aboveground production with increasing grazing is supported by studies showing that the grazing or clipping of the forage throughout the year results in an increased aboveground production (Biswell and Weaver 1933, Kelting 1954, Duvall 1962). Herferd (1951) noted that clipping after seedstalk formation increased foliage production while Jameson and Huss (1959) reported that during seed set in the early fall, the stems of little bluestem are grazed almost exclusively. Although the model results cannot be tested explicitly from existing data, these results warrant further investigation.

The decrease in cattle weight gain per head with greater than moderate grazing intensity is consistent with data from Harlan (1960), however, the model results greatly underestimate the decrease in weight gain. Model results also show that the N content of consumed forage declines with increasing grazing intervals. Decreased N content of the forage produces a decrease in the digestibility of the forage and results in a decrease in cattle weight gain. Harlan's data also show that the model overestimates weight gain per head at all of the grazing levels. Discrepencies result from the way the Brodie (1945) growth curve is used to control weight gain by the animals.

The peak total aboveground biomass and warm-season perennial-grass biomass increase as grazing levels increase to heavy and then decrease with extra heavy grazing. Cool-season annual-grass production decreases with increasing grazing pressures while warm-season forbs increase. Increasing grazing intensity from light to heavy results in the positive effect of increasing the desirable warm-season perennial grass and decreasing the cool-season annual grasses, while grazing intensities greater than heavy have the negative effect of decreasing warm-season grass production and greatly increasing the forbs which are of a low grazing preference.

The standing-crop parameters show that standing dead biomass decreases with grazing pressure, and that litter biomass is only slightly affected by grazing, while total root biomass has its maximum value with heavy grazing. Virtually all previous studies from the Osage site show a decrease in standing dead biomass under grazing conditions, while the decrease in root biomass under extra heavy grazing is supported by results of other studies (Weaver 1950). The Osage site data showed lower root production under grazed conditions in one of the three years.

The abiotic and nutrient data show that increasing grazing intensity produces an increase in transpiration, bare soil water loss, and nutrient (N and P) uptake by the live shoots, while water interception and the net N balance in the system decrease. The model output presented earlier also shows that soil water moisture decreases under grazing. Data to support the effect of grazing on water loss is lacking; however, other workers have shown a reduction of soil moisture under grazed conditions (Beebe and Hoffman 1968).

Field data to verify output results for the nutrient parameter do not exist; however, implications of the model results are very important. The simulation output shows that net accumulation of N in the grassland system is 0.89 g N · m^{-2} in ungrazed conditions and decreases to 0.06 g N · m^{-2} under heavy grazing, while extra heavy grazing causes a net loss of 0.5 g N · m^{-2} per year. These results suggest that grazing intensity less than or equal to heavy grazing (4.7 acres per animal) will result in net accumulation of N; however, extra heavy grazing will cause a depletion of N from the system. This suggests that shoot uptake of N under extra heavy grazing would decline with time as a result of the net loss from the system.

A positive effect of increased consumer uptake of nitrogen and phosphorus is to increase the rate of return of these nutrients to the soil pool. This is indicated by the fact that over 80% of the N consumed by a cow on a given day is returned within a week to the soil-plant system in the form of urine or feces. Nutrients contained in the urine and feces are returned to the soil nutrient pool much more rapidly than the nutrient contained in standing dead and litter biomass (Dahlman et al 1969, Wicklow 1975). However, up to 20% of the nitrogen in the feces and 50 to 90% of N in the urine is lost to the atmosphere through volitalization (see Chapter 7). The loss of nitrogen from animal feces and urine is the reason for the net loss of nitrogen from the system under extra heavy grazing.

Microbial activity was greater in the ungrazed pasture and decreased with increasing grazing intensity. This decrease in microbial activity with grazing is probably caused by the increased herbage biomass processed by the cattle and a reduction in the aboveground biomass available for microbial decomposition.

A summary of results shows that increasing the grazing intensity tends to increase net primary production and the uptake of nutrients by plants. A detailed analysis of the model structure and supporting research indicates that the reduction of light intercepted by the standing dead (reduced standing dead with grazing) and the accelerated nutrient release from aboveground biomass are the primary mechanisms responsible for increased primary production and nutrient uptake. Results also suggest that extra heavy grazing will cause long-term reduction of primary production and nitrogen uptake because of loss by volatilization of nitrogen from feces and urine. Another negative impact of increased grazing is a decrease in the nitrogen content of the forage which results in decreased cattle weight (digestibility generally decreases with lower nitrogen content).

Results for early-season steer grazing show that increasing the grazing intensity (light to extra heavy) has a similar impact on the output variables as changing grazing levels in the cow-calf system. The major differences are that maximum shoot uptake of nitrogen and maximum aboveground production in the wet years occur with heavy grazing while maximum values of both parameters occurred with extra heavy grazing in the cow-calf grazing runs.

Table 8.2. Three-Year Average Values for Output Parameters from the Grazing Simulations

	Primary production ($g \cdot m^{-2} \cdot yr^{-1}$)		Animal weight gain			Peak live (g biomass $\cdot m^{-2}$)			
Grazing runs	Net aboveground production	Net belowground production	Weight gain per head ($kg \cdot head^{-1}$)	Forage consumption ($g \cdot m^{-2} \cdot yr^{-1}$)	Average N content of forage consumed (% N)	Warm-season grass	Warm-season forbes	Cool-season annuals	Total aboveground
Cow-calf grazing									
Light	579	191	237	87	1.34	183	26	80	263
Moderate	594	229	237	139	1.29	210	33	55	277
Heavy	600	239	237	175	1.24	215	37	47	283
Extra heavy	611	240	236	280	1.22	165	64	28	245
Early steer grazing									
Light	522	124	83	75	1.20	143	23	126	257
Moderate	564	145	75	126	1.19	150	29	114	266
Heavy	581	166	71	161	1.19	163	35	96	265
Extra heavy	530	201	73	253	1.31	103	74	24	182
Late steer grazing									
Light	535	109	76	70	1.15	124	20	146	255
Moderate	553	121	67	117	1.13	225	25	150	269
Heavy	555	125	63	152	1.08	130	28	150	272

	Standing-crop (g biomass · m^{-2})			Abiotic (cm H_2O · yr^{-1})			Nutrients (g · m^{-2} · yr^{-1})			Microbial respiration
Grazing runs	Standing dead	Litter	Total roots	Transpiration	Bare soil water loss	Standing-crop interception	P shoot uptake	N shoot uptake	Net nitrogen balance	Biomass loss (g · m^{-2} · yr^{-1})
Cow-calf grazing										
Light	369	386	935	28.7	11.9	31.7	0.38	6.92	0.47	890
Moderate	361	364	979	29.0	12.9	30.2	0.41	7.00	0.22	883
Heavy	335	364	986	29.2	14.0	28.5	0.43	6.99	0.06	880
Extra heavy	248	370	947	30.4	18.7	20.7	0.48	7.27	−0.50	846
Early steer grazing										
Light	322	382	856	27.3	13.9	29.6	0.37	6.55	+0.60	913
Moderate	282	391	874	27.4	14.9	28.6	0.39	6.67	+0.37	898
Heavy	266	376	892	28.1	15.3	27.0	0.42	6.89	+0.20	889
Extra heavy	193	344	817	26.3	23.1	16.5	0.52	6.68	−0.40	778
Late steer grazing										
Light	296	402	827	26.5	14.7	28.6	0.35	6.30	+0.64	917
Moderate	247	400	831	26.6	16.1	26.4	0.33	6.26	+0.53	929
Heavy	208	382	825	26.9	17.3	24.6	0.36	6.34	+0.28	934

A probable explanation for the reduction of primary production under extra heavy grazing is that the removal of shoot biomass by cattle causes a reduction in net photosynthesis which is not compensated for by the increase in photosynthesis rate resulting from a decrease in standing-dead light interception. When one compares the cow-calf and steer-grazing runs, it is important to note that grazing intensities and assorted forage consumption rates for the growing season (April to October) are greater for seasonal steer grazing with annual forage removal under comparable grazing levels similar for both treatments. Results also showed that the decline in weight gain per head with increased steer grazing was more rapid than field data indicate (Harlan 1960). A general comparison of the cow-calf and early steer-grazing runs shows cow-calf grazing is more beneficial because above- and belowground production, warm-season perennial production, and average N content of the forage are lower with steer grazing, while production of the undesirable cool-season annual grass increased with steer grazing. There are no adequate field results available to compare with the simulation results. Data from the Osage site indicate that animal gains are realized under both systems, but year-round grazing requires supplements during the winter. Herbel and Anderson (1959) found that, at a moderate stocking rate, greater beef production resulted from seasonal grazing compared to a deferred rotation system. However, herbage production was greater under the deferred rotation scheme which suggests that greater utilization may have been possible. McIlvain and Shoop (1969) concluded that five different grazing systems were not superior to continuous year-long grazing at the same stocking rates and gave a number of possible explanations for their conclusions.

Comparison of the early and late steer-grazing simulations shows that delaying the initiation of grazing by 15 days in the spring produces reductions in above- and belowground production, in cattle weight gain per head, in N content of the forage, and in production of desirable warm season perennial grasses. The undesirable cool-season annual grass increased by 33%. Results show that changing from year-round cow-calf grazing to seasonal steer grazing and delaying the initiation of steer grazing in the spring cause a reduction in total aboveground and warm-season perennial grass production and increases the cool-season annual grass production.

Range management at the Osage site indicates that increasing the production of cool-season annual grass and decreasing the production of warm-season perennial grasses degrades range conditions because of the short season of the forage production afforded by the cool-season annuals. It is also interesting to note that the simulated decrease in warm-season perennial grasses is associated with an increase in cool-season annual grasses and that there is a decrease in net primary production of the grassland. This, of course, is the usual sequence under field conditions (Herbel and Anderson 1959). The model results suggest that an effective way to control cool-season annual grass is to graze early in the spring.

Cool-season grasses are a relatively small component of the total annual production in southern tallgrass prairie. Although these species capitalize opportunistically on the early-season conditions of adequate moisture, they do not flourish in the dense canopy of perennial warm-season grasses. However, when the integrity of the canopy is diminished by grazing, cool-season grasses compete much better and become correspondingly more important. For example, during the early 1970 growing season at the Osage site, there was almost ten times as much live biomass of cool-season grass on the grazed treatment as on the ungrazed treatment. The cool-season grass biomass was mostly Japanese brome *(Bromus japonicus)* and reached peak biomass in the sample of 17 June.

The simulated production of seeds for three years showed an average production of 38, 40, and 27 $g \cdot m^{-2}$ for the ungrazed, moderately steer-grazed, and moderately cow-calf grazed treatments. Measured values are somewhat lower than the simulated ones. In general, seed production on the grazed treatments is attributable to the increase in cool-season species. The warm-season perennial grasses do not normally produce large amounts of seed because the immature fruits are selectively grazed.

The results for the grazing simulations indicates that:

1. Compared to seasonal (April to October) steer grazing, year-round cow-calf grazing is more beneficial to the grassland because it increases above- and belowground production, nutrient uptake by plants, and nitrogen content of the forage while production of the undesirable cool-season annual grass is suppressed.
2. Weight gain per head, nitrogen content of the forage, standing dead, soil water content, and the net N balance all decrease with increasing grazing intensity, while with extra heavy grazing there is a net loss of N from the system.
3. Aboveground production is maximized with light grazing in years with below-normal rainfall, while heavy or extra heavy grazing maximized production in years with above-normal rainfall.
4. Production of cool-season annual grass under the seasonal steer-grazing regime can be reduced by grazing early in the spring.

Species Manipulations

The range-management experience at the Osage site indicates that cool-season annual grass and warm-season forbs are relatively undesirable species. The impact of removing these species on moderate cow-calf grazing and moderate early steer grazing is shown by a series of computer simulations, results of which are summarized in Table 8.3. Removing cool-season annual grass from the cow-calf grazing regime increased belowground production and production of warm-season perennial grass and forbs, while net aboveground production, weight gain per head, N uptake by the shoots, and N content of the consumed forage decreased. Aboveground cool-season annual grass production was replaced by warm-season grass production. The reduction in N content of consumed forage and in weight gain per head indicate that cool-season annual grasses provide high-quality forage early in the growing season, before the growth of warm-season grass is initiated.

The removal of warm season perennial forbs in the cow-calf grazing simulation reduces aboveground production and shoot uptake of N, while belowground production and warm season grass production is increased. Removal of the forbs

Table 8.3. Three-Year Average Values of the Output Variables for the Species-Manipulation Simulation

	Primary production ($g \cdot m^{-2} \cdot yr^{-1}$)		Animal weight gain			Peak live (g biomass $\cdot m^{-2}$)			
Species manipulation	Net aboveground production	Net belowground production	Weight gain per head ($kg \cdot head^{-1}$)	Forage consumption $g \cdot m^{-2} \cdot yr^{-1}$	Average N content of forage consumed (% N)	Warm-season grass	Warm-season forbes	Cool-season annuals	Total aboveground
Moderate cow-calf grazing									
Control	594	229	237	139	1.29	210	33	55	277
Cool-season annuals	583	307	235	142	1.18	257	48	0	310
Warm-season forbes	586	240	237	139	1.29	232	0	55	267
Moderate early steer grazing									
Control	564	145	75	125	1.19	150	29	114	266
Cool-season annuals	555	277	89	126	1.20	218	60	0	281
Warm-season forbes	544	140	79	125	1.21	152	0	118	256

	Standing-crop (g biomass $\cdot m^{-2}$)			Abiotic ($cm\ H_2O \cdot yr^{-1}$)			Nutrients ($g \cdot m^{-2} \cdot yr^{-1}$)			Microbial respiration
Species manipulation	Standing dead	Litter	Total roots	Transpiration	Bare soil water loss	Standing-crop interception	P shoot uptake	N shoot uptake	Net nitrogen balance	Biomass loss ($g \cdot m^{-2} \cdot yr^{-1}$)
Moderate cow-calf grazing										
Control	361	361	979	29.0	12.9	30.2	0.42	7.00	+0.22	883
Cool-season annuals	435	343	1065	27.1	13.2	30.3	0.48	6.51	+0.27	846
Warm-season forbes	354	363	956	28.9	13.3	29.7	0.39	6.88	+0.22	867
Moderate early steer grazing										
Control	282	391	874	27.4	14.9	28.0	0.39	6.67	+0.37	898
Cool-season annuals	413	323	1002	25.9	13.8	30.7	0.50	6.43	+0.37	828
Warm-season forbes	260	387	827	26.5	16.0	29.8	0.38	6.25	+0.36	888

has little effect upon the system; however, it is possible that the impact would be greater with heavy and extra heavy grazing since the production of forbs is increased with these grazing levels.

Removing cool-season annuals from the steer-grazing simulation increased belowground production, cattle weight gain, N content of consumed forage, and warm-season grass and forb production. Eliminating the forbs reduced above- and belowground production while the cattle weight gain and N content of the consumed forage increased.

A summary of results indicates that the removal of cool-season annuals has the positive effect of increasing cattle weight gain and N content of the consumed forage for seasonal steer grazing, while the opposite is true for year-round cow-calf grazing. The elimination of forbs has little impact upon cow-calf grazing; however, seasonal steer grazing responds favorably as a result of increased cattle weight gain. Results for both grazing strategies showed that removal of forbs or cool-season annual grasses increased the growth of the warm-season perennial grass.

Fire Simulations

Fire has been used to control the buildup of standing dead vegetation and litter in the tallgrass prairie and to control production of cool-season annual grasses. Computer runs were set up to simulate the effect of varying fire frequency on seasonally grazed (April 15 to October 31) pastures, from once every year to once every three years. The results indicate that fire once every three years increases net above- and belowground production, cattle weight gain per head, production of warm-season perennials and forbs, and shoot uptake of N and P, but decreases production of cool-season annuals and perhaps the N content of consumed forage (Table 8.4). Thus, fire has the positive effect of increasing primary production and cattle weight gain, and of decreasing production of cool-season annual grasses. It has a negative impact of slightly decreasing N content of consumed forage and producing a net loss of N from the system.

The impact of increasing frequency of fire from once every three years to once a year is to increase above- and belowground net primary production, cattle weight gain, production of warm season grass and to decrease N content of consumed forage. It produces a greater net loss of N from the system. The three year average N shoot uptake was increased; however, the total shoot uptake of N for the third year was lower with increased fire frequency. This suggests that the use of fire on a yearly basis will have a long-term negative impact on the grassland by decreasing the nutrient condition of the forage, which could possibly result in a decrease in net primary production after many years of annual burning. Decreased N content of consumed forage resulted because the aboveground net production increased more rapidly than N uptake by shoots.

The large net loss of nitrogen from the system (0.97 and 3.29 $g\ N \cdot m^{-2} \cdot yr^{-1}$ for frequencies of three years and one year, respectively) was surprising; however, it is important to note that the model results are dependent upon the

Table 8.4. Three-Year Average Values of the Output Variables for the Fire Simulation

Fire runs	Primary production ($g \cdot m^{-2} \cdot yr^{-1}$)		Animal weight gain			Peak live biomass ($g \cdot m^{-2}$)			
	Net above-ground production	Net belowground production	Weight gain per head ($kg \cdot head^{-1}$)	Forage consumption (g biomass $\cdot m^{-2} \cdot y^{-1}$)	Average N content of forage consumed (% N)	Warm season grass	Warm season forbes	Cool season annuals	Total aboveground
Moderate early steer grazing									
Control	564	145	75	125	1.19	150	29	114	266
1 fire every 3 years	621	212	84	124	1.18	187	43	57	265
1 fire every year	681	334	86	125	1.13	229	63	17	298

Fire runs	Standing-crop biomass ($g \cdot m^{-2}$)			Abiotic (cm $H_2O \cdot yr^{-1}$)			Nutrients ($g \cdot m^{-2} \cdot yr^{-1}$)			Microbial respiration
	Standing dead	Litter	Total roots	Transpiration	Soil water loss	Bare standing crop interception	P shoot uptake	N shoot uptake	Net nitrogen balance	Biomass loss ($g \cdot m^{-2} \cdot yr^{-1}$)
Moderate early steer grazing										
Control	282	391	874	27.4	14.9	28.0	0.39	6.67	+0.37	898
1 fire every 3 years	343	247	964	29.8	15.5	27.0	0.46	7.18	−0.97	748
1 fire every year	354	141	1059	31.4	20.2	20.6	0.49	7.51	−3.29	594

assumption that 68% of the aboveground N is lost in each fire. Nitrogen losses from a fire are poorly documented and could range from 25 to over 80%. Assuming that the net increase in N is 0.37 g N · m^{-2} · yr^{-1} without fire (see Table 8.4 and Chapter 7) and N loss per fire is 3.0 g N · m^{-2}, then the fire frequency that would result in neutral N balance in the system is one every nine years. A summary of literature data indicates that burning once every three or four years is the recommended frequency. Model results would be consistent with this burning frequency if nitrogen loss per fire was reduced to 34%.

The simulated increase in primary production with spring fire is consistent with results of numerous investigators who have observed increased primary production after burning in Illinois (Hadley and Kieckhefer 1963, Old 1969) and in Iowa (Ehrenreich and Aikman 1963). However, Anderson et al (1970) reported a small decrease in forage yield in Kansas after burning, while Gay and Dwyer (1965) showed no change after a single burning in Oklahoma. In central Kansas, McMurphy and Anderson (1965) recorded reduced production in 16 of 26 years, the reductions coinciding with years of low precipitation. These results suggest that fire once every three or four years will increase production for the following three years or so, if adequate moisture is available. The simulated reduction in production of cool-season annual grasses with spring burning is consistent with literature results, while the steady decrease of N in plant content with annual burning and the hypothesized long-term decrease in primary production are consistent with results of eight years of annual burning in Oklahoma, which reduced forage production by 53% (Elwell et al 1941).

A summary of simulated model results from the fire studies indicates that the use of fire in spring for seasonally grazed (April to October) pastures has the positive effect of increasing aboveground and belowground net primary production while reducing the production of cool-season annual grasses, and has the negative impact of decreasing the N content of consumed forage and of producing a net loss of N from the system. Results also suggest that frequent fire on a tallgrass prairie could lead to a decrease in productivity of the prairie as a result of decreased shoot uptake of N.

Nutrient Simulations

The effect of adding nitrogen and phosphorus to the grassland was simulated for pastures grazed seasonally with steers and for year-round cow-calf grazing. The results show that adding fertilizer to pasture grazed by a cow-calf operation caused the above- and belowground production, the warm-season perennial grass production, shoot uptake of nutrients, and N content of the consumed forage to increase (Table 8.5). Belowground production increased more rapidly than aboveground production (24 and 9%, respectively). Field studies have shown a similar response (McKell et al 1962, Lorenz and Rogler 1966). The simulated increase in primary production is supported by several field trials (Harper 1957, Reardon and Huss 1965; Chapter 3, this volume) at other sites. Gay and Dwyer (1965) had similar results from the Osage site. Prior experience

Table 8.5. Three-Year Average Value for Output Parameters for the Fertilization and Irrigation Simulations

Water and fertilizer	Primary production ($g \cdot m^{-2} \cdot yr^{-1}$)		Animal weight gain			Peak live biomass ($g \cdot m^{-2}$)			
	Net aboveground production	Net belowground production	Weight gain per head ($kg \cdot head^{-1}$)	Forage consumption (g biomass $\cdot m^{-2} \cdot yr^{-1}$)	Average N content of forage consumed (% N)	Warm season grass	Warm season forbes	Cool season annuals	Total aboveground
Moderate cow-calf grazing									
Control	594	229	237	139	1.29	210	33	35	277
Fertilizer	649	283	237	133	2.14	222	34	47	278
Water	954	446	237	138	1.24	265	51	54	332
Water and fertilizer	1077	595	237	134	1.85	330	65	51	401
Moderate seasonal steer grazing									
Control	564	145	75	125	1.19	150	29	114	266
Fertilizer	658	192	92	115	1.78	143	30	158	263
Water	634	357	89	123	1.11	212	50	159	295
Water and fertilizer	1164	458	97	116	1.76	58	58	162	345

Water and fertilizer	Standing-crop biomass ($g \cdot m^{-2}$)			Abiotic ($cm\ H_2O \cdot yr^{-1}$)			Nutrients ($g \cdot m^{-2} \cdot yr^{-1}$)			Microbial respiration
	Standing dead	Litter	Total roots	Transpiration	Soil water loss	Bare standing crop interception	P shoot uptake	N shoot uptake	Net nitrogen balance	Biomass loss ($g \cdot m^{-2} \cdot yr^{-1}$)
Moderate cow-calf grazing										
Control	361	361	979	29.0	12.9	30.2	0.41	7.0	+0.22	883
Fertilizer	399	381	1018	29.4	11.5	31.8	1.19	12.4	+6.50	908
Water	640	253	1276	39.4	7.5	48.1	0.55	10.03	+0.64	1208
Water and fertilizer	761	387	1465	39.1	6.5	49.5	1.76	16.37	+7.06	1309
Moderate seasonal steer grazing										
Control	285	391	856	27.4	14.9	28.0	0.37	6.67	+0.39	898
Fertilizer	309	416	890	29.5	13.0	29.9	0.99	11.69	+6.83	952
Water	552	341	1222	43.9	6.5	49.2	0.42	10.95	+0.70	1305
Water and fertilizer	644	381	1381	43.6	5.2	51.3	1.77	18.43	+7.37	1377

would indicate that adding fertilizer would increase cattle weight gains. These results were not simulated because the present model structure does not allow variations in nutrient quality and forage availability to greatly influence weight gain for calves. The model correctly predicted that the nutrient uptake by consumers and nutrient content of plants were increased by adding fertilizer, which is consistent with field results reported by Owensby et al (1970) and field and laboratory experiments by Zedler and Zedler (1969).

The effect of adding fertilizers to a pasture that is seasonally grazed at moderate levels by steers was to decrease the production of warm-season perennial grasses while nutrient uptake by consumers and plants, cattle weight gain, and production of cool-season annual grasses were increased. The model correctly predicted increased weight gain with added fertilizer under steer grazing, and also indicated that adding fertilizer has the adverse effect of increasing cool-season annual-grass production and slightly decreases warm-season perennial grasses. This is a common response demonstrated by Huffine and Elder (1960) in Oklahoma and by Owensby et al. (1970) in Kansas.

The simulated results suggest that adding fertilizer to pasture grazed throughout the year with a cow-calf operation generally has a positive impact on the system. Adding fertilizer to seasonally grazed pasture has the positive effect of increasing cattle weight gain; however, the desirable warm-season perennial grass is decreased while the undesirable cool-season annuals are greatly increased.

ELM Irrigation Simulations

The impact of irrigating the tallgrass prairie is simulated by adding water to a moderately grazed pasture that was grazed year-round with a cow-calf operation or seasonally with yearling steers (Table 8.5). Water was added from May through September. If the soil water tension in the 10 to 15 cm soil layers was less than −5 bars, irrigation added 1.25 cm of water. The total amount of water added to the grassland averaged 27.5 cm per year for the three-year simulation. Model results for both grazing regimes showed that adding water caused increases in above- and belowground production, the production of warm-season perennial grasses and forbs, microbial activity, the standing dead and root biomass, and the shoot uptake of nutrients, while the N content of the consumed forage decreased. The largest increase in aboveground production as a result of irrigation occurred during the drier year (148% year-round; 156% seasonal) while aboveground production was increased by 30% and 56%, respectively, for year-round and seasonal grazing during the wet year (13% above-normal growing-season rainfall). These responses are supported by the increased herbage production observed under field conditions (Owensby et al 1970). These authors also found that, with above-normal precipitation, moisture augmentation did not enhance primary production.

Comparison of the simulated impact of irrigation on seasonal and year-round grazing showed that irrigation slightly reduced cool-season annual production for year-round grazing while cool-season annual production was increased with seasonal grazing. Irrigation produces an increase in cattle weight gain with seasonal steer grazing; however, irrigation has little impact upon weight gain for year-round cow-calf grazing.

The simulated results suggest that irrigation generally has a positive effect upon the grassland, except for the decrease in the N content of the consumed forage. This decrease is caused by the fact that adding water stimulates an increase in aboveground net production which is greater than the increase in the nutrient uptake by the plants.

More information about the impact of water on the grassland can be gained by comparing yearly values of the output variables with annual rainfall. Results show that most variables are only slightly correlated with yearly rainfall. This suggests that the effect of yearly rainfall is confounded with the impact of the management scheme simulated and with variations of other climatic variables. Results for both grazing schemes showed that an increase in yearly rainfall caused an increase in shoot uptake of N and P, in total N and P in the standing dead, in transpired water loss, and in standing-crop H_2O interception for most of the computer runs. Output from the simulations with year-round grazing showed that above- and belowground production, live root biomass and total root biomass all increased with increased rainfall.

A comparison of the simulated impact of irrigation and fertilization at the Osage site shows that the increase in primary production with irrigation is much greater (61 to 83%) compared to the effect of fertilizer (9 to 17%). This suggests that water is the primary limiting factor for primary production at the Osage site. Cattle weight gains are increased more with added fertilizer than with irrigation. This is probably a result of the fact that adding fertilizer increases the nutrient content of the forage while adding water slightly reduces the nutrient content. Irrigation primarily increases production of warm-season perennials, while fertilizer can actually reduce the production of warm-season grass with seasonal steer grazing. These results indicate that adding fertilizer is the best strategy for increasing cattle weight gain, while adding water will produce the greatest increase in primary production.

The greatest increases in primary production and cattle weight gain are achieved by adding both fertilizer and water. Interestingly, the combined effect upon primary production of adding both fertilizer and water is closely approximated by summing the independent effects of adding fertlizer and water separately. The combined effect of both treatments is not additive for cool-season annual grass production since the independent effect of both treatments is very similar to the combined effect of both treatments. Warm-season perennial-grass production is greatly enhanced by the combined effect of both treatments.

Summary

Utilizing the ELM grassland model with parameters for the tallgrass prairie, this study simulated the effects of different management practices on (1) total primary production above and below ground, (2) animal weight gain, forage quality, and quantity consumed, (3) on warm- and cool-season grasses and forbs, (4) water and nutrient losses, and (5) decomposition under two grazing conditions. The management practices included grazing manipulation, plant-species manipulation, burning, fertilizing, and irrigating.

Results show that the Osage site version of the ELM grassland model can successfully simulate the impact of management practices upon tallgrass prairie. The simulated model results were compared with published data from the true prairie region and, in general, the model results are verified by field data. The major deficiency is that the model fails to correctly predict the impact of different management practices upon the weight gain of calves.

A summary of results for the grazing simulations shows that year-round cow-calf grazing is superior to seasonal steer grazing and that the production of undesirable cool-season annual grass under seasonal steer grazing can be reduced by grazing earlier in the spring. The species-manipulation simulations show that removing cool-season annuals has the positive effect of increasing primary production and cattle weight gain with seasonal steer grazing, while cattle weight gains are reduced for year-round cow-calf grazing. Spring burning once every three years reduces the production of cool-season annuals and increases cattle weight gain and total primary production. Adding fertilizer increases primary production and cattle weight gain for seasonal and year-round grazing, but has the negative impact of increasing cool-season annual production with seasonal steer grazing. Irrigation during dry periods in the growing season has the positive effect increasing cattle weight gain and primary production; however, irrigation has the negative impact of decreasing the nutrient content of forage.

References

Anderson, K. L., E. F. Smith, and C. E. Owensby. 1970. Burning bluestem range. *J. Range Manag.* **23**:81–91.

Beebe, J. D. and G. R. Hoffman. 1968. Effects of grazing on vegetation and soils in southeastern South Dakota. *Am. Midl. Nat.* **80**:96–110.

Birney, E. C. 1974. Dynamics of small mammal populations at Cottonwood and Osage Sites, 1972, *US/IBP Grassland Biome Tech. Rep. No. 257.* Fort Collins: Colorado State Univ.

Biswell, H. H. and J. E. Weaver. 1933. Effect of frequent clipping on the development of roots and tops of grasses in prairie sod. *Ecology* **14**:368–390.

Blocker, H. D. and R. Reed. 1971. Insect studies at the Osage Comprehensive site, *US/IBP Grassland Biome Tech. Rep. No. 93.* Fort Collins: Colorado State Univ.

Brodie, S. 1945. *Bioenergetics and Growth.* New York: Reinhold Publishing Co.

Cole, C. V., G. S. Innis, and J. W. B. Stewart. 1977. Simulation of phosphorus cycling in semiarid grasslands. *Ecology* **58**:1–15.

Dahlman, R. C., J. S. Olson, and K. Doxtader. 1969. The nitrogen economy of grasslands and dune soils. *In* Proc. Conf. Biology and Ecology of Nitrogen. Washington, D.C.: National Academy of Sciences, pp. 54–82.

Duvall, V. L. 1962. Burning and grazing increase herbage on slender blue-stem range. *J. Range Manag.* **15**:14–16.

Ehrenreich, J. H. and J. M. Aikman. 1963. An ecological study of certain management practices on mature plants in Iowa. *Ecol. Monogr.* **33**:113–130.

Elwell, H. M., H. A. Daniel, and F. A. Enton. 1941. The effect of burning pasture and natural woodland vegetation, *Okla. Agric. Exp. Stn. Bull. B-247:* Stillwater: Oklahoma State Univ.

French, N. R., W. E. Grant, W. Grodzinski, and D. M. Swift. 1976. Small mammal energetics in grassland ecosystems. *Ecol. Monogr.* **46**:201–220.

Gay, C. W., and D. D. Dwyer. 1975. Effect of one years nitrogen fertilization on mature vegetation under clipping and burning. *J. Range Mang.* **18**:273–277.

Hadley, E. B., and B. J. Kieckhefer. 1963. Productivity of two prairie grasses in relation to fire frequency. *Ecology* **44**:389–395.

Harlan, J. R. 1960. Grasslands of Oklahoma (memo report). Stillwater: Agron. Dep., Oklahoma State Univ.

Harper, A. J. 1957. Effect of fertilization and climatic conditions on prairie hay, *Oklahoma Agric. Exp. Stn. Bull. 492.* Stillwater: Oklahoma State Univ.

Herbel, C. H. and K. L. Anderson. 1959. Response of true prairie vegetation on major Flint Hills range site to grazing treatments. *Ecol. Monogr.* **29**:171–186.

Herferd, L. R. 1951. The effect of different intensities and frequency of clipping on forage yield of *Andropogon scoparius* Michx. and *Paspalum plicatulum* Michx (memo report) College Station: Texas A&M Univ.

Huffine, W. W. and W. C. Elder. 1960. Effect of fertilizer on mature grass pasture in Oklahoma. *J. Range Manag.* **13**:34–36.

Hunt, H. W. 1977. A simulation model for decomposition in grasslands. *Ecology* **58**:469–484.

Innis, G. S. 1978. *Grassland Simulation Model.* Ecological Studies, 26. New York: Springer-Verlag.

Jameson, D. A. and D. L. Huss. 1959. The effect of clipping leaves and stems on number of tillers, herbage weights, root weights and food reserves of litter bluestem. *J. Range Manag.* **12**:122–126.

Kelting, R. W. 1954. Effect of moderate grazing on composition and plant production of a mature tallgrass prairie in central Oklahoma. *Ecology* **35**:200–207.

Lorenz, R. J. and G. A. Rogler. 1966. Root growth of northern plains grasses under various fertilizer and management treatments. Proc. Am. Forage and Grassland Council.

May, S. W., and P. G. Risser. 1973. Microbial decomposition and carbon dioxide evolution at Osage Site, 1972, *US/IBP Grassland Biome Tech. Rep. No. 222.* Fort Collins: Colorado State Univ.

McKell, C. M., M. B. Jones, and B. R. Perrier. 1962. Root production and accumulation of root materials on fertilized range. *Agron. J.* **59**:459–461.

McIlvain, E. H., and M. C. Shoop. 1969. Grazing systems in the southern Great Plains. *In* Proc. 22nd Annual Meeting of American Society Range Management, pp. 21–22. Denver: Am. Soc. Range Management

McMurphy, W. E., and K. L. Anderson. 1965. Burning Flint Hills range. *J. Range Manage.* **18**:265–269.

Old, S. M. 1969. Microclimate, fire and plant production in an Illinois prairie. *Ecol. Monogr.* **39**:355–384.

Owensby, C. E., R. M. Hyde, and K. L. Anderson. 1970. Effect of clipping and supplemental nitrogen and water on loamy upland bluestem range. *J. Range Manage.* **23**:341–346.

Parton, W. J. and P. G. Risser. 1976. Osage Site version of the ELM grassland model. *In* Proceedings of the 1976 Summer Computer Simulation Conference, pp. 536–543. La Jolla, Calif. Simulation Councils Inc.

Reardon, P. O. and D. L. Huss. 1965. Effect of fertilization on little bluestem community. *J. Range Manag.* **18**:238–241.

Reuss, J. O. and G. S. Innis. 1977. A grassland nitrogen flow simulation model. *Ecology* **58**:379–388.

Risser, P. G. 1971. Osage Site, 1970 report, primary production, *US/IBP Grassland Biome Tech. Rep. No. 80*. Fort Collins: Colorado State Univ.

Risser, P. G. and R. K. Kennedy. 1972. Herbage dynamics of a tallgrass prairie, Osage, 1971, *US/IBP Grassland Biome Tech. Rep. No. 173*. Fort Collins: Colorado State Univ.

Risser, P. G. and R. K. Kennedy. 1975. Herbage dynamics of an Oklahoma tallgrass prairie, Osage 1972, *US/IBP Grassland Biome Tech. Rep. No. 273*. Fort Collins: Colorado State Univ.

Rodell, C. F. 1977. A grasshopper model for a grassland ecosystem. *Ecology* **58**:227–245.

Swift, D. M. and N. R. French. 1972. Basic field data collection procedures for the Grassland Biome 1972 season, *US/IBP Grassland Biome Tech. Rep. No. 145*. Fort Collins: Colorado State Univ.

Weaver, J. E. 1950. Effect of different intensities of grazing in depth and quantity of roots and grasses. *J. Range Manag.* **2**:100–113.

Wicklow, J. R. 1975. Comparative expense to nitrogen deficiency of a tropical and temperate grass in the interrelationship between photosynthesis, growth and accumulation of non-structural carbohydrates. *Neth. J. Agric. Sci.* **23**:104–112.

Zedler, J. B. and G. H. Zedler. 1969. Association of species and their relationships to microtopography with old fields. *Ecology* **50**:432–441.

9. Data-Based, Empirical, Dynamic Matrix Modeling of Rangeland Grazing Systems

KEITH A. REDETZKE and GEORGE M. VAN DYNE

Introduction

The objectives of the present chapter are (1) to describe a matrix-model approach for studying rangeland grazing systems, (2) to compare it to other dynamic modeling approaches, (3) to review the development of matrix models for case examples of shortgrass and mixed-prairie grazing lands, (4) to evaluate the models through verification and validation tests, and (5) to use the models in experimenting with concepts about succession and grazing management. The data referred to in this study are reported by Redetzke and Paur (1975) and a preliminary paper on the methodology has been presented by Redetzke and Van Dyne (1976).

Modeling Systems

The general approach to matrix modeling of a dynamic system requires the definition of a *state vector* and a *transition matrix*. The state vector expresses the main properties of the system at a given time in discrete categories. A transition matrix is composed of probabilities of change from one element to another in the state vector. Change is calculated in discrete time steps such as one week or one year. The matrix system, expressing the dynamics, may be compared to other dynamic modeling methodologies as follows:

Matrix models	$\mathbf{x}_t = \mathbf{T}_i\mathbf{x}_{t-1}$ where $\mathbf{T}_i = f(\mathbf{z}, t)$	(9.1)
Linear, first-order, constant-coefficient differential equation systems	$\dot{\mathbf{x}} = \mathbf{A}\mathbf{x} + \mathbf{B}\mathbf{z}$	(9.2)
General, nonlinear difference equation systems with lags and discontinuities	$\mathbf{x}_t = \mathbf{x}_{t-1} + \Sigma f(\mathbf{x}, \mathbf{z}, t)\Delta t$	(9.3)
Lag regression model	$X_t = b_0\lambda + b_1\lambda Y_t + b_2(1 - \lambda)Y_{t-1} + \epsilon_t$	(9.4)

In the above equations the vector **x,** represents the state vector with elements $x_1, x_2, x_3, \ldots, x_n$. These are the main expressible properties of the system such as cover composition, biomass, or numbers.

In the matrix model system Equation (9.1), the transition matrix **T** can vary and can be selected depending upon external or driving conditions, **z,** thus we can have $\mathbf{T}_i$.

In the general state-variable equation system for linear, first-order, constant-coefficient differential equation systems, Equation (9.2), the differentials $\dot{\mathbf{x}}$, can be calculated as a function of the state vector **x,** the driving variable vector **z,** and matrices of coefficients **A** and **B,** which are time-varying, thus $\mathbf{A}(t)$ and $\mathbf{B}(t)$.

Much of the recent simulation modeling work on large-scale systems, including the ELM model discussed in Chapter 8 and documented in Innis (1978), utilizes a difference equation approach. The general notation for this approach, Equation (9.3) shows that the values of the state variable at a given time are calculated from those of the past step in time plus a series of flows into and out of each compartment for that particular time step, Δt. The expressions for flows may be very general in form and can be nonlinear, with lag effects, and may have discontinuities. They are calculated as a function of the state variables, the driving variables, and time.

Equation (9.4) is the simplest form of a lag regression model. It assumes that the value of variable X at time t can be calculated from the value of variable Y at time t and the value of variable X at the previous time, t-1. This requires regression coefficients b_0, b_1, and b_2 and lag parameter λ. It assumes the error, ϵ_t, is normally and identically independently distributed. The lag regression model system may be expanded to include lags on other parameters, unlagged variables, multiple variables associated with a given lag parameter, and autocorrelated error terms. For all this potential diversity, however, the equation system seems to have been little used in ecological work.

Each of the above equation systems for dynamic models has its advantages and disadvantages. The matrix-model method has long been used in animal population biology and more recently it has been adapted to a variety of biological systems; its early use in animal population biology was by Lewis (1942) and Leslie (1945). Numerous developments since that time have included applications to forest management (Usher 1966) and timber supply projections (Peden 1972). Other applications of the technique include that of Olson and Christofolini (1965) and Waggoner (1969), both of whom looked at forest succession.

The first application of the matrix model technique to grazinglands seems to have been by Singh and Swartzman (1974) who described succession in a tropical grassland. They based their transition matrices on percent cover changes calculated from charted quadrants for different grazing periods over a three-year time span. The matrix methodology generally requires analyzing existing data collected from the field to determine the transitions of categories over periods of time. Thus, the system may be highly data-based. The transition matrix shows the probability that each category of the state vector will change to another category in one unit of time. The transition matrix then includes, in a complex way, a great deal of information on what has happened in the system over time. The transition matrix elements may be entirely empirically derived and do not necessarily have mechanistic meaning.

Since the probabilities in a transition matrix are generally calculated from observation of past events, there are stringent data requirements for development of such models. To provide an adequate data base from which to calculate transition probabilities, a sufficiently large number of samples should enter into the description of the system in any given year and a sufficient number of years should be available. In many instances, it may be necessary to subdivide the system according to geographic, edaphic, or topographic units in any given year, thus requiring more plots or points from which to estimate transition probabilities.

The matrix-model system has an advantage that, by assuming a single transition matrix and utilizing the eigenvalues and eigenvectors of the transition matrices, one can predict the long-term or steady-state conditions for the system. If there are several transition matrices selected from any given point in time, according to the conditions of external or driving variables, then a different approach must be used. Here, if the probability of utilizing a given transition matrix can be calculated, then an overall "average" transition matrix can be calculated and its Eigenvalues and Eigenvectors utilized to predict the long-term conditions.

Model Development

We discuss here the development of a matrix model for two grazing-land case examples: (1) a mixed-prairie grazing land at Akron, Colorado, on the Eastern Colorado Range Station (ECRS) of the Colorado Agricultural Experiment Station, and (2) a shortgrass prairie grazing land 20 km north of Nunn, Colorado, on the Central Plains Experimental Range (CPER) of the USDA Agricultural Research Service. The Pawnee site of the US/IBP Grassland Biome study was located in part on the CPER. Descriptions of the ECRS grazingland and its dynamics are reported by Hervey and Dahl (1959), Dahl (1963), and Sims et al (1976). Numerous references are available from USDA and US/IBP Grassland Biome study investigations on the CPER, but the key references are those of Costello (1944), Klipple and Costello (1960), and Hyder et al. (1966, 1975).

Mixed-Prairie Case Study

Data from the Eastern Colorado Range Station are used as a mixed-prairie example, although the vegetation is dominated by both shortgrass and midgrass species, such as blue grama *(Bouteloua gracilis)* and western wheatgrass *(Agropyron smithii)*. On the deep sandy dunes there are more tall grasses, such as sandhill bluestem *(Andropogon halii)* mixed with midgrasses and shortgrasses. The area is located about 30 km north of Akron, Colorado, at an elevation of 1310 m above sea level. Soils vary from loamy sand to sandy loam on level to slightly rolling dune topography of sandhill formations. Annual precipitation is about 41 cm with predominant precipitation during the summer growing season.

A grazing-intensity experiment was initiated at Akron in 1954 in two replicates of three intensities—light grazing at 0.81 ha per steer per month, moderate grazing at 0.41 ha, and heavy grazing at 0.28 ha. Pasture sizes range from 18 to 21 ha. Utilization, meaning total disappearence, of available herbage aboveground averaged 30, 50, and 70% for light, moderate, and heavy grazing. Yearling hereford steers were grazed generally from 1 May through 1 October. Animals were weighed at the beginning of each season and at one-month intervals from 1955 through 1966.

Vegetation measurements included basal cover taken by the Parker loop method using 6.1-m transects; 15 to 25 of these transects were located in each pasture. Cover data were taken generally at the end of the growing season in most years from 1956 through 1966. All species except annuals were included in the cover measurements. Biomass was measured and estimated, using a double-sampling technique, on 0.45-m^2 plots inside and outside cages according to major grass species and other plant-group categories.

Climatic data collected included precipitation, maximum and minimum temperatures, and average wind velocity at the station headquarters. Soils include a deep loamy sand with high substrata permeability, a deep sandy loam with moderate substrata permeability, and a deep dune sand. It was possible to determine from the records the location of each transect and plot on a given soil type in each intensity of grazing.

Shortgrass Prairie Case Study

The Central Plains Experimental Range is about 1650 m above sea level, topography is rolling, and soils are primarily clay loams to sandy loams. Some 70% of the annual precipitation of 30 cm comes during the growing season. This produces a vegetation dominated by the shortgrasses blue grama and buffalograss *(Buchloe dactyloides)* and midgrasses such as western wheatgrass and needle-and-thread *(Stipa comata)*. Other important species include fringed sagewort *(Artemisia frigida)*, broom snakeweed *(Gutierrezia sarothrae)*, winterfat *(Eurotia lanata)*, and prickly-pear cactus *(Opuntia polyacantha)*.

Grazing-intensity studies have been conducted since 1939 on three 130-ha pastures for the six months from May through October. Stocking rates were 2.1, 3.3, and 5.9 ha per yearling heifer per six months for heavy, moderate, and light grazing, respectively. Average utilization of aboveground, current-season herbage was 54, 37, and 21% for the heavy, moderate, and light grazing treatments.

Animals on each pasture were weighed at one-month intervals. The above schema was used in 1940 through 1953, no grazing was done in 1954 and 1955 because of drought, and in 1956 animals were rotated among pastures although the grazing intensities were maintained.

The percentage of ground-surface cover for all species of plants was determined by the square-foot density method. Visual estimation was used in plots 1.52 m square. Some 40 permanent plots were located in each pasture. Additionally, biomass was measured by double-sampling on 40 plots with the herbage divided into two categories.

Monthly weather records were available from the station headquarters for average temperature and total precipitation. Total kilometers of wind and centimeters of pan evaporation per month were available from the U.S. Weather Bureau Station at Cheyenne, Wyoming, less than 20 km north. Detailed soils maps of the area were used to identify soils for the permanent study plots. These were aggregated into Vona and Ascalon soils, Shingle and Renohill soils, and undifferentiated soils.

Model Structure

Classification of Transition Matrices. Precipitation and temperature data were used to characterize the years, first on the basis of total weather, and second on the basis of seasonal distribution. Weather records from May of the previous year through September of the particular year were used. A lag effect of weather from the previous growing season has been observed in cover changes for arid and semiarid grasslands (e.g., Reed and Peterson 1961, Paulsen and Ares 1962). For this 17-month period, potential evaporation was calculated according to the method of Thornthwaite (1948). The monthly moisture deficits for the 17-month interval were summed and mean and standard deviation values were calculated from long-term data. The year was classified as "dry" if annual moisture was less than the mean minus the standard deviation, "normal" if within the range of the mean plus or minus the standard deviation, and "wet" if greater than the mean plus the standard deviation. Thus, separate transition matrices were derived for transitions between different climatic situations.

Cover Classification Procedure. Within any given year, a state vector was developed which classified a given plot or transect into five categories of vegetation ground cover: 0 to 5%, 5 to 10%, 10 to 20%, 20 to 50%, and 51 to 100%. For each plot or transect, it was determined whether the cover category changed between successive years, and if so to what other category. Thus, we represent the vegetation of the range site in a particular pasture for a particular year by a 5-element state vector ($\mathbf{v}_{k,1}$) of cover categories, composed of the proportions of total plots falling into each of these categories on the basis of total plant cover for soil type k and grazing intensity l. A 5-by-5 transition matrix ($\mathbf{P}_{k,l,m}$) was calculated from the field data for each combination of soil type, grazing intensity, and weather m.

Species composition of the cover denoted in $\mathbf{v}_{k,l}$ is given by the matrix $\mathbf{S}_{k,l}$ (see Table 9.1). From the analysis of the changes in species composition under each cover-class category which occurred from year to year for each soil type, climatic condition, and grazing intensity, average percent changes of $\mathbf{C}_{k,l,m}$ were derived. The change in species composition, $c_{i,j,k,l,m}$ is added to the existing species composition $s_{i,j,k,l}$ to give an estimate of the cover composition for the next year. The cover composition for that year is normalized to produce the new estimate of species-cover composition $s_{i,j,k,l}$ $(t + 1)$. This is done because the

Table 9.1. Definition of Elements Used in the Matrix Model.

$$\mathbf{v}_{k,l} = \begin{Bmatrix} v_{1k,l} \\ v_{2k,l} \\ v_{3k,l} \\ v_{4k,l} \\ v_{5k,l} \end{Bmatrix} =$$

proportion of plots with total ground cover of vegetation falling into each of five cover categories on the k-th soil type in the l-th grazing intensity; such that $\Sigma v_i = 1$ for all k and l.

$$\mathbf{P}_{k,l,m} = \begin{Bmatrix} p_{11k,l,m}\, p_{12k,l,m} \cdot \cdot \cdot\, p_{15k,l,m} \\ \cdot \\ \cdot \\ \cdot \\ p_{51k,l,m} p_{52,k,l,m} \cdot \cdot \cdot\, p_{55k,l,m} \end{Bmatrix} =$$

proportion of plots changing in one year under weather category m from one cover class to another, or remaining in the same cover class; such that $\sum_j p_{ij} = 1$ for all k, l, and m.

$$\mathbf{S}_{k,l} = \begin{Bmatrix} s_{11k,l}\, s_{12k,l} \cdot \cdot \cdot\, s_{1nk,l} \\ \cdot \\ \cdot \\ \cdot \\ s_{51k,l}\, s_{5,2k,l} \cdot \cdot \cdot\, s_{5,nk,1} \end{Bmatrix} =$$

species $s_{i,j,k,l}$ percentage contribution to the total cover $(v_{i,k,l})$ for species j = 1, . . . , n for cover category i on the k-th soil type in the l-th grazing treatment; such that $\sum_j s_{i,j,k,l} = 1$ for all i, k, and l.

$$\mathbf{C}_{k,l,m} = \begin{Bmatrix} c_{11k,l,m} c_{12k,l,m} \cdot \cdot \cdot\, c_{n,k,l,m} \\ \cdot \\ \cdot \\ \cdot \\ c_{51k,l,m= rb\, c_{\mathrm{R\,1\,m}}} \cdot \cdot \cdot\, c_{5n,k,l,m} \end{Bmatrix} =$$

where $c_{i,j,k,l,m}$ average change in one year of cover percentage for species j = 1, . . . , n species in i = 1, . . . 5 cover classes in the k-th soil type in the l-th grazing treatment under the m-th climatic condition.

---

average cover change is added to the existing composition. The resultant sum does not necessarily add to 1 and some elements may be negative. Negative elements are set equal to zero and the remaining elements are normalized.

In summary, the model is identified by the following equation operations:

$$\mathbf{v}\,(\mathrm{t}+1)_{k,l} = \mathbf{P}_{k,l,m}\mathbf{v}\,(\mathrm{t})_{k,l} \tag{9.5}$$

$$\mathbf{U}\,(\mathrm{t}+1)_{k,l} = \mathbf{S}(\mathrm{t})_{k,l} + \mathbf{C}_{k,l,m} \tag{9.6}$$

$$\mathrm{s}\,(\mathrm{t}+1)_{k,l} = [\mu(\mathrm{t}+1)_{k,l}] / \left[\sum_{j=1}^{n} \mu(\mathrm{t}+1)_{i,j,k,l}\right], \text{ if } \mu(\mathrm{t}+1)_{i,j,k,l} \geqslant 0 \tag{9.7}$$

The basic matrix model, Equation (9.5), shows that the total plant-cover vector at time t + 1 can be calculated by multiplying the plant-cover vector at time t by the appropriate transition matrix for the particular climatic, soil, and grazing intensity combination. To get the species composition of that total cover requires the use of Equations (9.6) and (9.7), utilizing information on the average change in species composition, within a total cover class, in one year under one of the various soil, grazing, and climatic conditions.

Given initial conditions of total cover categories and of species composition within cover categories, the change in total cover and the species composition within cover categories can be predicted year by year. Knowing the percentage of the total pasture area covered by each soil type, one then can calculate changes in total cover categories and changes in species composition within cover categories for each grazing-intensity treatment. We can also take the product of the proportion of the plots in a given cover category times the average percent total cover in that category times the species composition within that cover category to get the species cover on each soil type and on each pasture.

Animal Gains Predicted From Climate. Within-year records of days grazed, number of animals, initial and final weights, and economic values were used to relate to climate. Climatic categories of wet, normal, and dry (as defined above) were used. Grazing records were analyzed to determine days grazed, number of animals, initial and final weights, and economic values. Seasonal and daily weight gains were calculated for each weather category and grazing intensity. These average values were then used as model predictions of production.

Use of Separate Data Sets. In developing and testing these models, the same data set is not specifically used both to evaluate or test the model's output and to develop the model's transition matrices. Basically, the information in the model is structured in the matrices $\mathbf{P}_{k,l,m}$ and $\mathbf{C}_{k,l,m}$. In the field experiments there were two sets of three pastures in each study. In each study, the matrices **P** and **C** were derived from data from one set of pastures. A separate set of three pastures was available in each case study, and these separate data were used to test the results of the model. Obviously, the same set of weather data applied to the plant and animal data from both sets of pastures within each case study.

Model Testing

The present study distinguishes between model testing verification and validation in model testing. In verification is tested whether the model will predict the general results over time which existed within the set of pastures from which the data were taken. The initial conditions in such tests were derived from the first year's data that provided data over all years to derive transition matrices. In the verification tests the predictions of total cover fell within 95% simultaneous-confidence intervals calculated from the field data for each of the pastures in all of the years. Individual plant-species cover was within the 95% simultaneous-confidence intervals about 98% of the time. The confidence intervals calculated from field data are, however, fairly large.

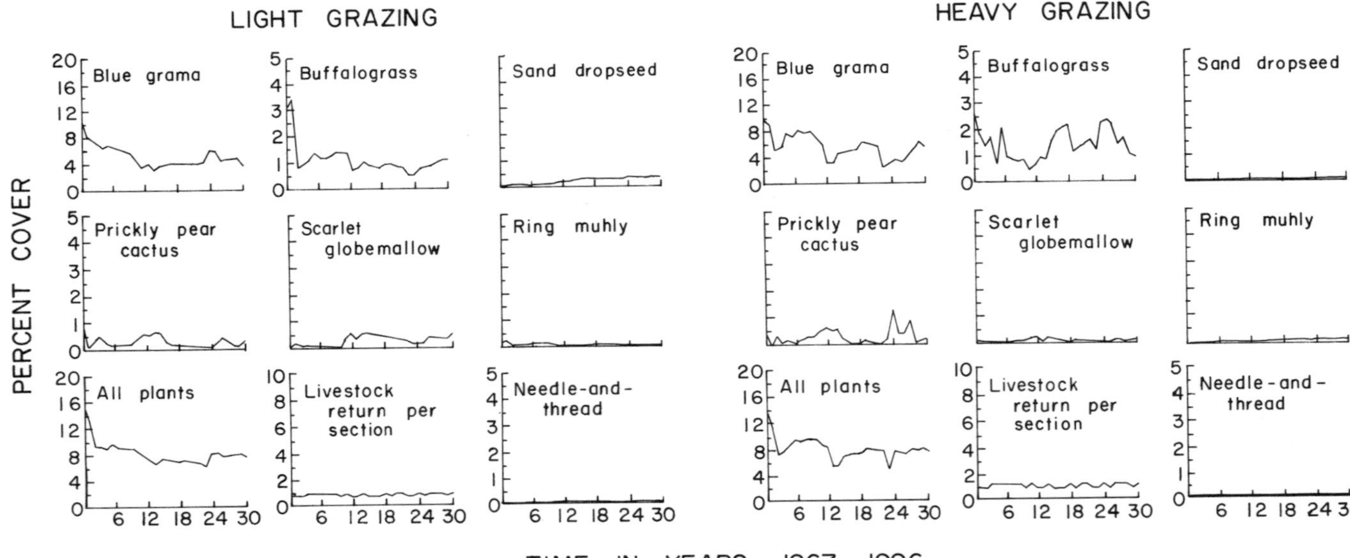

Figure 9.1. Results of a long-term (30-year) simulation under light and heavy grazing intensity for which the sequence of dry (D), normal (N), and wet (W) weather years was as follows: D,N,N,N,N,W,N,N,N,N,N,N,N,N,N,N,N,N,N,N,N,N,N,D, N,N,N,N,N,N.

In the validation tests, the initial conditions derived from the first year's data from the second, separate set of pastures were used. The model was driven or forced with the climatic conditions and generated values to compare with the independent field-measured values. This type of validation test serves to measure the model's accuracy in applications which are similar to the specific set of data from which the model's transition matrices were derived. Predictions of total cover of species cover fell within the 95% simultaneous-confidence intervals calculated from the field data for each set of grazing-intensity pastures as shown in Figure 9.1 (Redetzke and Van Dyne 1976). Predictions of average daily weight gain of animals were within the 95% simultaneous-confidence intervals for the field data 96% of the time for the independent validation test.

Model Experimentation and Analyses

The verification and validation tests of the basic matrix model provided good results in both case studies so a variety of analyses were undertaken to test management and theoretical hypotheses. These analyses were made with the model for the shortgrass prairie.

Management Question Analyses

An important question is; which grazing intensity will produce the highest net revenue consistent with maintaining a stable resource base of cover of desired forage plants? It is necessary to answer this question under long-term weather conditions. Available weather records were analyzed to determine the relative frequencies of what had been categorized as wet, normal, and dry years. A "probable-return function" was developed as follows:

$$R_i = \frac{A}{260} \sum_{m=1}^{3} p_m r_{i,m} \tag{9.8}$$

where $i = 1, \ldots, 3$ grazing intensities, $A = 130$ ha pasture^{-1}, p_m is the probability of weather condition m, and $r_{i,m}$ is the return for grazing intensity i and weather condition m. The value $r_{i,m}$ is calculated from the model run. The above function gives the expected annual return in dollars from 260 ha (one square mile) of pasture.

We want to find the maximum value subject to maintaining cover of the key forage plants. Based on dietary studies of livestock on these ranges (Rice and Vavra 1971), five key forage species were selected—blue grama grass, buffalograss, needleleaf sedge *(Carex stenophylla),* scarlet globemallow *(Sphaeralcea coccinea),* and needle-and-thread grass.

The expected values of livestock return and plant cover are shown in Table 9.2. The initial cover based on 1964 values is given. It is shown for each of three major soil types and for a pasture average what the expected percent cover of the

Table 9.2. Expected Values of Livestock Return and Plant Cover for Five Major Forage Species on Three Soils for Applications of Light, Moderate, and Heavy Grazing, and Initial Cover

Species	Expected cover (%)			Initial cover (%)[1]
	Light	Moderate	Heavy	
	Shingle-Renohill Soils (49 ha)			
Blue grama	6.8	7.1	5.1	6.0
	0.8	0.8	1.3	1.0
Buffalograss	0.8	0.8	1.3	1.3
Needleleaf sedge	0.1	0.1	0.1	0.0
Scarlet globemallow	0.0	0.2	t	0.2
Needle-and-thread	0.0	0.0	0.0	0.0
Total	7.7	8.2	6.5	7.5
	Vona-Ascalon soils (10 ha)			
Blue grama	6.8	7.1	6.2	6.3
Buffalograss	0.6	1.8	2.0	0.9
Needleleaf sedge	t	t	t	0.0
Scarlet globemallow	0.1	0.1	0.1	0.1
Needle-and-thread	0.1	0.0	0.0	t
Total	7.6	9.0	8.3	7.3
	Undifferentiated soils (69 ha)			
Blue grama	6.6	5.6	0.7	4.1
Buffalograss	0.8	2.6	5.8	4.5
Needleleaf sedge	t	0.0	0.0	0.0
Scarlet globemallow	0.0	0.1	t	0.0
Needle-and-thread	t	t	0.0	0.2
Total	7.4	8.3	6.5	8.8
	Pasture average (129 ha)			
Blue grama	6.7	6.3	2.8	5.0
Buffalograss	0.8	1.9	3.8	2.5
Needleleaf sedge	t	t	t	0.0
Scarlet globemallow	t	.1	t	0.1
Needle-and-thread	t	t	0.0	0.1
Total	7.6	8.3	6.6	7.7
Expected return	\$418	\$680	\$658	

[1] t = trace amount less than 0.1%.

five key species would be over a long period of time under three different grazing intensities. The largest expected economic return is given by moderate grazing. This return is only a few percent higher than that expected under heavy grazing, but it is about 63% higher than that expected under light grazing. However, one must consider both the expected cover composition and the expected animal production, since future returns depend on maintaining the resource base. Total cover of the five key species on a pasture average would be 7.6, 8.3, and 6.6% for light, moderate, and heavy grazing. Relatively, expected cover of the key plants under moderate grazing is about 10% higher than under light grazing but about 30% higher than under heavy grazing. These differences in plant cover occurred under all three soil types.

Graphic analysis of the data in Table 9.2 suggests that the optimal stocking rate would be about 3.16 ha per yearling heifer per six months, resulting in 39%

utilization of the herbage. This is somewhat lower than the stocking rate Bement (1969) suggested for maximum pounds of gain per acre and the projected stocking rate for maximum secondary production derived by Van Dyne et al (1977) from simulation-model experiments with a difference equation system. Bement's estimate is based on analysis of data from a 19-year interval of experimental grazing studies; Van Dyne et al (1977) estimated optimal production from a one-year simulation utilizing a semimechanistic simulation model.

Model Experiments in Grassland Succession

Experiments with the model were conducted to see if the output supported current knowledge of grassland succession. A list of testable hypotheses was generated based on a general knowledge of the pertinent literature. For each hypothesis, a matrix model simulation was designed with initial vegetation conditions, soil, weather, and grazing treatment to suit the hypothesized situation. The simulation results were then compared with the hypothesized outcome to see if the model output and the theory agreed.

Hypothesis 1. Heavy grazing can alter the species composition of mixed-grass sites to favor shortgrasses and inhibit midgrasses.

For this simulation, the model was run for a 30-year period using weather generated as normal random variates from the long-term monthly average temperature and precipitation means. The performance of the model tends to support this hypothesis (Figure 9.2). The heavy-use pasture had higher levels of buffalograss, although the levels of blue grama were fairly similar (note the magnitudes

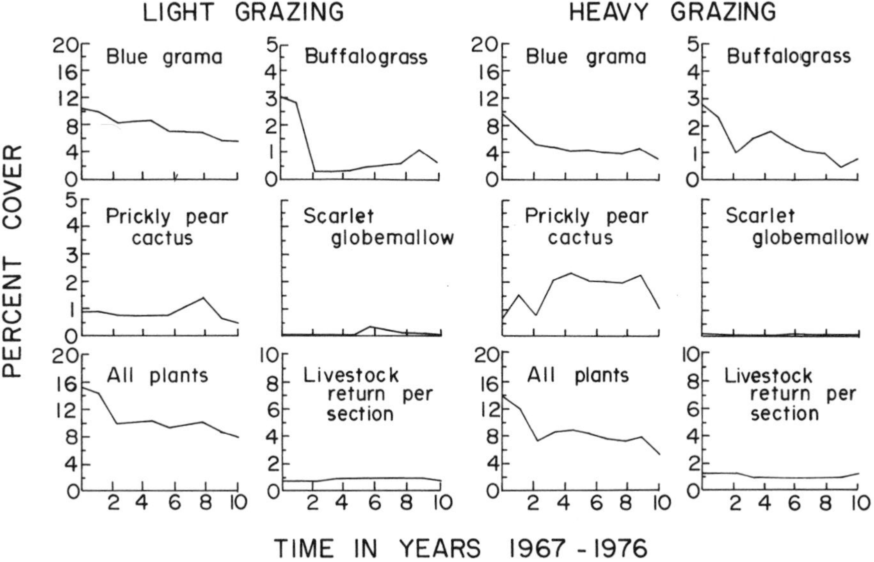

Figure 9.2. Results of a drought simulation of 10 years for which the sequence of dry (D) and normal (N) weather years was as follows: D,D,D,D,D,N,D,D,N,N.

of each vertical scale in Figure 9.2). Also, the lightly grazed pasture maintained higher levels of sand dropseed (*Sporobolus cryptandrus*) and ring muhly (*Muhlenbergia torreyi*). This same trend can be seen in the expected values of needle-and-thread and buffalograss shown in Table 9.2. The expected values of buffalograss cover were greatest and needle-and-thread lowest for the heavy-use pasture.

Hypothesis 2. Most of the damage to range resources occurs because of combined effects of overgrazing and drought.

For the drought simulation, the model was run for 10 years with generated weather, having precipitation reduced by 30% and temperatures increased by 10%. The model output tends to support the hypothesis. The loss of plant cover, primarily blue grama, was greatest for heavy grazing in the 10-year drought simulation (note that there are some differences in the vertical scales between light and heavy grazing in Figure 9.3). Also, the increase in plains prickly pear during drought was greatest for the heavy use pasture.

Hypothesis 3. Heavy grazing alters community structure by eliminating species that are less resistant to grazing and promoting resistant dominants, thereby reducing diversity.

This in effect is an extension or generalization of the first hypothesis tested. Figure 9.2 shows that needle-and-thread was essentially eliminated on the heavy use pasture during the 30-year simulation; the cover predicted for this species went to near zero early in the simulation and remained there for the duration. Other species were reduced in cover by heavy use but not eliminated. Prickly-pear cactus was increased in cover under heavy grazing after about 20 years. The results offer only slight support to the hypothesis, as the loss of a single species represents only a slight reduction in diversity. Perhaps changing the word "eliminating" in this hypothesis statement to "reducing" would result in greater support for the hypothesis.

Hypothesis 4. Drought never removes a dominant species entirely.

This hypothesis also was supported. The drought-simulation results (Figure 9.3) shows that none of the dominant species was eliminated.

Hypothesis 5. Recovery following drought is more rapid for lightly or moderately grazed range than for heavily grazed range.

The model was run with five years of precipitation reduced by 30% and temperatures increased by 10% to simulate drought conditions followed by five years of standard generated weather. This hypothesis was not supported by the model output. Blue grama, the major forage species, continued to decline in the lightly grazed pasture following the initial drought period, while in the heavily grazed pasture nearly half of the initial losses were made up by the end of 10 years (Figure 9.4).

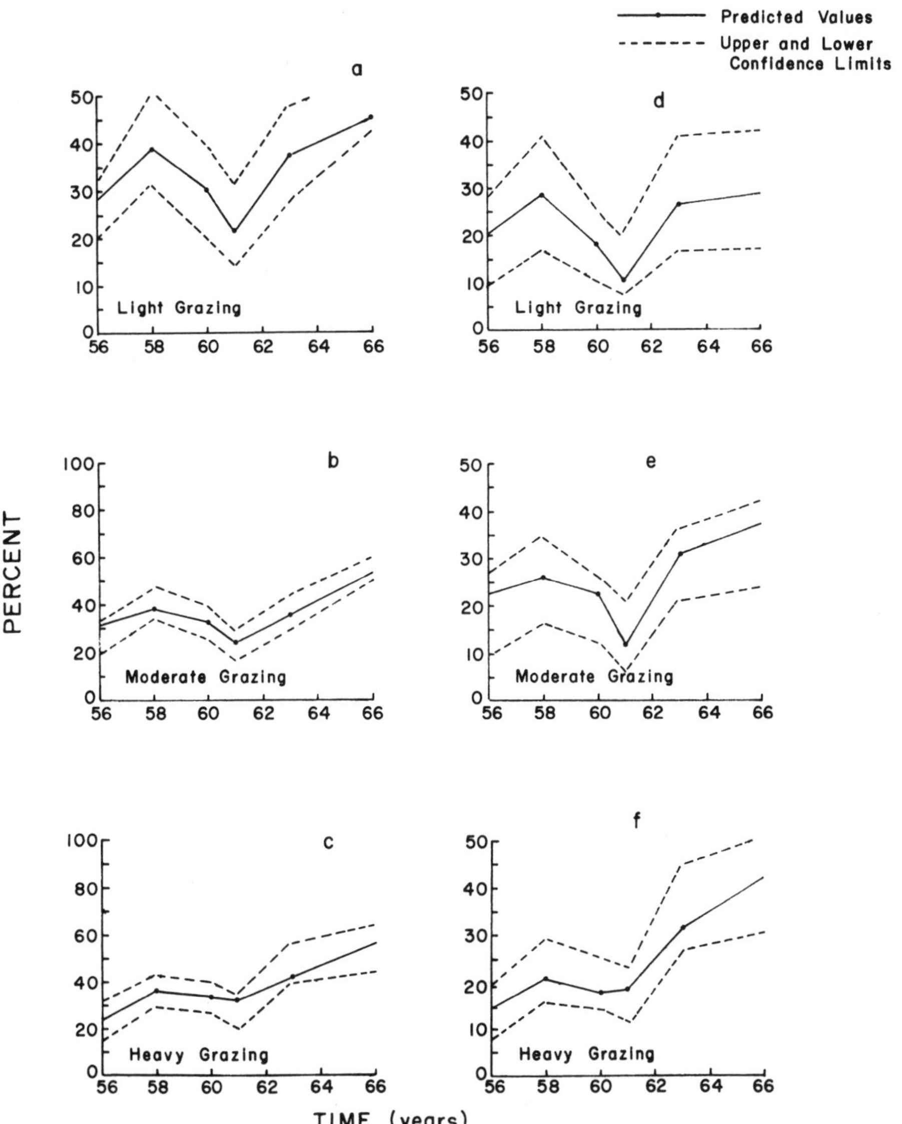

Figure 9.3. Graphs of mean cover predicted by the matrix model and $\alpha = 0.05$ simultaneous confidence limits.
Calculated from the data for total cover and blue grama from the Akron study on years that data were available. Graphs, a, b, and c present cover for all plants; in graphs d, e, and f, blue grama grass cover is presented (Redetzke and Van Dyne 1976).

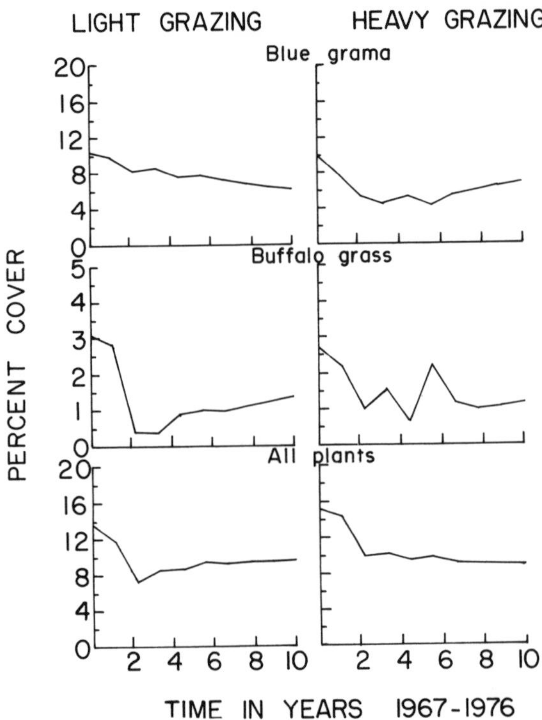

Figure 9.4. Results of a simulated drought recovery situation of 10 years for which the sequence of dry (D), wet (W), and normal (N) years was as follows: D,D,D,D,N, W,N,N,N,N.

Hypotheses Suggested from Model Experiment Results

Two hypotheses were suggested by observations of model output. The first was that the seasonal distribution of precipitation has an important influence on plant cover response. Supporting evidence for this hypothesis can be seen in the variability of response for years of simulation having the same annual weather category. In the drought simulation with the model, for example, plant cover increased in some of the dry years (Figure 9.3). This happened because within each of the major weather categories of the model there were several sets of transition matrices, each of which was derived from a year having a particular distribution of precipitation and temperatures. The selection of transition matrices to use in simulating a particular year was based first on the total weather and second on the distribution. Years with different weather distributions did show different plant-cover responses, even though they had the same annual weather categories.

The second hypothesis suggested was that patterns of change initiated during stress periods may be perpetuated after the stress is removed. Evidence of this is seen in the continued decline in blue grama and total plant cover on the light-grazing simulation of drought recovery with the model shown in Figure 9.4.

Summary

Vegetation cover, animal yield, and climatic data from long-term grazing studies were used to derive transition matrices and change matrices which interrelated vegetation-cover change from year to year with climatic conditions. Livestock production also was predicted from climatic conditions. Data were categorized by soil type, grazing intensity, and wet, normal, or dry climatic influences. Matrix models were developed for shortgrass prairie and mixed prairie grazing situations. The models were validated by making runs starting with conditions based on a separate data set. In both verification and validation tests, the predicted values of total plant cover, species composition, and animal production fell within the 95% simultaneous-confidence intervals about the field data over 95% of the time.

A management-application exercise was done to determine the practical utility of the model. The management objective assumed was to maximize net revenue consistent with maintaining a stable resource base. The probabilities of weather categories occurring were used to solve the predictive equations of the model for the expected mean values of revenue return and ground cover of major forage species. This was done for applications of light, moderate, and heavy grazing on a pasture of known acreages in each of the soil types and known initial plant cover. The largest dollar return and the greatest forage cover for the pasture in the coming year both were predicted for moderate grazing.

Experiments with the model determined if results would support current theories of vegetation change in grasslands. Of the five hypotheses tested, the following were supported: (1) heavy grazing can alter the composition of mixed-grass sites to favor the shortgrasses; (2) most of the damage to range resources occurs as a result of the combined effects of overgrazing and drought; and (3) drought never removes a dominant species entirely. The hypothesis that recovery following drought is more rapid for light or moderately grazed range than for heavily grazed range was not supported by model output. The model suggested greater support for the hypothesis which states that heavy grazing alters community structure by "reducing", rather than "eliminating" species that are less resistant to grazing and promoting resistant dominants. Two hypotheses were suggested by the model output: (1) seasonal distribution of precipitation has an important influence on the patterns of plant-cover response, and (2) patterns of change initiated during stress periods are perpetuated after the stress is removed.

References

Bement, R. E. 1969. A stocking-rate guide for beef production on blue-grama ramge. *J. Range Manag.* **22**:83–86.

Costello, D. F. 1944. Efficient cattle production on Colorado ranges, *Colorado Agric. Exp. Stn. Bull. 383-A*. Fort Collins: Colorado State Univ.

Dahl, B. E. 1963. Soil moisture as a predictive index to forage yield for the sandhill range type. *J. Range Manag.* **16**:128–132.

Hervey, D. F. and B. E. Dahl. 1959. Intensity of grazing study. *In Animal Nutrition and Range Management Research at the Eastern Colorado Range Station,* General Ser. 712, pp. 1–3. Fort Collins: Colorado State Univ. Exp. Stn.

Hyder, D. N., R. E. Bement, D. E. Remmenga, and C. Terwilliger. 1966. Vegetation-soils and vegetation-grazing relations from frequency data. *J. Range Manag.* **19**:11–17.

Hyder, D. N., R. E. Bement, E. E. Remmenga, and D. F. Hervey. 1975. Ecological responses of native plants and guidelines for management of shortgrass range, *USDA Tech. Bull. 1503.* Washington, D.C.: U.S. Government Printing Office.

Innis, G. S. 1978. *Grassland Simulation Model.* Ecological Studies, 26. New York: Springer-Verlag.

Klipple, G. E. and D. F. Costello. 1960. Vegetation and cattle responses to different intensities of grazing on short-grass ranges of the Central Great Plains, *USDA Tech. Bull. 1216.* Washington, D.C.: U.S. Government Printing Office.

Leslie, P. H. 1945. On the use of matrices in certain population mathematics. *Biometrika* **35**:183–212.

Lewis, E. G. 1942. On generation and growth of population. *Sankhya* (Ser. B) **6**:93–96.

Olson, J. S. and S. Christofolini. 1965. Succession of Oak Ridge vegetation, p. 76–77. *In Oak Ridge Nat. Lab. Rep. ORNL-3849.* Oak Ridge, Tenn.

Paulsen, H. A., Jr. and F. N. Ares. 1962. Grazing values and management of black grama and tobosa grasslands and associated shrub ranges of the Southwest, *USDA Tech. Bull. 1270.* Washington, D.C.: U.S. Government Printing Office.

Peden, L. M. 1972. A Markov model for timber-supply projections (M.S. thesis). Fort Collins: Colorado State Univ.

Redetzke, K. A. and L. F. Paur. 1975. Long-term grazing intensity data from the Great Plains, *US/IBP Grassland Biome Tech. Rep. No. 272.* Fort Collins: Colorado State Univ.

Redetzke, K. A. and G. M. Van Dyne. 1976. A matrix model of a rangeland grazing system. *J. Range Manag.* **29**:425–430.

Reed, M. and R. A. Peterson. 1961. Vegetation, soil, and cattle responses to grazing on northern Great Plains range, *USDA Tech. Bull. 1252.* Washington, D.C.: U.S. Government Printing Office.

Rice, R. W. and M. Vavra. 1971. Botanical species of plants eaten and intake of cattle and sheep grazing shortgrass prairie. *US/IBP Grassland Biome Tech. Rep. No. 103.* Fort Collins: Colorado State Univ.

Sims, P. L., B. E. Dahl, and A. H. Derham. 1976. Vegetation and livestock response at three grazing intensities on sandhill rangeland in eastern Colorado, *Colorado Agr. Exp. Stn. Tech. Bull. 130.* Fort Collins: Colorado State Univ.

Singh, J. S. and G. S. Swartzman. 1974. A dynamic programming approach to optimal grazing strategies using a succession model for a tropical grassland. *J. Appl. Ecol.* **11**:537–548.

Thornwaite, C. W. 1948. An approach toward a rational classification of climate. *Geogr. Rev.* **38**:55–94.

Usher, M. B. 1966. A matrix approach to the management of renewable resources, with special reference to selection forests. *J. Appl. Ecol.* **3**:355–367.

Van Dyne, G. M., L. A. Joyce, and B. K. Williams. 1977. Models and the formulation and testing of hypotheses in grazingland ecosystem management, pp. 41–84 in M. Holdgate and M. Woodman (eds). *Ecosystem Restoration—Principles and Case Studies.* London: Plenum Press.

Waggoner, P. E. 1969. Computer, forests, and fungus. *Frontiers in Plant Science,* **21**:6–7.

10. Principal Subsystem Interactions in Grasslands

Norman R. French

Introduction

This chapter reviews the important factors controlling primary and secondary production in grasslands, particularly at the subsystem level of organization. This evidence is drawn largely from the previous chapters and from the experience and data accumulated under the IBP Grassland Biome studies conducted from 1968 through 1976.

Subsystems are basic interacting units of the ecosystem. Thus, the grassland ecosystem has an energy-fixing primary production base composed of populations of autotrophic organisms. These populations function by distinctly different strategies, but collectively constitute the subsystem which provides the energy base that allows the ecosystem to persist. Various categories of consumers operate on this energy base and may be classified into primary consumer, secondary consumer, and detrivore subsystems according to their modes of energy utilization. The abiotic factors that directly or indirectly affect processes within subsystems may be considered a separate subsystem.

The functioning of various subsystem components of the grassland ecosystem are controlled directly by abiotic driving variables or indirectly through the moderation of these variables by other subsystem processes. In order to evaluate the total functioning of the ecosystem and to estimate the effects of modified input parameters on system functions it is essential to focus on these key factors controlling subsystem functions.

Producer-Environment Relationships

Temperature

That temperature is an important controlling factor of system function in grasslands is indicated by the characteristic photosynthetic mechanisms of their different plant species. Different species of grassland plants can be separated according to physiological and biochemical characteristics associated with photosynthesis. These are the cool-season (C_3) plants and the warm-season (C_4) plants. Maximum photosynthetic rate (Black 1971) is achieved at temperatures of

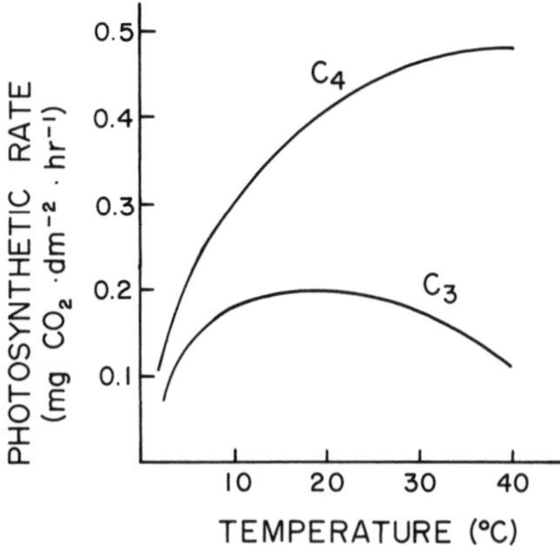

Figure 10.1. Characteristic rates of photosynthesis in relation to temperature for plants with the C_3 and C_4 carbon pathways (Adapted from Black 1971).

10 to 25°C in C_3 plants, but at 30 to 45°C in C_4 plants (Figure 10.1). *Agropyron smithii* (western wheatgrass) is a cool-season plant with a Calvin-cycle (C_3) photosynthetic type, and it grows and develops in the cooler months of spring and early summer. *Bouteloua gracilis* (blue grama) is a warm-season plant characterized by the dicarboxylic acid (C_4) photosynthetic type, which begins active growth in early summer and grows in hotter months whenever moisture is available (Williams 1974). The results presented in Chapter 2 demonstrate a high degree of temporal variability associated with the moisture relationship. As soil dries following summer rainfall, the photosynthetic rate may decrease by 75% in 10 days.

Species composition at different grassland sites indicates the controlling effect of environmental temperatures on plant-species composition. As latitude (degrees north) increases, an increasing proportion of the plant species is of the

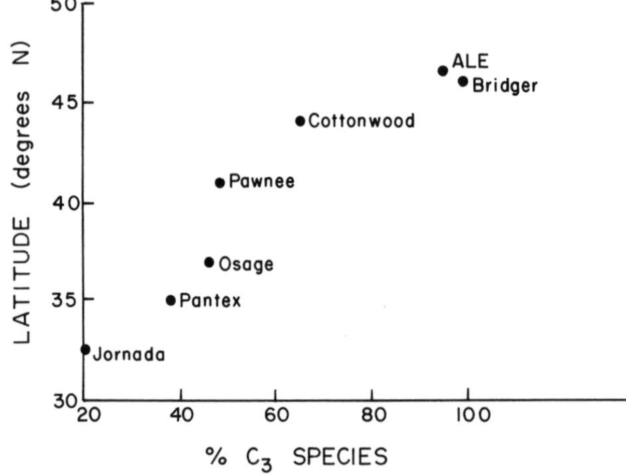

Figure 10.2. C_3-type species as a percentage of total plant species in comparison to latitude of field sites in the Grassland Biome program.

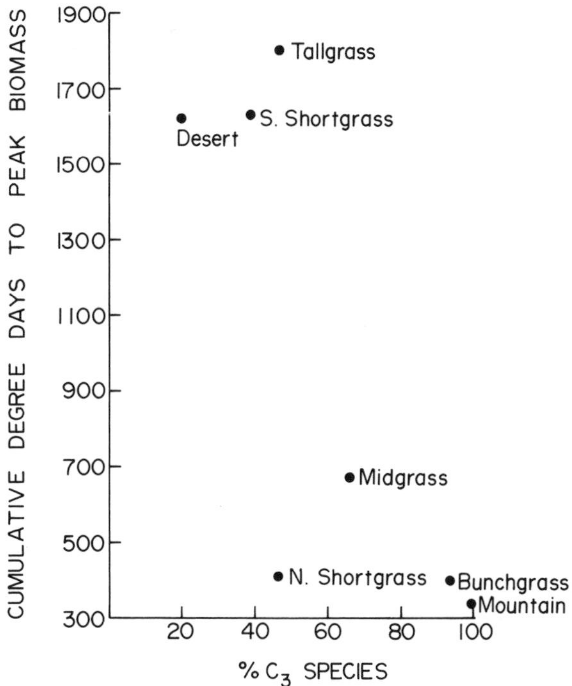

Figure 10.3. C_3-type species as a percentage of total plant species in comparison to temperature (cumulative degree days above 10°C to peak vegetation biomass).

cool-season type (Figure 10.2). That this is predominantly a response to temperature is indicated in Figure 10.3, which shows a decreasing proportion of C_3 plant species as cumulative degree days (total degrees above 10°C) increase in relation to the time of peak aboveground vegetation biomass. Such a comparison shows that the grassland sites fall into two distinct groups; those with short growing seasons and early-season peak biomass, and those with long growing seasons and late attainment of peak biomass. The northern shortgrass prairie site reached peak biomass after only 38% of the growing season was completed, while the southern shortgrass site reached peak biomass after the growing season was 65% complete. These relationships are also correlated with distribution of rainfall.

Water

Ares (1976) demonstrated that the maximum rate of root growth and of leaf expansion in blue grama occurs when soil water potential is high (Figure 10.4) by making detailed observations and measurements behind darkened subterranean windows in natural ungrazed shortgrass prairie. Young nonsuberized roots were shown to be most effective in water absorption, and this condition persisted for an individual root only during about 15 to 25 days of development. The nonsuberized roots occurred in a region of the soil where water potential was high, and most of them died and disappeared as the soil dried.

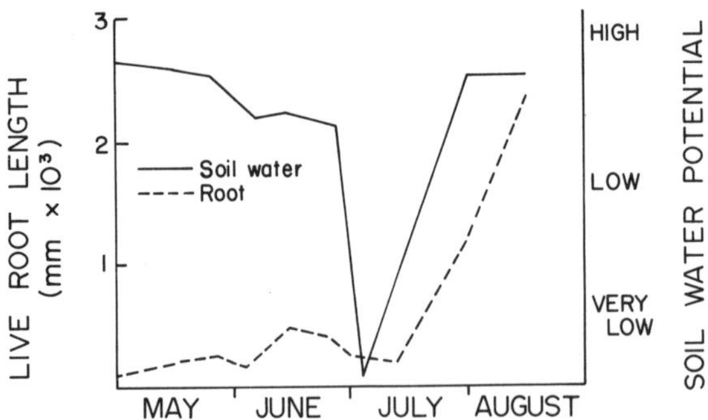

Figure 10.4. Soil water and length of live roots of *Bouteloua gracilis* during the growing season on the northern shortgrass prairie (Adapted from Ares 1976).

A somewhat less direct indication of the relationship between plant growth and soil water is demonstrated by the comparison of aboveground live plant biomass in natural, ungrazed shortgrass prairie and cumulative precipitation during the season. These comparisons are shown for four separate seasons (1972–1975) in Figure 10.5. In general, the first rapid increase in precipitation after 1 June is correlated with an increased rate of vegetative biomass production. Later in the season, precipitation is less effective in promoting increased primary production due to high evaporation rates. These relationships are not straightforward, however, and it is evident that other factors are interacting with precipitation to affect the rate of primary production. A much broader evaluation of the relationship between production and climatic variables is given in Chapter 1.

Regression analysis of vegetation biomass and mean annual precipitation for different U.S. grassland sites (Figure 10.6) indicates a very strong correlation for most sites. The exceptions are the mountain grassland, where the growing season is shortened by high elevation, and the mixed-prairie site where vegetation growth is highly dependent upon seasonal distribution of rainfall.

Long-term fluctuations in water availability influence the relative abundance of different species in different ways. In the northern Great Plains, after a period of above-normal precipitation during 1950–1954, there were important increases in the basal cover of mesic-type species such as *Agropyron dasystachyum* and *Stipa spartea*. There were corresponding decreases in *Stipa comata* and *Bouteloua gracilis* (Coupland 1959). In other regions, drought affected total cover but had little influence on species composition. Cover and density were approximately 100% greater in the post-drought period than during the drought (Whitman et al 1943). The one exception was *Poa secunda,* which increased in density and cover during the drought (Van Dyne 1975).

Nutrients

Results from an experimental plot to which nitrogen was added indicated that nutrients are an important controlling variable in grassland production (see

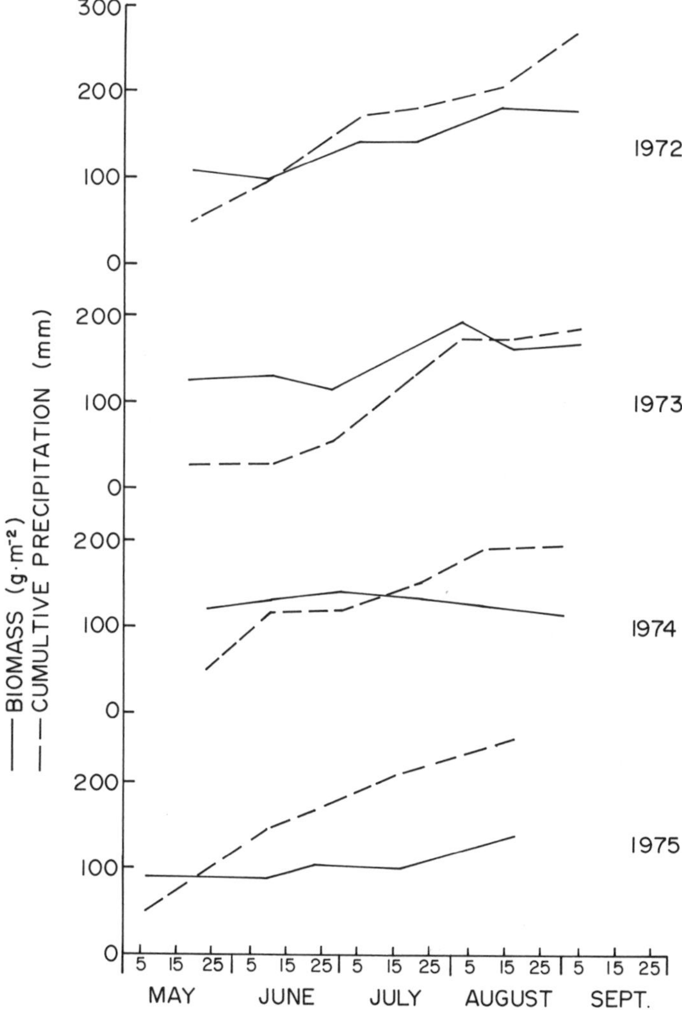

Figure 10.5. Vegetation biomass and cumulative precipitation at the northern shortgrass prairie site.

Chapter 4). The unfertilized control plot showed an irregular increase in plant biomass as cumulative precipitation for the season increased (Figure 10.7). The fertilized plot, however, although initially lower in vegetation biomass than the control plot, showed a considerable gain in biomass with the same cumulative precipitation as the control plot, finally attaining biomass approximately 75% greater than the biomass of the control plot. Woodmansee (Chapter 7) has summarized available information on input and output of nitrogen, demonstrating the critical level of this nutrient in grasslands.

The effect of nutrients is further amplified when water is nonlimiting. Although primary production in the shortgrass prairie is enhanced by nitrogen

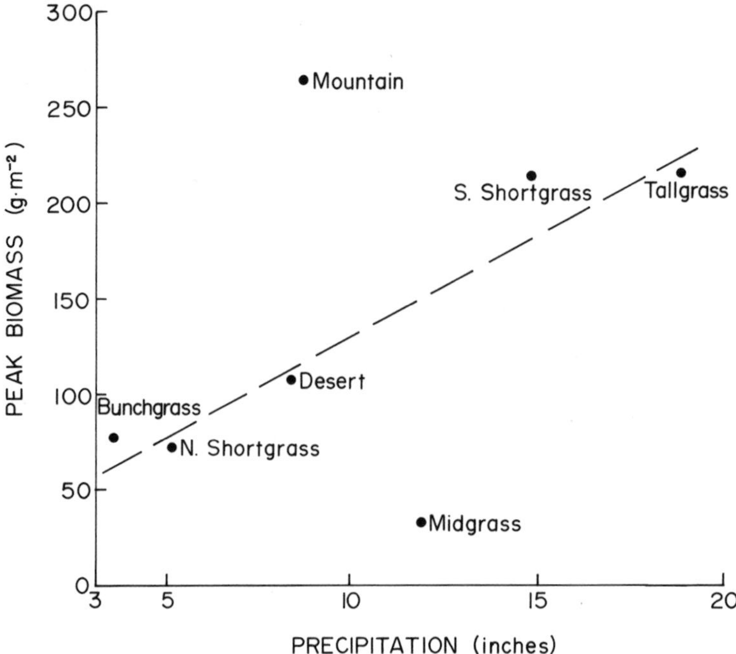

Figure 10.6. Peak vegetation biomass and mean annual precipitation at seven grassland sites (1972).

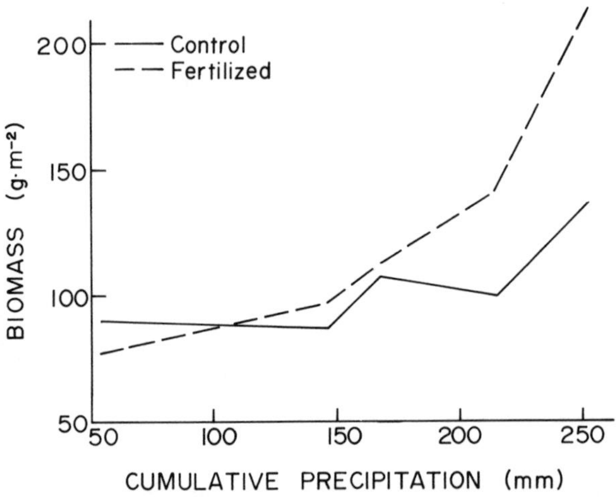

Figure 10.7. Vegetation biomass compared to cumulative precipitation through a single growing season (1975) in two shortgrass prairie plots, one of which had received supplemental nitrogen (maintained at 50 kg · ha^{-1} above normal) as a fertilizer.

application, the increase in plant biomass through the growing season, when water as well as nitrogen is supplemented, is spectacular (see Chapter 4).

Producer Interrelationships

Competition Within the Plant Community

Niche overlap is the joint use of a resource or resources. Joint use of a resource by two species does not necessarily imply competition between them (Colwell and Futyuma 1971). Competition occurs when resource use by one species restricts its use by other species.

Ares (1975) has explored some of the US/IBP Grassland Biome data for indications of competition between plant species by utilizing an equitability index to characterize biomass distribution among species. He interpreted intraseasonal variation in species dominance as an indication of the intensity of competition and overlap between species, competition being relaxed at the height of the growing season and becoming more intense as habitat width (or resource width) shrinks again at the end of the growing season. He presented a matrix model to depict a feasible explanation of the trends of such variation.

Torssell (1975) used a model which emphasized the processes taking place in the system rather than the state variables. This approach focused on the changes between life stages or phenophases in the life cycle of the plants. His results indicate the most variable factor (or "filter") is the establishment of seedlings during germination. This approach emphasizes a filter constant which is similar to alpha in the familiar competition equations. Whereas this approach considers only a two-species system, Ares' matrix model allows expression of competition between any pair of the total number of species present.

To determine competition experimentally, a reduction either in niche breadth, in the fraction of the total spectrum of resources utilized, or in niche overlap in the presence of the competing species must be demonstrated (Colwell and Futyuma 1971). In other words, the actual niche breadth and overlap will differ from the virtual niche breadth and overlap, which may be measured only in the absence of competition.

A comparison of niche breadth and niche overlap of the same species under normal undisturbed conditions, and under varying degrees of resource supplementation or abundance, can be used to evaluate the importance of competitive interactions among plant species in determining community structure of grasslands. Enrichment may have a destabilizing effect on competitive systems (Rosenzweig 1971). Release from physical (abiotic) limiting factors may allow the biotic interactions of a community to be emphasized.

Perturbations which have a direct detrimental effect on the majority of species involved (negative stresses) tend to emphasize only the responses of the least tolerant organisms. Chronic stress would allow slowly responding organisms to demonstrate their capabilities—acute stress only lets the fast responding types respond—and therefore may allow the ecosystem to reach a new equilibrium of community interactions (Kirchner 1977). Creating an oversupply of a scarce resource permits examination of the virtual niche by minimizing competition.

Response to Release from Competition

The response of shortgrass prairie plant species in the direction of expansion toward the virtual niche following partial release from competition, using the weighted relative values of niche breadth and niche overlap (Colwell and Futyuma 1971), was examined to indicate the degree of competition between these species in normal conditions. The niche breadth and overlap values are presented in Table 10.1 and results are diagrammed in Figure 10.8. The normal competition picture (resources limited) is derived from comparing control-treatment biomass values for major plant species across a series of five years (1971–1975) to represent normal variability under the existing climatic regime. Each year is taken to represent a sample of the response of plants, indicated by species biomass distribution at the time of peak plant biomass, to normal variations in driving variables of the system.

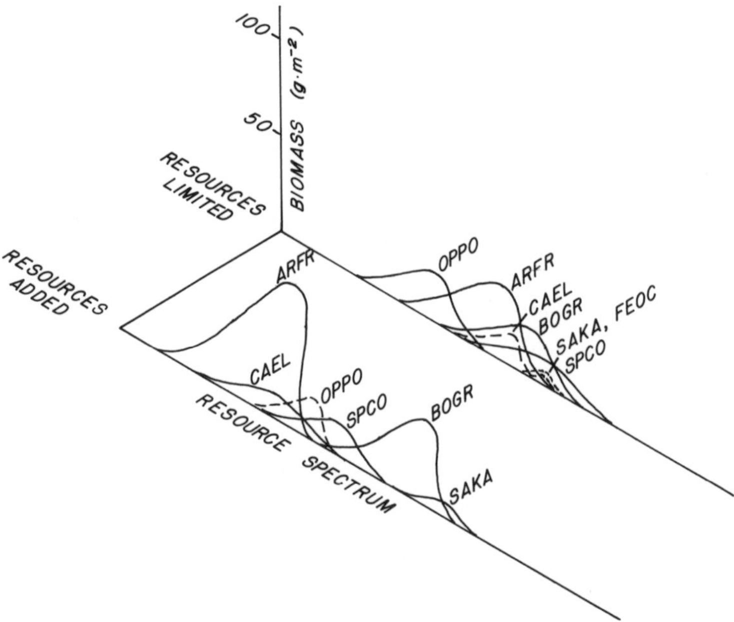

Figure 10.8. Diagrammatic representation of the relative niche breadth and niche overlap and mean biomass of selected species in the shortgrass prairie under normal conditions (Resources Limited) and under application of fertilizer and water (Resources Added). ARFR = *Artemisia frigida,* OPPO = *Opuntia polyacantha,* CAEL = *Carex eleocharis,* SPCO = *Sphaeralcea coccinea,* BOGR = *Bouteloua gracilis,* SAKA = *Salsola kali,* FEOC = *Festuca octoflora.*

Table 10.1. Ecosystem Stress Area Plant Biomass and Niche Analysis

Biomass ($g \cdot m^{-2}$)	Relative breadth	Overlap[1]						
			ARFR	BOGR	CAEL	FEOC	OPPO	SPCO
			Across years (1971–1975) control					
42.16 ± 14.23	.8915	ARFR						
25.60 ± 13.55	.8051	BOGR	.7403					
4.18 ± 3.78	.4759	CAEL	.6286	.5473				
1.09 ± 1.72	.4701	FEOC	.4968	.6952	.5244			
27.70 ± 15.27	.7466	OPPO	.7334	.5201	.4035	.2330		
1.97 ± 0.92	.8250	SPCO	.7082	.9073	.5072	.6636	.5499	
0.10 ± 0.16	.3578	SAKA	.5009	.4934	.3190	.3864	.4558	.5539
			Across treatments (1974)					
77.91 ± 33.35	.8647	ARFR						
45.11 ± 27.96	.7669	BOGR	.6186					
2.56 ± 0.57	.9689	CAEL	.8598	.6833				
0	–	FEOC	–	–	–			
15.59 ± 15.08	.5687	OPPO	.5454	.4401	.6209	–		
3.44 ± 2.12	.7686	SPCO	.8337	.7096	.7671	–	.4332	
0.37 ± 0.55	.4358	SAKA	.3455	.7269	.4102	–	.1980	.4434

[1] ARFR = *Artemisia frigida*, OPPO = *Opuntia polyacantha*, CAEL = *Carex eleocharis*, SPCO = *Sphaeralcea coccinea*, BOGR = *Bouteloua gracilis*, SAKA = *Salsola kali*, FEOC = *Festuca octoflora*.

Results of partial release from competition (resources added) are taken from the corresponding data in a single year (1974) by comparing across the treatments (treatments included the addition of nitrogen, of water, or both, as described in Chapter 3). In this case, each treatment area is considered as a separate sample of resource distribution. In response to release from nutrient and water stress, one plant expanded its niche breadth greatly and one showed a considerable reduction. *Carex* doubled its niche breadth but not its biomass. *Opuntia* decreased its niche breadth and also its biomass. Both *Artemisia* and *Bouteloua* increased greatly in biomass without a corresponding expansion of niche breadth. An introduced annual, *Salsola,* expanded its niche breadth and quadrupled its biomass. Another minor species, *Festuca (Vulpia),* vanished completely.

It is evident that release from competition is incomplete in this comparison. Some species benefited by expansion in biomass, niche breadth, or both, whereas others suffered perhaps due to competition for space and sunlight, or due to the fact that the more mesic environment was unsuitable for growth or germination.

C_4 species have higher photosynthetic rates and are more efficient in use of water than C_3 plants. That is, they require about half as much water per unit of biomass produced (Black 1971). Two C_4 species experienced the greatest biomass increase upon release from competition, *Bouteloua* and *Salsola.* The plant that disappeared completely, *Festuca,* is a C_3 plant. However, it is also an annual plant that may require special conditions for germination. The C_3 plants that persisted, like *Carex* and *Sphaeralcea,* responded more by a change in niche breadth than by change in biomass. However, *Artemisia frigida* has characteristics of a C_3 plant, yet increased in biomass without a change in niche breadth, much like *Bouteloua.* It has been pointed out in Chapter 2 that, as soil water increases, the optimal temperature for photosynthesis increases. Such interactions between temperature and soil water may result in a differential response by C_3 and C_4 plants.

With one exception, the changes in niche breadth were minor. This would indicate that the approach to the virtual niche condition was quite incomplete, and that an understanding of competition in this situation would require a multidimensional approach to niche analysis. Results suggest that these plants are in very close balance and that a highly competitive condition exists for a variety of resources that make up the total fundamental niche of these plant species.

Consumer-Producer Relationships

A number of studies indicate that herbivore activity stimulates primary production in grasslands. This may be accomplished by large domestic or wild grazing animals (Vickery 1972, McNaughton 1975), by rodents (Batzli 1975), or by grasshoppers (Dyer and Bokhari 1976). However, most forms of herbivory do not seem to have this effect. The timing and degree of utilization, as well as the plant parts utilized, may have significant effects on vegetation response. It is well known that activity of herbivores can influence the composition of the vegetation. There may be a link between rodent population density and primary production in grassland through nutrient cycling (Grant 1974). A striking vegetation response to redistribution of minerals by rodents has been shown by Batzli (1975).

Grazing may have important effects on nutrient cycling, as can other activities of grazers such as mechanical disturbance of the soil (Grant and French, in press). Grasshoppers contribute a sizeable fraction of green mulch to the soil as a by-product of their consumption activities (Mitchell 1975).

Primary production can have a direct effect on consumer populations. Although there is no evidence that the supply of vegetative food is limiting to small mammal populations in grasslands, there is evidence that the available supply of invertebrate food is fully utilized in grasslands (French et al 1976) and that seeds may be limiting in desert environments (French et al 1974). Aboveground invertebrate populations in grasslands show no indication of being limited by abiotic factors during the growing season, but show a close correlation with vegetation biomass (Figure 10.9).

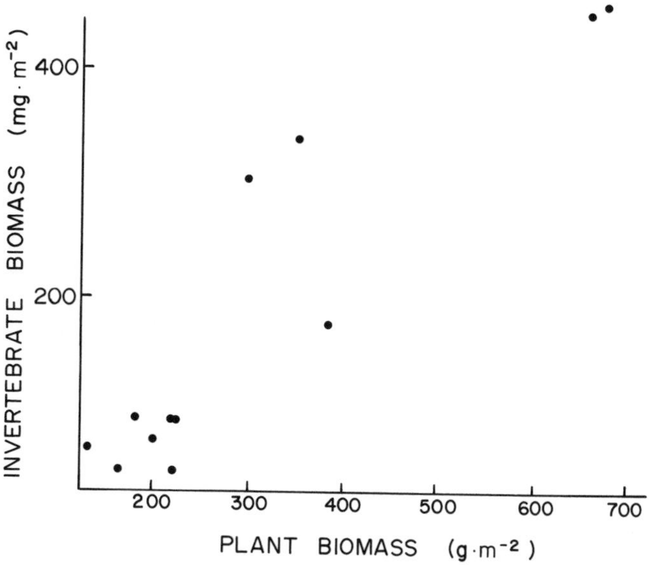

Figure 10.9. Biomass of invertebrates and of vegetation in various natural and treated plots in the shortgrass prairie.

Consumer Relationships

Consumers and Food Utilization

Through consumers the two major system properties of ecosystems are united. These two concepts, energy flow and nutrient cycling, are usually depicted separately. There are, however, important links between these system functions. Production of new organic matter requires both energy and nutrients and, since nutrients are limiting, the rate of energy flow can influence production by affecting the rate of nutrient cycling. This is perhaps the single most important feedback element of the ecosystem.

Herbivores consume producers, and in the process contribute to the system pool of dead organic material. Detrivores both consume and contribute to the pool of dead organic material. Thus, herbivores have the capability of directly affecting the production of their food, whereas detrivores do not have this capability. Wiegert and Owen (1971), and Heal and MacLean (1975), have discussed some of the implications of dual consumer pathways in ecosystems.

Consumers

The comparison of consumer activities in grasslands indicates a large proportion of this process is carried out below the surface of the ground. Since there is so much below ground activity, it would seem that perhaps these processes function more efficiently there than above ground. To address this question, data for all sites (from Chapter 5) were averaged and a standard error was computed (Figure 10.10). The comparison of the proportion of production in any trophic level to production in the next lower trophic level indicates that these values are indeed higher in the belowground portion of the system. Values of 0.034 for the proportion of primary consumer production relative to producer production, and 0.170 comparing the production of secondary consumers with that of primary consumers, are substantially higher than the corresponding aboveground figures (0.007 and 0.147). Therefore, a greater proportion of the production is utilized belowground at each step in the trophic pyramid. However, when efficiency is examined for the comparison of production relative to consumption at each trophic level, the values aboveground are little different from those belowground, the only exception being the secondary consumers belowground which are most efficient at converting energy to biomass. Most of the organisms are functioning similarly and belowground processes are essentially the same as aboveground processes.

The factors that account for the differences in aboveground and belowground biomass and energy flow are the large amount of primary production (the base of the trophic pyramid) that occurs belowground and the high degree of utilization of this material. In Chapter 2, it was indicated 70 to 85% of the photosynthate is translocated to storage belowground. Of this large amount of belowground production, 23% is utilized by consumers, compared to 5% utilized by above-

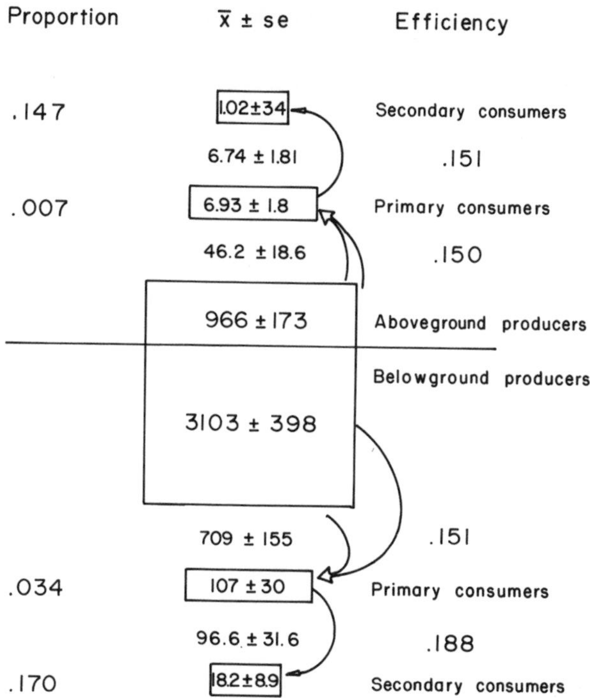

Figure 10.10. Grassland production (in boxes) and consumption (between boxes) representing means and standard errors for four sites (presented in Chapter 5). Production in one trophic level is represented as the proportion of production in the next lower trophic level, and efficiency as the ratio of production to consumption by each consumer trophic level.

ground consumers. A greater source of material on which to work results in greater production at each successive trophic level below the surface of the ground.

The relative importance of invertebrate consumers is likely to be a matter of efficiency. Comparison of the allometric relationship between body weight and unit metabolic rate for metazoan heterotherms and homeotherms shows that two such organisms of identical size would show a 20 to 35 times greater unit-metabolic rate in the homeotherm (Fenchel 1974). The metabolic cost of maintenance in the homeotherm is exceedingly high. Similarly, a comparison of the rates of increase for populations of two such animals indicates that the homeotherm population would have a rate of increase only about twice that of the heterotherm population. Thus, the heterotherms are far more efficient in using ecosystem energy. This is only partially offset by the approximately 200 percent greater assimilation efficiency of the homeotherms.

Trophic Relationships

Certain similarities and differences are apparent among the trophic pyramids for the different grassland types described in Chapter 4. Trophic pyramids representing biomass of different types of grasslands have a very broad base of primary producers supporting relatively narrow layers of primary consumers. The difference is great compared to the difference between the secondary consumer level and the base supporting it, and is likely to be an indication of the efficiency of energy transfer between respective levels. The magnitude of the difference between primary consumer and producer levels is surprising, considering the inclusion of detritus feeders in appropriate consumer categories. Another important feature is the greater amount of consumer biomass belowground than above. This is consistent for all grassland sites, and may be a generalization that applies to all primarily herbaceous terrestrial communities.

The most arid (seasonally) grassland sites, bunchgrass and desert, where growing conditions are limited more by rainfall distribution than by temperature, have evolved ecosystem structures distinct from other grassland types. The desert grassland has a low proportion of primary producer biomass in the belowground structures, and emphasizes opportunism in the form of seed production and persistence in the form of woody tissues. The bunchgrass type has a high proportion of primary producer biomass in belowground structures, thus emphasizing storage.

Total primary producer biomass is least in the desert, greater in the shortgrass prairie, still greater in the midgrass, and greatest in the tallgrass prairie. Primary producer biomass values of the bunchgrass and mountain grasslands are comparable to the shortgrass prairie.

Less striking are differences among the primary consumer biomass components. Primary consumer biomass of the midgrass and tallgrass prairies is somewhat higher than other grassland types. Aboveground primary consumer biomass is principally biophagic, whereas saprophagic consumers are more important belowground. Secondary consumer biomass is low in the desert grassland—but comparatively high when only aboveground biomass is considered—and is highest in the mixed-grass prairie.

Comparison of the trophic-level distribution of biomass at different grassland sites indicates that the southern Great Plains sites are somewhat more broadly based than the northern Great Plains sites. The mountain grassland is also of the northern type. This indicates a correlation with a temperature regime, and suggests that northern sites must turn over the primary producer biomass at a greater rate in order to maintain productivity, the consumers aiding in this turnover. Consumer biomass is proportionately higher at the colder sites, and is also proportionately higher at the arid sites. Under cold or dry conditions, activity of microorganisms responsible for decomposition is severely limited. These comparisons suggest the interesting hypothesis that higher consumers play a greater role in the reduction of organic matter and, hence, in nutrient cycling, under conditions which curtail microbial contribution.

Microbial Decomposition

There can be no doubt that the activities of microflora and microfauna in grasslands are important in the reduction or mineralization of organic compounds in the soil and surface layers, and that these actions promote primary production in nutrient-limited systems. Averaging the estimates of bacterial biomass reported in the literature, Clark and Paul (1970) gave a value of 54 g dry weight $\cdot$ m^{-2} of bacteria to a depth of 15 cm. Similarly, they estimated that an equivalent unit of soil would contain 38 g of fungal biomass. Their best estimates came from a Canadian grassland site (Matador), where April-to-October average values were 57 g dry weight $\cdot$ m^{-2} to 30 cm depth for the bacteria and actinomycetes, and 138 g for fungi. They therefore use 200 g as an estimate of the combined microfloral biomass of grassland soil. For shortgrass prairie soil, Sparrow and Doxtader (1973), as cited in Coleman et al. (1977), estimated microbial biomass as 65 g $\cdot$ m^{-2} to 30 cm. Chapter 5 estimated 80 g $\cdot$ m^{-2} of bacteria and protozoa, and 104 g $\cdot$ m^{-2} for fungi in the 0–60-cm soil layer of the shortgrass prairie.

Although total microbial biomass in the soil is comparatively large, their activity is not in proportion to biomass because they function only when abiotic conditions are appropriate. Coleman et al (1977) used an estimate of 20% for the active fraction. Clark and Paul (1970) present evidence that 1.5 to 3% activity would likely be an overestimate, because the data on soil respiration from which these estimates are derived also include the effects of root respiration.

Rates of decomposition processes in grasslands have been demonstrated to be significantly correlated with temperature and precipitation (Vossbrinck 1976). This is primarily a result of the influence of these factors on microbial activity. Soil fauna augment the process by mechanical reduction of the organic matrix. Unique experiments in the USSR suggest the importance of abiotic processes in decomposition (R. I. Zlotin, personal communication). In a series of small field plots, from which microflora as well as micro- and mesofauna were excluded, shading from direct sunlight or exposure to filtered sunlight markedly reduced the rate of decomposition of organic matter. The study of abiotic decomposition processes could prove important to understanding nutrient cycling in arid and semiarid grasslands.

Conclusions

The different approaches used in this volume to evaluate production, energy flow, and nutrient cycling demonstrate the high degree of interaction among factors controlling ecosystem processes. Primary production is dependent upon the interrelated abiotic factors of temperature and soil moisture (Chapters 1 and 2), and both of these effects, as well as their interactions, may be modified by grazing (Chapters 8 and 9). That no system process occurs in the absence of grazing by either large or small herbivores is demonstrated by the consumer studies (Chapters 5 and 6). Certain nutrients are in critical balance in ecosystems, particularly nitrogen (Chapters 3 and 7), but the effects of consumer-producer interrelationships on this balance is incompletely understood, and may be one of the most divergent characteristics to emerge from the comparison of different ecosystems.

The complexity of interactions and feedback within and between subsystem processes obviates the necessity of a modeling approach to augment our understanding of ecosystem dynamics. Multivariate statistical analyses serve to indicate related trends among sets of variables, but do little to enhance our understanding of the biological processes at work. Simulation modeling can be useful to indicate the dynamic relationships between key factors and subsystem or system processes. Its practical importance is indicated in the primary production model (Chapter 2), which demonstrates that the proportion of photosynthate going belowground can make a large difference in production, and in the grazing model (Chapter 8), which demonstrates that the trend of the system can be altered by the pattern of grazing. Corroborative results from modeling and data analysis, such as the estimates of 14% (Chapter 2) and 15% (Chapter 5) of net primary production aboveground heightens confidence in both procedures.

Modeling has been used in grassland investigations in various ways. *Data models* or interpolation models (Chapter 6) have been used to interpolate between, or extrapolate from, quantitative estimates based on field sampling. A data model might be viewed as several input-output models in series. Such a model, by design, follows and is constrained by the condition of the system as determined from direct observation. *Matrix models* (Chapter 9) start with a set of initial conditions for system state variables, usually determined by direct observation of the system. The state variables are operated on, and modified, according to a set of functions which represent the processes affecting the system state variables. Such models start with values representing the real system, but proceed without further reference to or constraints from real data about the system. *Simulation models* (Chapter 8), like matrix models, start with initial conditions derived from the real-world system. They then proceed by operating on the initial conditions through functions that incorporate dynamic conditions or stochastic processes.

These broad classes of models—data models, matrix models and simulation models—represent generally increasing degrees of mathematical sophistication and complexity, and a generally decreasing similarity to the real world. Their utility, however, increases when reference is made to the great difficulty of improving on existing data by additional detailed sampling or by improved field methodology.

Summary

Subsystem process rates, including those of primary production, primary and secondary consumption, and decomposition determine total production of grassland ecosystems. Temperature is important in controlling primary production, as evidenced by the proportion of C_3 and C_4 plants at different latitudes with different temperature regimes. The importance of water is indicated by a close correlation of soil water with root growth and of precipitation with vegetation biomass. Nutrients have been shown to be of critical importance, both theoretically and experimentally. Experimental manipulation has also demonstrated that plants exhibit a high degree of competition under natural conditions. After partial release from competition, grassland plants show varying degrees of niche breadth and niche overlap modification. Consumers are important in modifying the rates or pathways of nutrient cycling. Invertebrates are the most important consumers, perhaps due to their greater energetic efficiency than vertebrates. Belowground consumers account for more energy flow than aboveground consumers, because of the greater total available energy belowground and because of the relatively high ecological efficiency of belowground organisms. The biomass of soil microbial organisms is at times high, although their annual activity or function is comparatively low, due to their dependence upon rather narrow ranges of abiotic conditions. A combination of data analysis and modeling efforts offers the most practical approach to solution of ecosystem problems and processes.

References

Ares, J. 1975. A model and experimental data on changes in plant community structure during a growing season, *US/IBP Grassland Biome Tech. Rep. No. 295*. Fort Collins: Colorado State Univ.

Ares, J. 1976. Dynamics of the root system of blue grama. *J. Range Manag.* **29**:208–213.

Batzli, G. O. 1975. The role of small mammals in arctic ecosystems. *In* F. B. Golley, K. Petrusewicz, and L. Ryszkowski (eds.), Small Mammals: *Their Productivity and Population Dynamics,* pp. 243–68 Cambridge, England: Cambridge Univ. Press.

Black, C. C. 1971. Ecological implications of dividing plants into groups with distinct photosynthetic production capacities. *Adv. Ecol. Res.* **7**:87–114.

Clark, F. E., and E. A. Paul. 1970. The microflora of grassland. *Adv. Agron.* **22**:375–435.

Coleman, D. C., R. Andrews, J. E. Ellis, and J. S. Singh. 1977. Energy flow and partitioning in selected man-managed and natural ecosystems. *Agro-Ecosystems* **3**:45–54.

Colwell, R. K., and D. J. Futyma. 1971. On the measurement of niche breadth and overlap. *Ecology* **52**:567–576.

Coupland, R. T. 1959. Effects of changes in weather conditions upon grasslands in the northern Great Plains. *In* H. B. Sprague (ed.), *Grasslands,* pp. 291–306. New York: American Association for the Advancement of Science.

Dyer, M. I. and U. G. Bokhari. 1976. Plant-animal interactions: Studies of the effects of grasshopper grazing on blue grama grass. *Ecology* **57**:762–772.

Fenchel, T. 1974. Intrinsic rate of natural increase: The relationship with body size. *Oecologia* **14**:317–326.

French, N. R., W. E. Grant, W. Grodzinski, and D. M. Swift. 1976. Small mammal energetics in grassland ecosystems. *Ecol. Monogr.* **46**:201–220.

French, N. R., B. G. Maza, H. O. Hill, A. P. Aschwanden, and H. W. Kaaz. 1974. A population study of irradiated desert rodents. *Ecol. Monogr.* **44**:45–72.

Grant, W. E. 1974. The functional role of small mammals in grassland ecosystems (Ph.D. diss.). Fort Collins: Colorado State Univ.

Grant, W. E. and N. R. French. In press. The functional role of small mammals in grassland ecosystems. *Ecol. Model.*

Heal, O. W., and S. F. MacLean, Jr. 1975. Comparative productivity in ecosystems: Secondary productivity. *In* W. H. Van Dobben and R. H. Lowe-McConnell (eds.) *Unifying Concepts in Ecology,* pp. 89–108. The Hague: Dr. W. Junk.

Kirchner, T. 1977. The effects of resource enrichment on the diversity of plants and arthropods in a shortgrass prairie. *Ecology* **68**:1334–1344.

McNaughton, S. J. 1975. Serengeti migratory wildebeest: Facilitation of energy flow by grazing. *Science* **191**:92–94.

Mitchell, J. E. 1975. Variation in food preferences of three grasshopper species (Acrididae:Orthoptera) as a function of food availability. *Am. Midl. Nat.* **94**:267–283.

Rosenzweig, M. L. 1971. Paradox of enrichment: Destabilization of exploitation ecosystems in ecological time. *Science* **171**:387–388.

Sparrow, E. B., and K. G. Doxtader. 1973. Adenosine triphosphate (ATP) in grassland soil: Its relationship to microbial biomass and activity, *US/IBP Grassland Biome Tech. Rep. No. 224*. Fort Collins: Colorado State Univ.

Torsell, B. W. R. 1975. European, American and Australian approaches to the study of plant competition. *US/IBP Grassland Biome Tech. Rep. No. 276*. Fort Collins: Colorado State Univ.

Van Dyne, G. M. 1975. An overview of the ecology of the Great Plains grasslands with special reference to climate and its impact, *US/IBP Grassland Biome Tech. Rep. No. 290*. Fort Collins: Colorado State Univ.

Vickery, P. J. 1972. Grazing and net primary production of a temperate grassland. *J. Appl. Ecol.* **9**:307–314.

Vossbrinck, C. R. 1976. Partitioning the biotic and abiotic effects on decomposition and mineralization, *US/IBP Grassland Biome Tech. Rep. No. 303*. Fort Collins: Colorado State Univ.

Whitman, W. C., H. C. Hanson, and R. Peterson. 1943. Relation of drought and grazing to North Dakota range lands, *North Dakota Agr. Exp. Stn. Bull. No. 320*. Fargo: North Dakota Agricultural College

Wiegert, R. G., and D. F. Owen. 1971. Trophic structure, available resources and population density in terrestrial vs. aquatic ecosystems. *J. Theor. Biol.* **30**:69–81.

Williams, G. J., III. 1974. Photosynthetic adaptation to temperature in C_3 and C_4 grasses. *Plant Physiol.* **54**:709–711.

Index

C

D

E

F

G

H

I

J

L

M

N

O

P

R

S

Ecological Studies

Analysis and Synthesis

Edited by W. D. Billings, F. Golley, O. L. Lange, and J. S. Olson

Volume 1

Analysis of Temperate Forest Ecosystems
1st corrected reprint
Edited by D.E. Reichle
1973. xii, 304p. 91 illus. cloth

Volume 2 is out of print.

Volume 3

The Biology of the Indian Ocean
Edited by B. Zeitzschel in cooperation with S.A. Gerlach
1973. xiii, 549p. 286 illus. cloth

Volume 4

Physical Aspects of Soil Water and Salts in Ecosystems
Edited by A. Hadas et al.
1973. xvi, 460p. 221 illus. 61 tables. cloth

Volume 5

Arid Zone Irrigation
Edited by B. Yaron, E. Danfors, and Y. Vaadia
1973. x, 434p. 181 illus. cloth

Volume 6

Genetics of Forest Ecosystems
By K. Stern and L. Roche
1974. x, 330p. 70 illus. cloth

Volume 7

Mediterranean Type Ecosystems
Origin and Structure
Edited by F. di Castri and H.A. Mooney
1973. xii, 405p. 88 illus. cloth

Volume 8

Phenology and Seasonality Modeling
Edited by H. Lieth
1974. xvi, 444p. 120 illus. cloth

Volume 9

Methods of Studying Plant Water Relations
By B. Slavik
1974. xviii, 449p. 181 illus. cloth

Volume 10

Coupling of Land and Water Systems
Edited by A.D. Hasler
1975. xvi, 309p. 95 illus. cloth

Volume 11

Tropical Ecological Systems
Trends in Terrestrial and Aquatic Research
Edited by F.B. Golley and E. Medina
1975. xiii, 398p. 131 illus. cloth

Volume 12

Perspectives of Biophysical Ecology
Edited by D.M. Gates and R.B. Schmerl
1975. xiii, 609p. 215 illus. cloth

Volume 13

Epidemics of Plant Diseases
Mathematical Analysis and Modeling
Edited by J. Kranz
1974. x, 170p. 46 illus. cloth

Volume 14

Primary Productivity of the Biosphere
Edited by H. Lieth and R.H. Whittaker
1975. viii, 339p. 67 illus. cloth

Volume 15

Plants in Saline Environments
Edited by A. Poljakoff-Mayber and J. Gale
1975. vii, 213p. 54 illus. cloth

Volume 16

Fennoscandian Tundra Ecosystems
Part 1: **Plants and Microorganisms**
Edited by F.E. Wielgolaski
Editorial Board: P. Kallio and T. Rosswall
1975. xv, 366p. 90 illus. 90 tables. cloth

Volume 17

Fennoscandian Tundra Ecosystems
Part 2: **Animals and Systems Analysis**
Edited by F.E. Wielgolaski
Editorial Board: P. Kallio et al.
1975. xiii, 337p. 81 illus. 97 tables. cloth

Volume 18

Remote Sensing for Environmental Sciences
Edited by E. Schanda
1976. xiii, 367p. 178 illus. 31 tables. cloth

Volume 19

Water and Plant Life
Problems and Modern Approaches
Edited by O.L. Lange, L. Kappen, and E.D. Schulze
1976. xx, 536p. 178 illus. 66 tables. cloth

Volume 20

Theories of Populations in Biological Communities
By F.B. Christiansen and T.M. Fenchel
1977. x, 144p. 68 illus. 5 tables. cloth

Volume 21

Cells, Macromolecules, and Temperature
Conformational Flexibility of Macromolecules and Ecological Adaptation
By V.Y. Alexandrov
Translated from the Russian by V.A. Bernstam
1977. xi, 330p 74 illus. 30 tables. cloth

Volume 22

Air Pollution
Phytotoxicity of Acidic Gases and Its Significance in Air Pollution Control
By B. Guderian
1977. viii, 127p. 40 illus. (4 in color) 26 tables. cloth

Volume 23

Lessepian Migration
The Influx of Red Sea Biota into the Mediterranean by Way of the Suez Canal
By F.D. Por
1978. approx. 250p. 47 illus. 2 maps. 10 plates. cloth

Volume 24

A Coastal Marine Ecosystem
Simulation and Analysis
By J. Kremer and S.W. Nixon
1978. xi, 217p. 80 illus. 13 tables. cloth

Volume 25

Microbial Ecology of a Brackish Water Environment
Edited by G. Rheinheimer
1978. xi, 291p. 77 illus. 84 tables. cloth

Volume 26

Grassland Simulation Model
Edited by G.S. Innis
1977. xxvi, 298p. 87 illus. cloth

Volume 27

Production Ecology of Some British Moors and Montane Grasslands
Edited by O.W. Heal, D.F. Perkins and W.M. Brown
1978. xii, 426p. 130 illus. 148 tables. cloth

Volume 28

Pond Littoral Ecosystems
Methods and Results of Quantitative Ecosystem Research in the Czechoslovakian IBP Project
Edited by D. Dykyjová and J. Květ
1978. xiv, 464p. 183 illus. 87 tables. cloth

Volume 29

Vegetation and Production Ecology of an Alaskan Arctic Tundra
Edited by L.L. Tieszen
1978. approx. 450p. approx. 210 illus. cloth

Volume 30

Crassulacean Acid Metabolism
Analysis of an Ecological Adaptation
By M. Kluge and I.P. Ting
1978. approx. 250p. 112 illus. 21 tables. cloth